Practical Business Intelligence

Learn to get the most out of your business data to optimize your business

Ahmed Sherif

BIRMINGHAM - MUMBAI

Practical Business Intelligence

First published: December 2016

Production reference: 1161216

Published by Packt Publishing Ltd.
Livery Place
35 Livery Street
Birmingham
B3 2PB, UK.
ISBN 978-1-78588-543-3

www.packtpub.com

Credits

Author

Ahmed Sherif

Reviewer

Davide Moraschi

Commissioning Editor

Veena Pagare

Acquisition Editor

Tushar Gupta

Content Development Editor

Aishwarya Pandere

Technical Editor

Vivek Arora

Copy Editors

Safis Editing

Vikrant Phadkay

Project Coordinator

Nidhi Joshi

Proofreader

Safis Editing

Indexer

Mariammal Chettiyar

Production Coordinator

Arvindkumar Gupta

About the Author

Ahmed Sherif has been working in the business intelligence field for over 10 years. He has both an engineering and a business background, which helped him in his first job as a data analyst. Understanding business needs and translating them into technical requirements became second nature. Ahmed started digging into the backend SQL of business intelligence tools such as SAP BusinessObjects, where he started to understand the underlying data model behind the business layout. He used these skills build dashboards and data visualization applications as a consultant for customers who were in need of something more than just spreadsheets.

As a business intelligence consultant, Ahmed has had the opportunity to work with customers from all back end data types. He found a common theme across all of their needs. If the model for the data warehouse is poorly architected on the backend, then it doesn't matter how much technology on the fronted is spent to build a productive business intelligence application. Ahmed has made it his focus to help customers develop useful visualizations from their data.

In 2016 he competed a Masters in Predictive Analytics from Northwestern University, where he focused on machine learning and predictive modeling techniques using SAS, R, and Python.. As a data scientist, Ahmed strives to fuse predictive capabilities into business intelligence solutions so that organizations can leverage their data to understand the past as well as the future. He is fascinated by anything data visualization related, especially when it involves politics and sports.

You can follow Ahmed on twitter at `@TheAhmedSherif`.

I would like to thank Kajal, Vivek, Aishwarya, and Davide for all of their editorial feedback to help make this a high quality publication. Also, I would like to thank my colleague Dallas Marks for suggesting me as an author for this very interesting topic. I'd like to thank my father, Dr. SA Sherif, for helping me with my physics homework in the 11th grade. I'd like to thank my brother, Mohammad Sherif, for getting me into sports analytics with fantasy football. I'd like to thank Dr. Saeed and Patricia Khan for being very cool in-laws. Finally, I'd like to thank my beautiful wife, Dr. Ameena Khan, and my two lovely children, Safiya and Hamza, for all of their love and support as I worked long nights and weekends on this book. I would not have been able to do this without you guys!

About the Reviewer

Davide Moraschi is a consultant, writer, and trainer. He's been doing business intelligence projects with technologies such as MicroStrategy, SQL Server, Oracle, and others for more than 15 years now.

Experienced in several sectors including but not limited to healthcare, insurance, and consumer goods, he has been involved in data analysis projects with multinational companies (Microsoft, Novartis, and COTY), international organizations (European Commission and CNR) and non-profit organizations (RES and SevillaUP).

He maintains the website `http://moraschi.com/` and can be reached at `davidem@eurostrategy.net`.

Since 2012, he has been freelancing with clients in Europe and the US.

Among the many other positions that he has covered during his career, he jokingly adds that he has been the CED (Chief Executive Dishwasher) of his family during more than a decade now.

He is also author of the Packt Publishing book *Business Intelligence with MicroStrategy Cookbook*.

I would like to thank my son Angelo, LEGO© master and experienced Minecrafter. He keeps me busy with the best job of the world: being a parent.

www.PacktPub.com

For support files and downloads related to your book, please visit www.PacktPub.com.

Did you know that Packt offers eBook versions of every book published, with PDF and ePub files available? You can upgrade to the eBook version at www.PacktPub.com and as a print book customer, you are entitled to a discount on the eBook copy. Get in touch with us at service@packtpub.com for more details.

At www.PacktPub.com, you can also read a collection of free technical articles, sign up for a range of free newsletters and receive exclusive discounts and offers on Packt books and eBooks.

https://www.packtpub.com/mapt

Get the most in-demand software skills with Mapt. Mapt gives you full access to all Packt books and video courses, as well as industry-leading tools to help you plan your personal development and advance your career.

Why subscribe?

- Fully searchable across every book published by Packt
- Copy and paste, print, and bookmark content
- On demand and accessible via a web browser

Customer Feedback

Thank you for purchasing this Packt book. We take our commitment to improving our content and products to meet your needs seriously—that's why your feedback is so valuable. Whatever your feelings about your purchase, please consider leaving a review on this book's Amazon page. Not only will this help us, more importantly it will also help others in the community to make an informed decision about the resources that they invest in to learn.

You can also review for us on a regular basis by joining our reviewers' club. **If you're interested in joining, or would like to learn more about the benefits we offer, please contact us**: customerreviews@packtpub.com.

I'd like to dedicate this book to my mother, Azza Shamseldin. She passed away in 2011 but will never really leave me because she instilled in me a work ethic that got me through hurdles writing this book and as well as hurdles in life. I think about her all the time and miss her very much!

Table of Contents

Preface

Business intelligence is the process of delivering actionable business decisions from analytical manipulation and presentation of data within the confines of a business environment. Business intelligence can be delivered using many different tools, including some that were not even originally intended to be used for BI. This book will focus on building a separate BI application in each chapter using a different BI tool. Some of these tools require the use of open source software such as D3.js (JavaScript), R, and Python. Others require the use of popular data discovery desktop tools such as Microsoft Power BI, Tableau, and QlikSense.

What this book covers

Chapter 1, *Introduction to Practical Business Intelligence*, serves as the overall introduction to the book and gives a high-level understanding of what business intelligence is, the intended audience of this book, and a summary of the different technologies that will be used.

Chapter 2, *Web Scraping*, focuses on data extraction from the Web using web scraping libraries from both R and Python. We will also focus on importing data into our data into SQL Server.

Chapter 3, *Analysis with Excel and Creating Interactive Maps and Charts with Power BI*, focuses on using pivot tables and charts in Microsoft Excel to help with data analysis. Additionally, we build the first BI application using maps and graphs in Microsoft Power BI.

Chapter 4, *Creating Bar Charts with D3.js*, introduces D3.js and explains how this JavaScript library can be used to leverage visualizations developed with SVG elements as well as data from a CSV file. Ultimately, we will use both methods to develop a bar chart with SVG elements tied to data from a CSV file.

Chapter 5, *Forecasting with R*, introduces building line charts and time series with R. Additionally, we incorporate forecasting libraries within R to visualize them with existing time series. RStudio is used to deliver R code to business users.

Chapter 6, *Creating Histograms and Normal Distribution Plots with Python*, covers data visualizations developed with popular Python libraries, such as matplotlib and seaborn. The main goal of this chapter is to build a histogram and normal distribution plot with the Jupyter Notebook and Python.

Chapter 7, *Creating a Sales Dashboard with Tableau*, focuses on building a dashboard using Tableau Public against a sales and marketing dataset developed in SQL Server.

Chapter 8, *Creating an Inventory Dashboard with QlikSense*, focuses on building a dashboard using QlikSense against an inventory dataset developed in SQL Server.

Chapter 9, *Data Analysis with Microsoft SQL Server*, serves as a wrap-up of the technologies covered as well as focusing on advanced querying techniques that can be deployed in SQL Server.

What you need for this book

This book requires the use of a Windows 7/8/10 OS with at least 2 GB RAM and at least 100 GB of hard drive space. Additionally, the following software will need to be installed:

- Microsoft SQL Server Express 2014
- Python 3 and PyCharm
- R and RStudio
- Microsoft Power BI and Microsoft Excel
- Tableau Public
- QlikSense
- D3.js

Who this book is for

This book is intended for a wide range audience. Technical folks, whether they be BI developers, data scientists, or even data analysts, will find the chapters based on D3.js, Python, and R right up their alley as they are based heavily on building BI applications with open source technology. More business-savvy folks may find more interest in data discovery desktop tools such as Tableau, Power BI, and QlikSense that are not heavily reliant on code. If you are a business intelligence manager looking to establish a department with a variety of tools to help flesh out your requirements, this book could serve as a good source for interview questions to weed out unqualified candidates.

Conventions

In this book, you will find a number of text styles that distinguish between different kinds of information. Here are some examples of these styles and an explanation of their meaning.

Code words in text, database table names, folder names, filenames, file extensions, pathnames, dummy URLs, user input, and Twitter handles are shown as follows: "The next lines of code read the link and assign it to the to the `BeautifulSoup` function."

A block of code is set as follows:

```
#import packages into the project
from bs4 import BeautifulSoup
from urllib.request import urlopen
import pandas as pd
```

When we wish to draw your attention to a particular part of a code block, the relevant lines or items are set in bold:

```
<head>
<script src="d3.js" charset="utf-8"></script>
  <meta charset="utf-8">
  <meta name="viewport" content="width=device-width">
  <title>JS Bin</title>
</head>
```

Any command-line input or output is written as follows:

```
C:\Python34\Scripts> pip install –upgrade pip
C:\Python34\Scripts> pip install pandas
```

New terms and **important words** are shown in bold. Words that you see on the screen, for example, in menus or dialog boxes, appear in the text like this: "In order to download new modules, we will go to **Files** | **Settings** | **Project Name** | **Project Interpreter**."

Warnings or important notes appear in a box like this.

Tips and tricks appear like this.

Reader feedback

Feedback from our readers is always welcome. Let us know what you think about this book-what you liked or disliked. Reader feedback is important for us as it helps us develop titles that you will really get the most out of. To send us general feedback, simply e-mail `feedback@packtpub.com`, and mention the book's title in the subject of your message. If there is a topic that you have expertise in and you are interested in either writing or contributing to a book, see our author guide at `www.packtpub.com/authors`.

Customer support

Now that you are the proud owner of a Packt book, we have a number of things to help you to get the most from your purchase.

Downloading the example code

You can download the example code files for this book from your account at `http://www.p acktpub.com`. If you purchased this book elsewhere, you can visit `http://www.packtpub.c om/support` and register to have the files e-mailed directly to you.

You can download the code files by following these steps:

1. Log in or register to our website using your e-mail address and password.
2. Hover the mouse pointer on the **SUPPORT** tab at the top.
3. Click on **Code Downloads & Errata**.
4. Enter the name of the book in the **Search** box.
5. Select the book for which you're looking to download the code files.
6. Choose from the drop-down menu where you purchased this book from.
7. Click on **Code Download**.

Once the file is downloaded, please make sure that you unzip or extract the folder using the latest version of:

- WinRAR / 7-Zip for Windows
- Zipeg / iZip / UnRarX for Mac
- 7-Zip / PeaZip for Linux

The code bundle for the book is also hosted on GitHub at `https://github.com/asherif 844/PracticalBusinessIntelligence`. We also have other code bundles from our rich catalog of books and videos available at `https://github.com/PacktPublishing/`. Check them out!

Downloading the color images of this book

We also provide you with a PDF file that has color images of the screenshots/diagrams used in this book. The color images will help you better understand the changes in the output. You can download this file from `https://www.packtpub.com/sites/default/files/downloads/PracticalBusinessIntelli gence_ColorImages.pdf`.

Errata

Although we have taken every care to ensure the accuracy of our content, mistakes do happen. If you find a mistake in one of our books-maybe a mistake in the text or the code-we would be grateful if you could report this to us. By doing so, you can save other readers from frustration and help us improve subsequent versions of this book. If you find any errata, please report them by visiting `http://www.packtpub.com/submit-errata`, selecting your book, clicking on the **Errata Submission Form** link, and entering the details of your errata. Once your errata are verified, your submission will be accepted and the errata will be uploaded to our website or added to any list of existing errata under the Errata section of that title.

To view the previously submitted errata, go to `https://www.packtpub.com/books/conten t/support`and enter the name of the book in the search field. The required information will appear under the **Errata** section.

Piracy

Piracy of copyrighted material on the Internet is an ongoing problem across all media. At Packt, we take the protection of our copyright and licenses very seriously. If you come across any illegal copies of our works in any form on the Internet, please provide us with the location address or website name immediately so that we can pursue a remedy.

Please contact us at `copyright@packtpub.com` with a link to the suspected pirated material.

We appreciate your help in protecting our authors and our ability to bring you valuable content.

Questions

If you have a problem with any aspect of this book, you can contact us at `questions@packtpub.com`, and we will do our best to address the problem.

1
Introduction to Practical Business Intelligence

What is business intelligence? Before answering this question, I want to pose and answer another question. What isn't business intelligence? It is not spreadsheet analysis done with transactional data with hundreds of thousands of rows. One of the goals of **Business Intelligence** (**BI**) is to shield the users of the data from the intelligent logic lurking behind the scenes of the application that is delivering that same data to them. If the integrity of the data is compromised in any way by an individual not intimately familiar with the data source, then there cannot, by definition, be intelligence in the business decisions made with that same data. The following statement is a common theme that will be revisited frequently throughout the book:

> *Business intelligence works best when the intelligent logic and data delivery are isolated to ensure a single source of truth.*

This single source of truth is the key for any business intelligence operation whether it is a Mom-and-Pop soda shop or a Fortune 500 company. Any successfully built report, dashboard, or application that is delivering information to a user through a BI tool must allow transparency between the numbers available in the data source and those that appear in the final product. If the numbers cannot be traced back to the original source, trust between the user and the data will be compromised and this will ultimately defeat the overall purpose of business intelligence.

In my opinion, the most successful tools used for business intelligence directly shield the business user from the query logic used to display that same data in a visual manner of same kind. Business intelligence has taken many forms in terms of labels over the years. For the purposes of this book, we will use the following definition:

> *Business intelligence is the process of delivering actionable business decisions from analytical manipulation and presentation of data within the confines of a business environment.*

The delivery process mentioned in the definition is where the bulk of this book will focus its attention on. The beauty of BI is that it is not owned by any one particular tool that is proprietary to a specific industry or company. Business intelligence can be delivered using many different tools, including some that were not even originally intended to be used for BI. The tool itself should not be the source where the query logic is applied to generate the business logic of the data. The tool should primarily serve as the delivery mechanism of the query that is generated by the data warehouse that houses both the data as well as the logic.

Before we continue on with this chapter, a little bit about me may help understand where I'm coming from. I started out as a data analyst over 10 years ago in 2005 using-at that time-a very popular tool called BusinessObjects. I thought I knew what I was talking about and was quite confident in my skills as an analyst. One day I saw a position open in a department that I wanted to work in. I had thought the qualifications were within my wheelhouse, but apparently the interviewing manager didn't see it the same way. Initially, he was eager and excited to interview me. He must've thought that on paper I was a strong candidate. However, as he kept asking me question after question about my SQL skills his facial expressions showed frustration and disappointment. I will never forget what he said to me at the end, "You have glaring weaknesses". I was quite heartbroken at the time but ultimately used the opportunity to strengthen my technical skills so that I would never put myself in that position again.

I would dig behind the reports to understand the hidden query logic that is pushed out to users. I would then take the query logic (SQL) and connect directly to the data source to understand the logic behind the scenes, which was not directly evident in the final product. As a data analyst, I found my true passion in **data visualization (dataviz)**. Regardless of the data available, I found that I could tell a story with a chart or graph more effectively than a spreadsheet.

However, I didn't always have the relevant data available to do the visualizations that were needed or requested by the business. That ultimately took me down the path from a frontend developer to a backend developer. Only in the backend could I ensure that I have the necessary data available and the level of granularity needed for it to be properly visualized in the front end. As you go through this chapter and other chapters in this book, you will see that I place an emphasis on getting the data right at the earliest stage possible to prevent tedious workarounds for the end users. I love the field of business intelligence and hope to continue to work to bridge the gap between what a business needs and what IT can deliver. More and more now, business intelligence is becoming its own department within an organization as opposed to two separate silos that do not communicate using the same language... literally.

I find that the best way to learn a new tool or a programming language is to plunge in and begin developing right away. Performing basic tasks is good but they don't have to be the goal of an assignment; they should be the means to an end result. If you approach this book as more of a cookbook of recipes for delivering powerful BI applications, you will find much success. The way we will approach a design session is not necessarily the only way, but just one of many ways. Many of these tools are in their infancy and will change as new versions are released in the upcoming years, but they will only grow in their abilities to provide new insights to users. The goal of this book is to get you up and running in every chapter with downloading, installing, and developing a business intelligence application with a different tool. In the back of my mind, as I wrote each chapter, I couldn't help but think about that young aspiring BI developer who was humbled by that interview over 10 years ago and what would have helped him be better prepared for that job.

In this chapter, we will cover the following topics:

- Understanding the Kimball method
- Understanding business intelligence architecture
- Who will benefit from this book?
- Working with Data and SQL
- Working with business intelligence tools
- Downloading and installing MS SQL Server 2014
- Downloading and installing AdventureWorks

Understanding the Kimball method

As we discuss the data warehouse where our data is being housed, we will be remised not to bring up Ralph Kimball, one of the original architects of the data warehouse. Kimball's methodology incorporated dimensional modeling, which has become the standard for modeling a data warehouse for business intelligence purposes. Dimensional modeling incorporates joining tables that have detail data and tables that have lookup data.

A detail table is known as a fact table in dimensional modeling. An example of a fact table would be a table holding thousands of rows of transactional sales from a retail store. The table will house several IDs affiliated with the product, the sales person, the purchase date, and the purchaser, just to name a few. Additionally, the fact table will store numeric data for each individual transaction, such as the sales quantity for sales amount. These numeric values are generally referred to as measures.

While there is usually one fact table, there will also be several lookup or dimensional tables that will have one table for each ID that is used in a fact table. So, for example, there would be one dimensional table for the product name affiliated with a product ID. There would be one dimensional table for the month, week, day, and year of the ID affiliated with the date. These dimensional tables are also referred to as lookup tables, because they basically look up what the name of a dimension ID is affiliated with. Usually, you would find as many dimensional tables as there are IDs in the fact table. The dimensional tables will all be joined to one fact table creating something of a "star" look. Hence, the name for this table arrangement is star schema, as seen in the following screenshot:

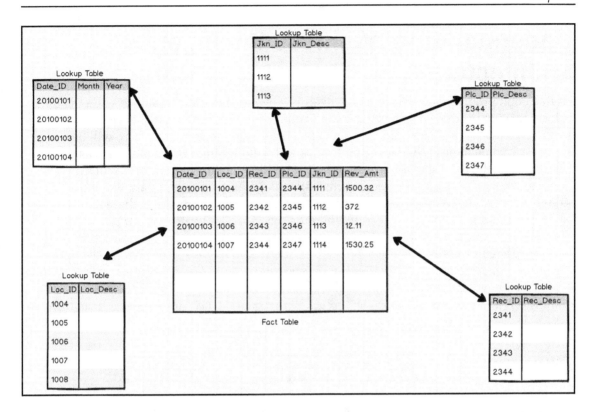

It is likely that the fact table will be the largest table in a data warehouse, while the lookup tables will most likely have fewer rows, some just one row. The tables are joined by keys, also known as foreign keys and primary keys. Foreign keys are referenced in fact tables to a unique identifier in a separate lookup table as primary keys. Foreign keys allow the most efficient join between a fact table and a dimensional table as they are usually a numeric data type. The purpose of a foreign key is to locate a single row in a lookup table to join to and establish a relationship. This rule is referred to as the referential integrity constraint and it exists to ensure that a key in a detail or fact table has a unique description to a lookup or dimensional table. As more and more rows are added to a lookup table, that new dimension is just given the next number of the identifier in line, usually starting with something like 1. Query performance between table joins suffers when we introduce non-numeric characters into the join, or worse, symbols (although most databases will not allow that).

Understanding business intelligence architecture

As this book progresses, I will continue to emphasize the benefits that arise when the bulk of logic used to produce datasets for visualization is pushed to the database level as opposed to the reporting level. There will always be exceptions, where there will be a need to produce some logic at the reporting level, and I will highlight those scenarios as they arise. Ultimately, the database is more adept at handling complex logic and will also be closer to the source of information, so this will make data quality and data validation more straightforward. If we minimize the number of locations where the logic that feeds a particular BI tool is applied, we can retain our single source of truth for our users. For example, if the requirement for a BI dashboard is to show the current and previous years' sales for US regions only, the filter for region code would be ideally applied in the data warehouse as opposed to within the BI tool. The following is a query written in SQL joining two tables from the AdventureWorks database; it highlights the difference between dimensions and measures. The region column is a dimension column and SalesYTD and SalesPY are measure columns:

```
Select
region.Name as Region, round(sum(sales.SalesYTD),2) as SalesYTD,
round(sum(sales.SalesLastYear),2) as SalesPY
FROM [AdventureWorks2014].[Sales].[SalesTerritory] region
left outer join [AdventureWorks2014].[Sales].[SalesPerson] sales on
sales.TerritoryID = region.TerritoryID
where region.CountryRegionCode = 'US'
Group by region.Name
order by region.Name asc
```

In this example, TerritoryID is serving as the key join between SalesTerritory and 'SalesPerson'. Since the measures are coming from the SalesPerson table, that table will serve as the fact table and SalesPerson.TerritoryID will serve as the foreign key. Since the Region column is dimensional and coming from the SalesTerritory table, that table will serve as the dimensional or lookup table and SalesTerritory.TerritoryID will serve as the dimension ID. In a finely tuned data warehouse, both the fact ID and the dimension ID would be indexed to allow efficient query performance. The output of the SQL statement can be seen in the following screenshot:

```
⊟Select
  region.Name as Region
  ,round(sum(sales.SalesYTD),2) as SalesYTD
  ,round(sum(sales.SalesLastYear),2) as SalesPY
  FROM [AdventureWorks2014].[Sales].[SalesTerritory] region
  left outer join [AdventureWorks2014].[Sales].[SalesPerson] sales on
  sales.TerritoryID = region.TerritoryID
  where region.CountryRegionCode = 'US'
  Group by region.Name
  order by region.Name asc
```

100 %   ▼

⊟ Results ⓑ Messages

	Region	SalesYTD	SalesPY
1	Central	3189418.37	1997186.20
2	Northeast	3763178.18	1750406.48
3	Northwest	4502152.27	3298694.49
4	Southeast	2315185.61	1849640.94
5	Southwest	6709904.17	3512662.03

This performance is obtained by sorting IDs numerically so that a row from one table that is being joined to another table does not have to be searched through the entire table but only a subset of that table. When the table is only a few hundred rows, it may not seem necessary to index columns, but when the table grows to a few hundred million rows, it may become necessary.

Why is it then that quite often the logic is not applied at the database level but instead at the reporting level on a Tableau dashboard or a Qlik application? Frequently a user of the dashboard will get a request to filter out parts of the results. The user will go to the dashboard developer and put in the request. Sometimes this request goes through an arduous ticketing process with IT that could take weeks or even months. So rather than rely on IT to make the change, the dashboard developer will apply the filter logic at the reporting level instead. If these filters are being performed to correct data quality issues, then applying the logic at the reporting level just masks a more serious issue that needs to be addressed across the entire data warehouse. You will be performing a disservice in the long run as you will be establishing a precedent for data quality being handled by the report developer as opposed to the database administrator. This can ultimately take an organization down a slippery slope towards multiple sources of truth.

Ideal BI tools will quickly connect to the data source and then allow for slicing and dicing of your dimensions and measures in a manner that will quickly inform the business of useful and practical information. Ultimately, the choice of a BI tool by an individual or an organization will come down to the ease of use of the tool as well as the flexibility to showcase data through various components such as graphs, charts, widgets, and infographics.

Who will benefit from this book?

As you are reading this book, you may be asking yourself, "How will this book benefit me if I'm too technical or if I'm not technical at all? Is the book geared towards managers rather than developers?" The answer to your questions is "Yes." Not every chapter of this book will be for everyone, but having spent the last 10 years in the Business Intelligence industry, I believe there is something for everyone in this book. Certain tools such as Tableau, Qlik, and Power BI allow for quick and flashy visualizations out of the box without much customization. Other tools such as R, Python, and D3.js require more of a programming background, which can lead to massive customization of a visualization but also more of a learning curve when it comes to producing something out of the box.

Manager

If you are a business intelligence manager looking to establish a department with a variety of tools to help flesh out your requirements, this book will serve as a good source of interview questions to weed out unqualified candidates. Additionally, the book will highlight specific tools more geared towards data scientists as opposed to data analysts, dashboard developers, and computer programmers. A manager could use this book to distinguish some of the nuances between these different skillsets and prioritize hiring based on immediate needs. In addition to hiring resources, managers are also tasked with licensing decisions based on new and existing software used by their department. At the last count, the Gartner BI Magic Quadrant listed 24 different BI platforms in the current market (`https://www.gartner.com/doc/reprints?id=1-2XXET8P&ct=160204`). That does not even take into account that some companies, such as SAP, offer multiple sub BI platforms within their main BI platform. This can be a daunting task for a BI manager when it comes to evaluating which platform tool is best suited to meet their organization's needs. With the emphasis on a different BI tool in each chapter, a manager can compare the similarities and differences for each one and evaluate which is more appropriate for them.

Data scientist

Data science is a relatively new position to fill within organizations and in 2012 was deemed the sexiest job of the 21st century by the Harvard Business Review (`https://hbr.org/2012/10/data-scientist-the-sexiest-job-of-the-21st-century`).

The term *data scientist* has been more often misused in the BI industry than any other position. It has been lumped in with *data analyst* as well as *BI developer*. Unfortunately, these three positions have separate skill sets and you will do yourself a disservice by assuming that one person can do multiple positions successfully. A data scientist will be able to apply statistical algorithms behind the data that is being extracted from the BI tools and make predictions about what will happen in the future with that same dataset. Due to this skill set, a data scientist may find the chapters focusing on R and Python to be of particular importance because of their abilities to leverage predictive capabilities within their BI delivery mechanisms. Very often data scientists find themselves doing the job of a BI developer to prepare the data that they need in a way that allows for statistical analysis. Ideally this task should be left to the BI developer with strong querying skills and allow the data scientist to focus on the hidden story behind the data.

Data analyst

Data analyst is probably the second most misused position behind a data scientist. Typically, a data analyst should be analyzing the data that is coming out of the BI tools that are connected to the data warehouse. Most data analysts are comfortable working with Microsoft Excel. Additionally, may have some working knowledge of how to build or alter existing SQL scripts. Often, they are asked to take on additional roles in developing dashboards that require programming skills outside their comfort level. This is where they would find some comfort using a tool such as Power BI, Tableau, or Qlik. These tools allow a data analyst to quickly develop a storyboard or visualization that allows a quick analysis with minimal programming skills.

Visualization developer

A *dataviz* developer is someone who can create complex visualizations out of data and showcase interesting interactions between different measures inside a dataset that cannot necessarily be seen with a traditional chart or graph. More often than not, these developers possess some programming background such as JavaScript, HTML, or CSS. These developers are also used to developing applications directly for the Web and therefore would find D3.js a comfortable environment to program in.

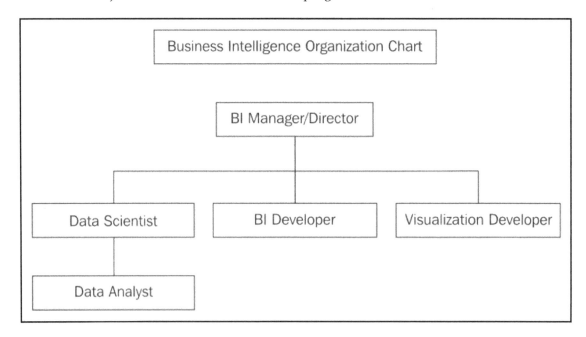

Working with data and SQL

The examples and exercises that will be utilized in this book will come from the
AdventureWorks database. This database has a comprehensive list of tables that mimics a
fictional bicycle retailer called AdventureWorks. The examples in this book will draw on
different tables from the database to highlight BI reporting from various segments
appropriate for the AdventureWorks organization. The areas that we will report on for the
AdventureWorks organization are the following:

- Human resources
- Inventory
- Sales
- Discounts

A different segment of the data will be highlighted in each chapter, utilizing a specific set of
tools. We've already mentioned SQL earlier on in this chapter. SQL or Structured Query
Language is the programming language used by databases to communicate relationships
between all of the tables in their system. The beauty of SQL is that is pretty much universal
with regard to how the tables communicate with each other. A cursory understanding of
SQL will be helpful to get a grasp of how data is being aggregated with dimensions and
measures. Additionally, an understanding of the SQL statements used will help with the
validation process to ensure a single source of truth between the source data and the output
inside the BI tool of choice.

Every database environment, whether it is Oracle, Teradata, SAP, or Microsoft, will use a
slightly modified version of SQL syntax. The essence is the same but the formatting may be
slightly different. Since we will be using Microsoft SQL Server to develop our SQL
statements, it will be important for us to become familiar with its formatting and syntax. For
more information about learning Microsoft SQL syntax, visit the following website:
https://www.techonthenet.com/sql_server/select.php.

Working with business intelligence tools

Over the course of the last 20 years, there have been a growing number of software products released that were geared towards business intelligence. In addition, there have been a number of software products and programming languages that were not initially built for BI but later on became a staple for the industry. The tools used in this book were chosen based on the fact that they were either built on open source technology or products from companies that provided free versions of their software for development purposes. Many big enterprise firms have their own BI tools and they are quite popular. However, unless you have a license with them, it is unlikely that you will be able to use their tool without having to shell out a small fortune. The tools that we will cover in this book will fall under one of these two general categories:

- Traditional programming languages such as R, Python, and D3.js (JavaScript)
- Data discovery desktop applications such as Tableau, Qlik, and Power BI

Power BI and Excel

Power BI is one of the relatively newer BI tools from Microsoft. It is known as a self-service solution and integrates seamlessly with other data sources such as Microsoft Excel and Microsoft SQL Server. Our primary purpose in using Power BI will be to generate interactive dashboards, reports, and datasets for users.

In addition to using Power BI, we will also focus on utilizing Microsoft Excel to assist with some data analysis and the validation of results pulled from our data warehouse. Pivot tables are very popular within MS Excel and will be used to validate aggregations done inside the data warehouse.

D3.js

D3.js, also known as data-driven documents, is a JavaScript library known for its delivery of beautiful visualizations by manipulating documents based on data. Since D3 is rooted in JavaScript, all visualizations make a seamless transition to the Web. D3 allows major customization to any part of a visualization, and because of this flexibility it will require a steeper learning curve that probably any other software program discussed in this book. D3 can consume data easily as a `.json` or a `.csv` file. Additionally, the data can be imbedded directly within the JavaScript code that renders the visualization on the Web.

R

R is a free and open source statistical programming language that produces beautiful graphics. The R language has been widely used among the statistical community, and more recently in the data science and machine learning community as well. Due to this fact, it has gathered momentum in recent years as a platform for displaying and delivering effective and practical BI. In addition to visualizing BI, R has the ability to visualize predictive analyses with algorithms and forecasts. While R is a bit raw in its interface, some **IDEs** (**Integrated Development Environments**) have been developed to ease the user experience. For the purposes of this book, RStudio will be used to deliver visualizations developed within R.

Python

Python is considered the most traditional programming language of all the different languages that will be covered in this book. It is a widely used in general-purpose programming language with several modules that are very powerful in analyzing and visualizing data. Similar to R, Python is a bit raw in its own form for delivering beautiful graphics as a BI tool; however, with the incorporation of an IDE, the user interface becomes a much more pleasurable development experience. PyCharm will be the IDE used to develop BI with Python. PyCharm is free to use and allows the creation of the IPython (now called Jupyter) notebook, which delivers seamless integration between Python and the powerful modules that will assist with BI.

As a note, for the purposes of this book all code in Python will be developed using the Python 3 syntax.

Qlik

Qlik is a software company specializing in delivering business intelligence solutions using their desktop tool. Qlik is one of the leaders in delivering quick visualizations based on data and queries through their desktop application. They advertise themselves as a self-service BI for business users. While they do offer solutions that target more enterprise organizations, they also offer a free version of their tool for personal use. It is this version that will be discussed in this book. Tableau is probably the closest competitor to Qlik in terms of delivering similar BI solutions.

Tableau

Tableau is a software company specializing in delivering business intelligence solutions using their desktop tool. If this sounds familiar to Qlik, it's probably because it's true. Both are leaders in the field of establishing a delivery mechanism with easy installation, setup, and connectivity to the available data. Tableau has a free version of their desktop tool, which will be primarily used in discussions in this book. Again, Tableau excels at delivering both quick, beautiful visualizations as well as self-service data discovery to more advanced business users.

Microsoft SQL Server

Microsoft SQL Server 2014 will serve as the data warehouse for the examples that we will use with the BI Tools discussed previously in this book. Microsoft SQL Server is relatively simple to install and set up, and it is free to download. Additionally, there are example databases that configure seamlessly with it, such as the `AdventureWorks` database.

Downloading and installing MS SQL Server 2014

First things first. We will need to get started with getting our database and data warehouse up and running so that we can begin to develop our BI environment.

We will visit this Microsoft link to start the download selection process:
`https://www.microsoft.com/en-us/download/details.aspx?id=42299.`

Select the specified language that is applicable to you and also select the MS SQL Server Express version with advanced features, that is, the 64-bit edition, as shown in the following screenshot:

Ideally you'll want to be working in the 64-bit edition when dealing with servers. After selecting the file, the download process should begin. Depending on your connection speed, it could take some time as the file is slightly larger than 1 GB.

The next step in the process is selecting a new standalone instance of SQL Server 2014, as shown in the following screenshot:

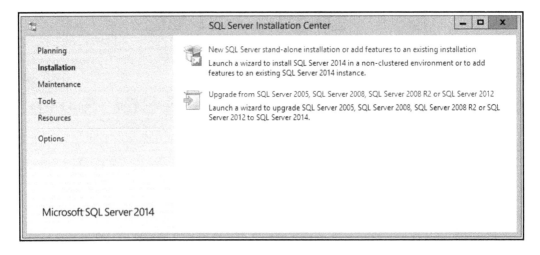

After accepting the license terms, continue through the steps in **Global Rules**, as well as **Product Updates**, to get to the setup installation files.

For the **Features** selection tab, make sure that the following features are selected for your installation:

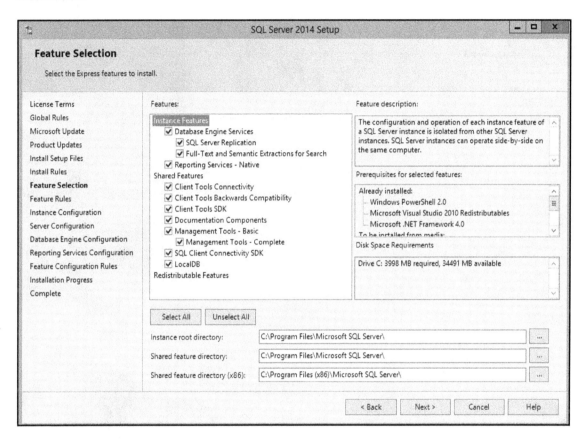

Our preference is to label a **Named instance** of this database with something related to the environment we will be developing in. Since this will be used for business intelligence, I went ahead and named this instance SQLBI, as shown in the following screenshot:

The default **Server Configuration** settings are sufficient for now; there is no need for further configuration:

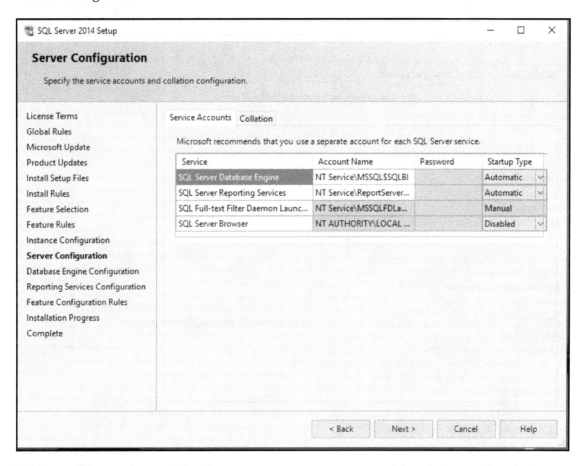

Unless you are required to do so within your company or organization, for personal use it is sufficient to just go with **Windows authentication mode** for sign-on, as shown in the following screenshot:

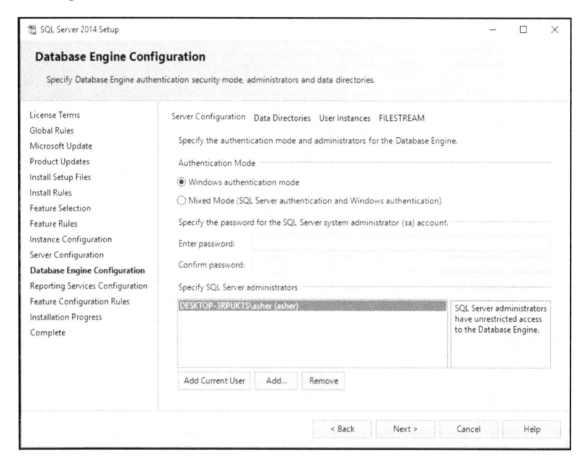

We will not need to do any configuring of reporting services, so it is sufficient for our purposes to just proceed with installing **Reporting Services Native mode** without any need for configuration at this time.

At this point, the installation will proceed and may take anywhere between 20-30 minutes, depending on available resources.

 If you have issues with your installation, you can visit the following website from Microsoft for additional help:
http://social.technet.microsoft.com/wiki/contents/articles/23878.installing-sql-server-2014-step-by-step-tutorial.aspx.

Ultimately, if everything goes well with the installation, you'll want to verify that all portions of the installation have a check mark next to their name and be labeled **Succeeded**, as shown in the following screenshot:

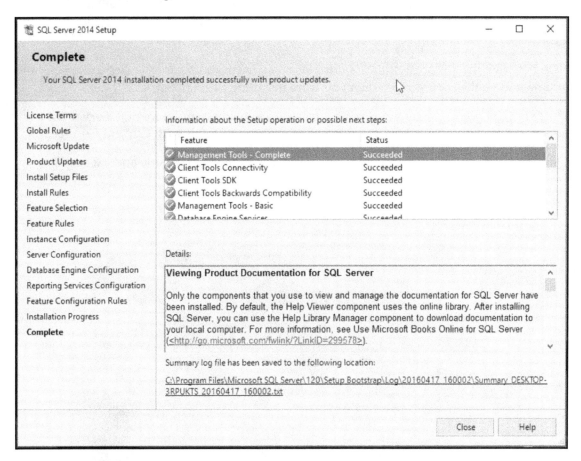

Downloading and installing AdventureWorks

We are almost finished with establishing our business intelligence data warehouse. We are now at the stage where we will extract and load data into our data warehouse. The last part is to download and install the AdventureWorks database from Microsoft. The zipped file for AdventureWorks 2014 is located at the following link:

https://msftdbprodsamples.codeplex.com/downloads/get/880661.

Once the file is downloaded and unzipped, you will find a file named `AdventureWorks2014.bak`.

Copy the aforementioned file and paste it in the following folder, where it will be incorporated with your Microsoft SQL Server 2014 Express Edition: `C:\Program Files\Microsoft SQL Server\MSSQL12.SQLBI\MSSQL\Backup`.

Also note that the `MSSQL12.SQLBI` subfolder will vary from user to user depending on how you named your SQL instance when you were installing MS SQL Server 2014.

Once that has been copied over, we can fire up Management Studio for SQL Server 2014 and start up a blank new query by going to **File | New | Query with Current Connection**.

Once you have a blank query set up, copy and paste the following code and execute it:

```
use [master]
Restore database AdventureWorks2014

from disk = 'C:\Program Files\Microsoft SQL
Server\MSSQL12.SQLBI\MSSQL\Backup\AdventureWorks2014.bak'

with move 'AdventureWorks2014_data'

to 'C:\Program Files\Microsoft SQL
Server\MSSQL12.SQLBI\MSSQL\DATA\AdventureWorks2014.mdf',

Move 'AdventureWorks2014_log'

to 'C:\Program Files\Microsoft SQL
Server\MSSQL12.SQLBI\MSSQL\DATA\AdventureWorks2014.ldf'
, replace
```

Once again, note that the MSSQL12.SQLBI subfolder will vary from user to user depending on how you named your SQL instance when you were installing MS SQL Server 2014.

At this point, within the database you should have received a message saying that Microsoft SQL Server has **Processed 24248 pages for database 'AdventureWorks2014'**. Once you have refreshed your database tab in the upper-left corner of SQL Server, the AdventureWorks database will become visible, and so will all the appropriate tables, as shown in this screenshot:

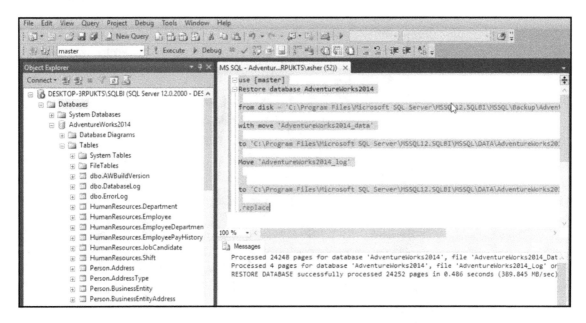

One more step that we will need is to verify that our login account has all the appropriate server settings. We right-click on the SQL Server name in the upper-left portion of Management Studio, select the properties, and then select **Permissions** inside **Properties**.

Find your username and check all the rights under the **Grant** column, as shown in the following screenshot:

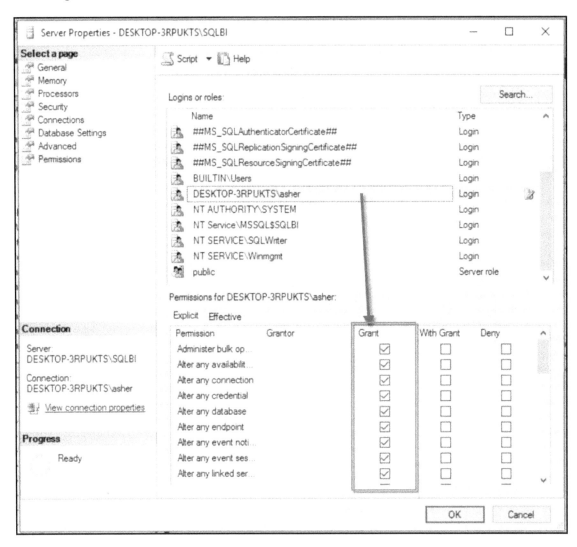

Finally, we need to ensure that the folder that houses Microsoft SQL Server 2014 also has the appropriate rights enabled for our current user. That specific folder is located at `C:\Program Files\Microsoft SQL Server\.`

For the purposes of our exercises, we will assign all rights for the user or group that will connect to SQL Server to the following folder:

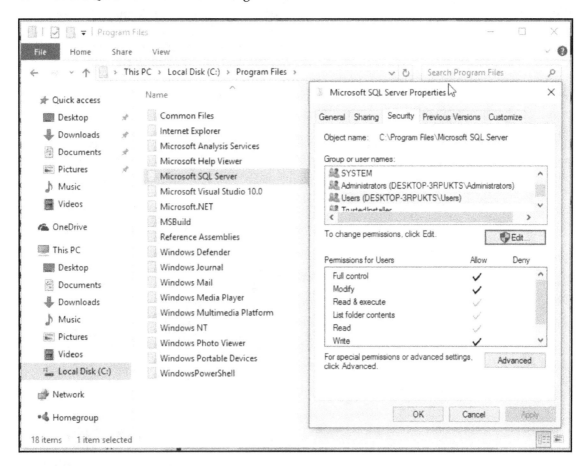

We are finished with installing our data warehouse infrastructure as well as adding our `AdventureWorks` database to our data warehouse. We are now ready to connect our data warehouse directly to our BI tools.

Summary

We have come to the conclusion of the first chapter and we have covered quite a bit of ground. We summarized the core material regarding the data modeling methodology with the Kimball method. We established our definition of business intelligence, which will be applied throughout the book. We also summarized the various tools that we will be using to implement business intelligence with. Our main emphasis will be placed on implementing business intelligence best practices within various tools that will be used based on the data available to us within the `AdventureWorks` database.

In the next chapter, we will cover extracting additional data from the Web, which will then be added to the `AdventureWorks` database. This process is known as web scraping and can be performed with great success using tools such as Python and R. In addition to collecting data, we will focus on transforming the collected data for optimal query performance.

2
Web Scraping

The amount of data created each day on the Internet is quite staggering. Much of this data is created on social media websites as well as individual blogs. We also have data that we create from our cell phones, tablets, and wearable devices. According to the following website (`http://www.livevault.com/2-5-quintillion-bytes-of-data-are-created-every-day/`) in 2015 IBM reported that the average amount of data created per day is approximately 2.5 quintillion bytes. It would be useful to any organization to get their hands on this data and make sense out of it. This is where web scraping comes into play.

Simply put web scraping is a technique to extract data from different websites, manipulate the data into a structured format, and then save the data to local files for consumption and reporting. We've all probably done some form of web scraping in the past even though we may not have known it as the time.

In the previous chapter, *Introduction to Practical Business Intelligence,* we focused on designing and configuring our data warehouse for reporting on `AdventureWorks` data, and we highlighted all of the different tools that we would use to report that data. Two of those tools we discussed were R and Python. While both are software programs that can be used for reporting, they also serve a different purpose: gathering data. Both tools have packages that make it convenient to extract large sizes of datasets from the Web to your local computer or server. This process will be the main focus of the chapter.

If a website updates a table on a regular basis, it may make sense to set up a few lines of code to extract the data. For example, a stock broker who is interested in analyzing stock prices for a company throughout the day may want to set up a web scraping application to pull the latest stock price from Yahoo! Finance (`http://finance.yahoo.com`) on an hourly basis. For the purposes of this book, we will extract tabular data that will assist us with our `AdventureWorks` database from GitHub (`https://github.com/`). GitHub is a web-based repository service that hosts code and data and can be displayed in a *wiki* format. Once the data is extracted using either R or Python, the data will be formatted into a tabular format known as a *data frame*, exported to a spreadsheet, and uploaded to the SQL Server database along with the existing AdventureWorks tables.

It is important to note that, when scraping data from a specific website, you make sure that you are scraping within their guidelines without infringing on any of their proprietary data. While web scraping is a powerful tool, it is still undergoing some legal issues and these are constantly changing. It is always a good idea to check beforehand.

We will cover the following topics in the chapter:

- Getting started with R
- Web scraping with R
- Getting started with Python
- Web scraping with Python
- Uploading data frames to Microsoft SQL Server

Getting started with R

In order for us to begin scraping websites with R, we must first get our environment set up with R, as well as RStudio. R and RStudio are available to download on many different platforms whether it be Windows, Mac, or Linux. As with everything else in this book, the environment will be set up in a Microsoft Windows 10 64-bit environment.

Downloading and installing R

R is quite easy to download and install. Any online search for **CRAN** (**Comprehensive R Archive Network**) will lead you to the latest version of R to download from the location that is closest to you. The search for R led me to the following website:
`https://cran.r-project.org/bin/windows/base/`.

At the time of writing this book, the latest version of R is version 3.3.2 for Windows 32/64-bit, as can be seen in the following screenshot:

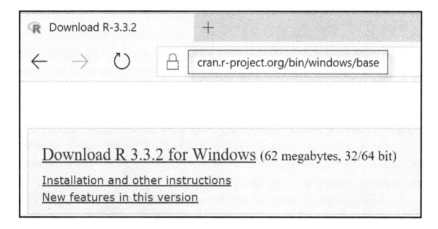

Once the file has been downloaded, the next step is to begin the installation of the executable file as shown in the following screenshot:

Select the default destination where **R for Windows 3.3.2** should be installed, as shown in the following screenshot:

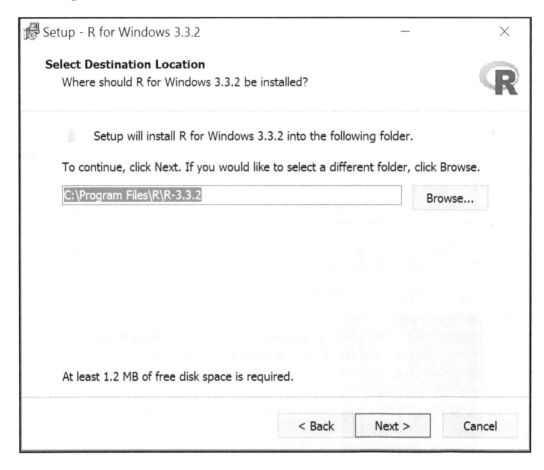

At least 1.2 MB of free disk space is required.

Select all of the components to be installed in the user installation as shown in the following screenshot:

Additionally, for our purposes, there is no need to customize the startup options as the default settings are sufficient. Feel free to check all the additional tasks to be performed, such as these:

- Create a desktop icon
- Create a Quick Launch icon
- Save the version number in the registry
- Associate R with `.RData` files

Now your installation process should begin and should complete without any issues as long as you see what is shown in the following screenshot:

While R is a great tool to use, some find it to be a bit raw within its user interface. This is mainly because R is known as a statistical programming language created by statisticians, for statisticians. While statisticians are great at creating algorithms they may not have developed R with a business user in mind. This is where RStudio comes into play. RStudio is known as an **IDE**, short for **Integrated Development Environment**. An IDE is developed to facilitate and centralize development tools for the developers. R can be used by itself just fine and RStudio will just be a shell without a prior installation of R, but the combination of the two can provide a powerful work environment. Also, RStudio has additional resources that allow delivery of charts and graphs in line with data. We will cover these topics in more depth in Chapter 5, *Forecasting with R.*

Downloading and installing RStudio

RStudio can be downloaded from the following website:
`https://www.rstudio.com/products/rstudio/download/`.

Select the installation file for **Windows Vista/7/8/10** and begin the download process as shown in the following screenshot:

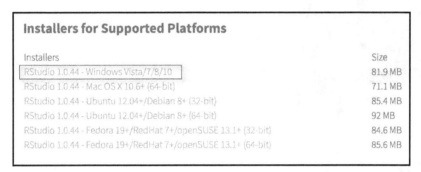

Next, choose the installation location for RStudio, as seen in the following screenshot:

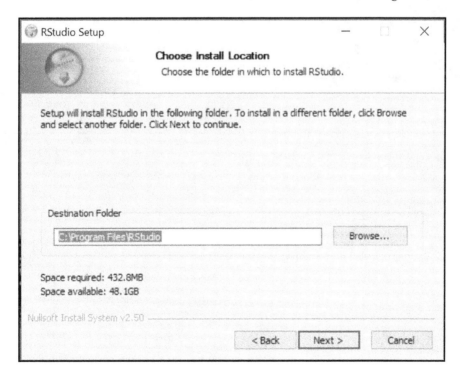

Select **Next** and let the installation process begin. Assuming that everything went smoothly with the installation process, you should see this:

We are now ready to begin web scraping with R.

Web scraping with R

When we first open up RStudio, the first thing that we see is four main quadrants. These four quadrants represent our coding input as well as coding output, as shown in the following screenshot:

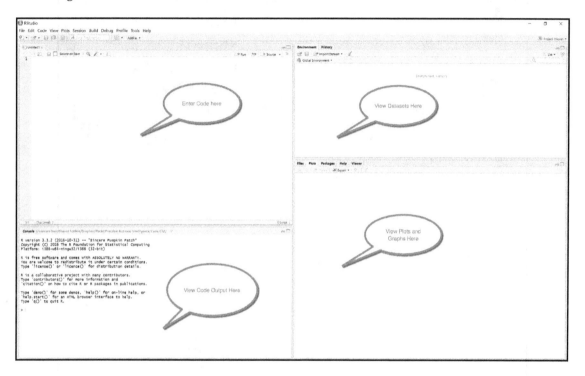

Let's now set up a new file, which we will use to get our web scraper up and running, by going to **File** | **New File** | **R Script**, as seen in the following screenshot:

We now have a blank R file to begin our coding. The next step is identifying the website data that will be the source of our web scraping exercise.

The following link
(`https://github.com/asherif844/PracticalBusinessIntelligence/wiki/AdventureWork s—Weekly-Data-by-Discount`) within GitHub has a useful table that we can scrape from to incorporate into our database.

WeekInYear	DiscountCode
01	38
02	14
03	4
04	16
05	10

The full data in the table can also be seen in the following screenshot:

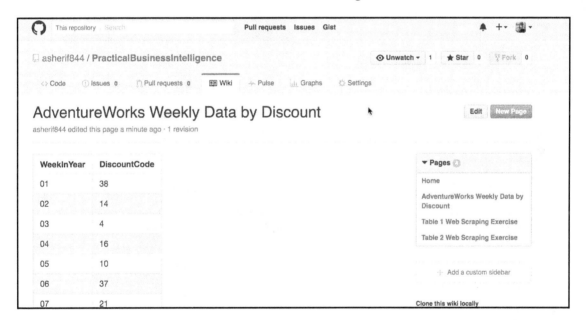

In order to scrape this Wikipedia table from R, we will need to install a couple of libraries within our R framework to facilitate the scraping process. Libraries are generally straightforward to download and install through RStudio. First we will select on main bar and select **Tools**. Then we select **Install Packages**. We should then see this:

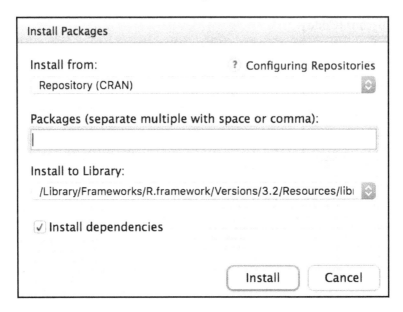

To avoid any issues with installing packages and libraries inside RStudio, always run the program as an administrator.

We are only interested in two packages for our scraping exercise. The first is XML and the second is RCurl. We can type them in both, separate each one with a comma, and then select the **Install** button to begin the download and installation path for both packages:

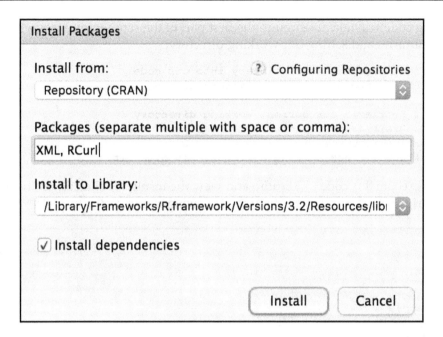

If everything is successful, the following message should be displayed inside the console box within RStudio:

```
package 'XML' successfully unpacked and MD5 sums checked

The downloaded binary packages are in
        C:\Users\asher\AppData\Local\Temp\Rtmpc9isgv\downloaded_packages
>
```

We are now ready to run our code to extract the tables from our website.

R uses the <- syntax for assignment instead of =. If you are new to R, this may take a bit of getting used to, but ultimately it will become second nature. For more information regarding R syntax, please visit the following website:
https://cran.r-project.org/doc/manuals/r-release/R-lang.html#Syntax-and-examples

The following code will take us through the first part of the scraping process where we are loading our libraries and setting our working directory:

```
library(XML) #Loads the XML library into our code
library(RCurl) #Loads the RCurl library into our code

getwd() # Retrieves our current working directory
setwd('C:/Users/asher/Desktop')
#sets working directory to necessary location
getwd() # confirm new working directory has been set
```

We can then execute this code in RStudio and view the results by clicking on the **Run** icon in the upper right-hand corner, as seen in the following screenshot:

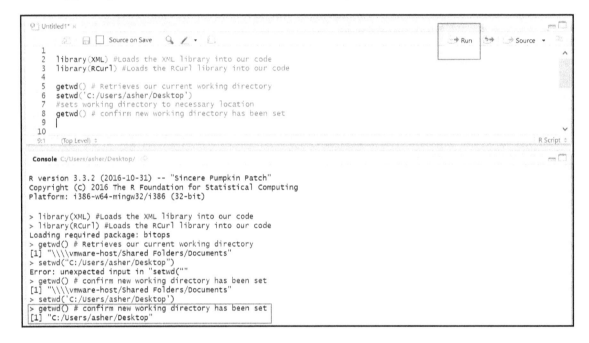

Keep in mind that the `setwd()` location will be different for each user looking to set their current working directory. For my environment, I used the following location:

```
setwd('C:/Users/asher/Desktop')
```

Make sure that you are setting your output to a directory that you have access to.

Our next few lines of code will be aimed at linking to the website of our data source, capturing the data, formatting it into a tabular structure, and previewing the first five rows of the table.

```
url <-
"https://github.com/asherif844/PracticalBusinessIntelligence/wiki/Adventure
Works---Weekly-Data-by-Discount"
# defines the url value to be set to the URL link of our choice

get_URL <- getURL(url) # Leverages the RCurl library to bring the
#link back as a string
str(get_URL) #displays the structure of the variable, which in this
#case is the link to the website

retrieveTable <- readHTMLTable(get_URL, which = 1)
#reads the table in an HTML format
#and which specifies the order of the table if there was more than one
head(retrieveTable)
#returns the first five rows of the table
```

We can now view the output of the first five rows using the head() function as shown in the following screenshot:

```
> head(retrieveTable) #returns the first five rows of the table
  WeekInYear DiscountCode
1       01           38
2       02           14
3       03            4
4       04           16
5       05           10
6       06           37
>
```

We can also view the structure of the data frame, retrieveTable, to confirm the column data types. In order to find out the structure of the data frame, we execute the str(retrieveTable) function to return the following output:

```
> str(retrieveTable)
'data.frame':    52 obs. of  2 variables:
 $ WeekInYear   : Factor w/ 52 levels "01","02","03",..: 1 2 3 4 5 6 7 8 9 10 ...
 $ DiscountCode : Factor w/ 32 levels "10","12","13",..: 22 4 24 5 1 21 11 1 12 18 ...
```

WeekInYear and DiscountCode both return a data type of Factor. A factor functions as a categorical variable, which is basically a fancy statistical term for a non-numeric data type. Categorical variables are quite common in statistical modeling when assigning dummy variables as predictor variables. However, they are non-numeric and non-numeric data types cannot be aggregated. This may be sufficient for the WeekInYear column but not for the DiscountCode column. Therefore, we must convert the DiscountCode column from a factor to a numeric value using the following script:

```
getTable$DiscountCode <- as.numeric(getTable$DiscountCode)
#Convert factor fields to Numeric
```

The new structure of the data frame, when executing str(retrieveTable), looks like this:

```
> str(retrieveTable)
'data.frame':   52 obs. of  2 variables:
 $ WeekInYear  : Factor w/ 52 levels "01","02","03",..: 1 2 3 4 5 6 7 8 9 10 ...
 $ DiscountCode: num  22 4 24 5 1 21 11 1 12 18 ...
```

The DiscountCode column now shows a numeric data type instead of the factor data type shown previously. Once we are satisfied with the data frame, we can export it to a .csv file using the write.csv() function as seen in the following script:

```
write.csv(retrieveTable, file = "DiscountCodebyWeek.csv")
#writes #the data frame to a csv file to your directory
```

The exported file will be saved to your default working directory with R code. The file is called DiscountCodebyWeek.csv. We will revisit this file later on in this chapter when we import it into MS SQL Server.

 The complete code for this exercise, as well as all other exercises performed in this book, will be downloadable directly from Packt (https://www.packtpub.com).

Getting started with Python

Chances are that you already have some version of Python installed on your machine, especially if you have a Mac. For the purposes of this exercise, we will be downloading Python 3 onto our Windows machine. At the time of writing this book, Python 3.5.1 is available for download; however, for the purposes of this book, we will go with the more reliable version, 3.4.4.

Downloading and installing Python

Similar to R, Python has a dedicated website for downloading appropriate versions of Python: `https://www.python.org/downloads/`

Once the executable file has been downloaded, run it to get the installation process started, as shown in the following screenshot:

Select the appropriate directory for the installation of Python 3.4.4. When asked to customize Python during the installation, allow all the features to be selected, especially **Add python.exe to Path**, as this function will allow you to just type python in a command prompt without having to type in the full path.

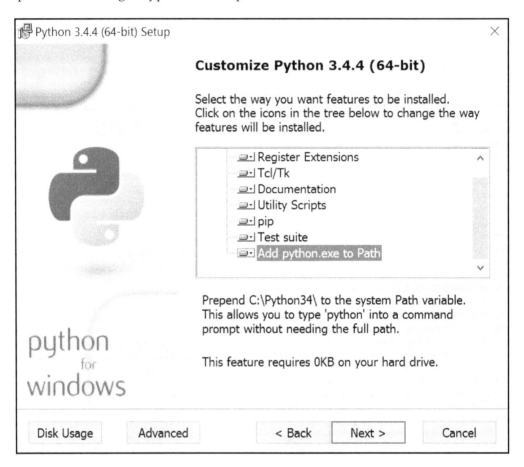

Once you've selected all the features, the installation process will begin. If everything has been installed properly, the following message should appear:

Downloading and installing PyCharm

Just as R has RStudio as an IDE, Python has several popular IDEs to use as well. I personally have a preference for PyCharm. I find it easy to use in terms of navigating the interface, installing Python modules, and incorporating IPython (Jupyter) notebooks.

PyCharm is developed by a company called JetBrains and the community version of PyCharm can be downloaded from the following website:
`https://www.jetbrains.com/pycharm/download/`.

Once the executable file has been downloaded, go ahead and begin the installation process. If everything with the installation is successful, the following screen should appear:

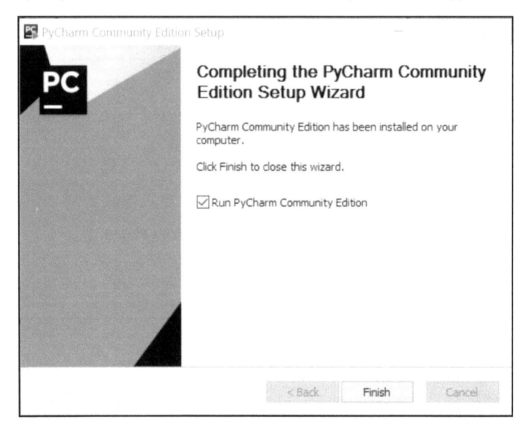

Once the installation is complete, run the PyCharm Community Edition and select **I do not have a previous version of PyCharm or I do not want to import my settings**, as shown in the following screenshot:

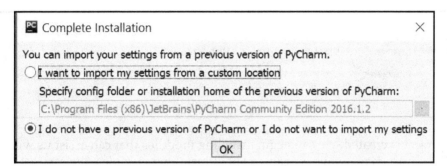

Once that is done, you will be prompted with the following screenshot to indicate whether or not you wish to start a new project. Go ahead and select **Create New Project**, as seen in the following screenshot:

Select the location for the folder path you wish to associate your new project with and select an interpreter to be `Python34` folder; it should already be the default selection, as seen in the following screenshot:

Once the project is created, we can begin installing modules that can assist us with web scraping. There are many ways we can go about installing modules. We can install them manually, using the command prompt, or directly through PyCharm. Our first option will be to install through PyCharm as it is the most straightforward process.

In order to download new modules, we will go to **Files** | **Settings** | **Project Name** | **Project Interpreter**.

There may be some default packages/modules already installed such as `pip` and `setuptools`, as seen in the following screenshot:

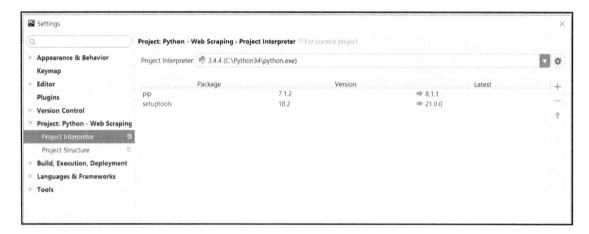

`pip` is a Python package manager used to install other modules. It is important to always keep `pip` updated with the latest version. As we can see, our current version is at **7.1.2** and the latest version is **8.1.1**. Before we can install any module we will need to update our `pip` to the latest version. This can easily be done by clicking on `pip` under **Project Interpreter**, selecting **Install Package**, and then **Specify version** as seen in the following screenshot:

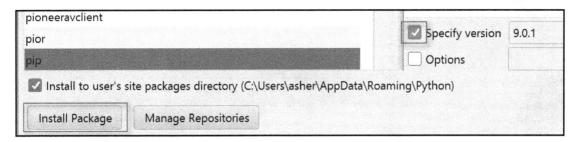

If our package was successfully installed, we should see the following message:

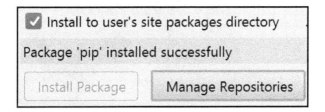

We will now go ahead and download the following modules into our environment to help us with our web scraping exercise:

- pandas
- bs4
- Jupyter

 bs4 (BeautifulSoup4) is one of the most powerful web scraping packages within Python, and more information about it can be found at the following link: `https://www.crummy.com/software/BeautifulSoup/`.

Our next step is to click on the plus sign on the right-hand side and type `pandas` in the
Available Packages selection list, as seen in the following screenshot.

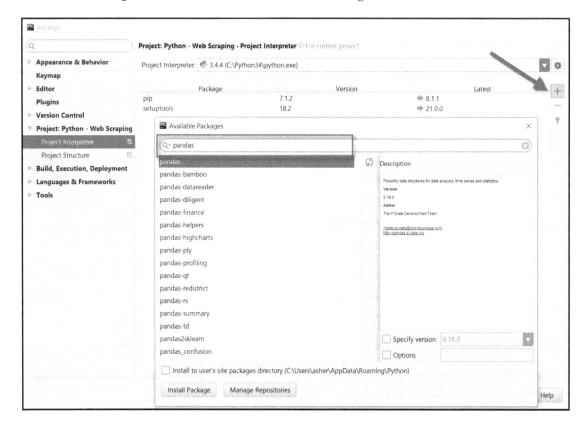

Once the appropriate package has been selected, click on the **Install Package** button at the
bottom left. Repeat the same steps for the other modules individually as you can only install
one package at a time.

While this may be the easiest way to install new packages for Python, it is not without some
flaws. From time to time, you may encounter errors with installing packages when using
this method. Another method can be used (as a backup) to pull in packages using the old-
school command prompt. For example, if we chose to upgrade `pip` and install `pandas`
through the command prompt, we would type in the following commands:

```
C:\Python34\Scripts> pip install –upgrade pip
C:\Python34\Scripts> pip install pandas
```

A general rule of thumb is to first try and install the package using PyCharm; otherwise, utilize the command prompt for Windows.

The first execution command ensures that `pip` for Python has been upgraded to the latest version, and the subsequent command will recreate the process of installing the same package for `pandas` as we used PyCharm. We will go through more in depth with installing Python modules in more depth in `Chapter 6`, *Creating Histograms and Normal Distribution Plots with Python*.

A quick refresh of the package modules in PyCharm should reflect the new modules installed, as seen in the following screenshot:

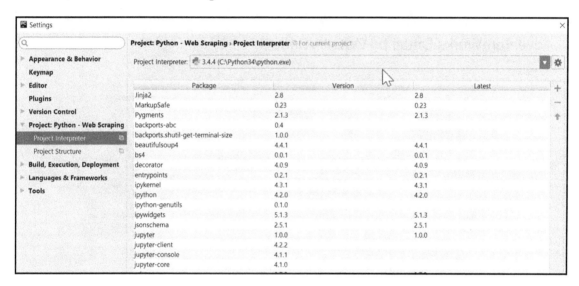

We are now ready to begin web scraping with Python.

Web scraping with Python

Let's start a new Python notebook by going to **File** and selecting **New Jupyter Notebook**. We can assign it the following name: PercentBikeRiders by Country. We will scrape a table from the following Wikipedia website:
`https://github.com/asherif844/PracticalBusinessIntelligence/wiki/AdventureWorks`
`—Detail-by-CountryCode`.

This table lists country codes with the percentage of bicycle riders, as seen in the following screenshot:

In our new notebook, our first lines of code will import all of the required modules that we just finished installing, as seen in the following script:

```
#import packages into the project
from bs4 import BeautifulSoup
from urllib.request import urlopen
import pandas as pd
```

Once those have been imported, click on the play symbol button on the toolbar to execute the code inside of the cells.

At this point, you can continue to work inside of PyCharm directly, or you can copy the server IP address (`http://127.0.0.1:8888`) that pops up when you execute the first line of code. You can then paste that code into a browser and work inside of the notebook within the browser instead, as shown in the following screenshot:

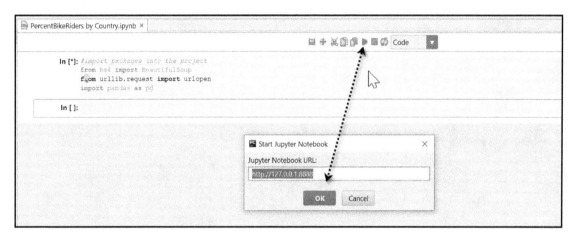

To ensure that the Jupyter Notebook has been activated, we will need to click on the **OK** button. The next lines of code read the link and assign it to the to the `BeautifulSoup` function:

```
html =
urlopen('https://github.com/asherif844/PracticalBusinessIntelligence/wiki/A
dventureWorks---Detail-by-CountryCode')

soup = BeautifulSoup(html.read())
```

If we inspect the element of the browser, we can find the class and table associated with the <tag> we want to scrape. Using a browser such as Google Chrome, we find that the appropriate tag inside of the GitHub link is called `table`. This is also the only tag called table on this webpage. In future, the name of the table may not be as literal and may vary. However, hovering over the object in the browser will highlight the technical name given to the selected item, as seen in the following screenshot:

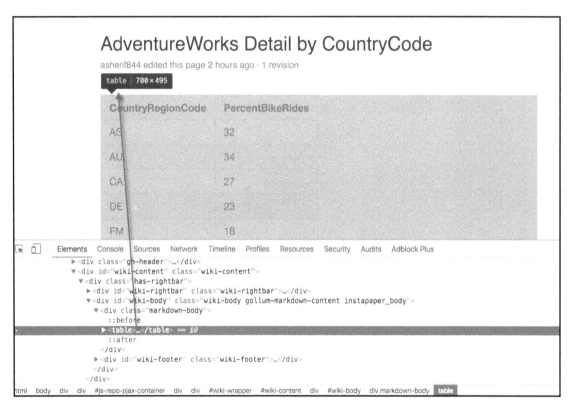

The following code will return all the HTML rows and columns associated with the table holding the values that we need:

```
title_1=soup.findAll("table")
print(title_1)
```

We now need to create our data frame with two columns for `CountryRegionCode` and `PercentBikeRides`. Our next lines of code will create two empty columns and then assign the data to these two columns by looping through the data with the row tags, `<tr>`, and the column tags, `<td>`:

```
CountryRegionCode = []
PercentBikeRides = []
final_table = soup.find('table')

#Begin loop
for row in final_table.find_all('tr')[1:]:
    col = row.find_all('td')
    column_1 = col[0].string.strip()
    CountryRegionCode.append(column_1)
    column_2 = col[1].string.strip()
    PercentBikeRides.append(column_2)
```

Once the columns have been created and appended to each other, we are almost finished, with just a few final steps to give the column headers a more database-friendly name:

```
columns = {'CountryRegionCode':CountryRegionCode,
'PercentBikeRides':PercentBikeRides}
```

We now need to convert our `columns` array into a data frame.

```
dataframe=pd.DataFrame(columns)
```

Once we are finished building our data frame structure, we can preview the first five rows using the following code. The result is shown in the next screenshot:

dataframe.head()

In [15]:	dataframe.head()	
Out[15]:		
	CountryRegionCode	**PercentBikeRides**
0	AS	32
1	AU	34
2	CA	27
3	DE	23
4	FM	18

Additionally, we can rename both "WeekinYear" as well as "DiscountCode" to
WeekInYear and DiscountCode by selecting each one and removing the quotes. We also
want to change the data type of DiscountCode from string [DT_STR] to numeric
[DT_NUMERIC] to confirm that the database will treat DiscountCode as a number and not a
character. Next we want to specify our destination, which will be **Microsoft OLE DB
Provider for SQL Server**. Enter the necessary credentials if needed and make sure that the
AdventureWorks2014 database is selected as seen in the following screenshot:

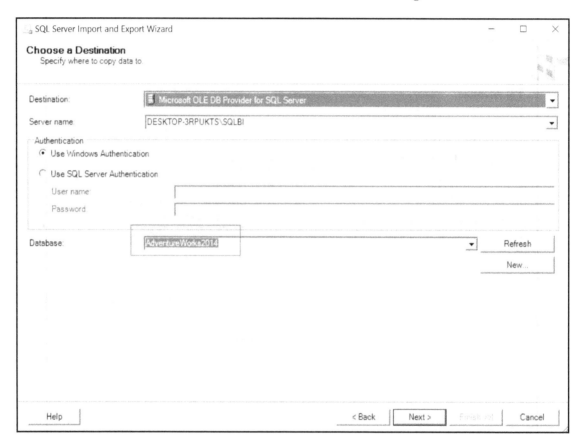

Once that has been set, we can begin the transfer process to upload the data to AdventureWorks2014. If everything executed successfully, we should be able to see the following **Success** message:

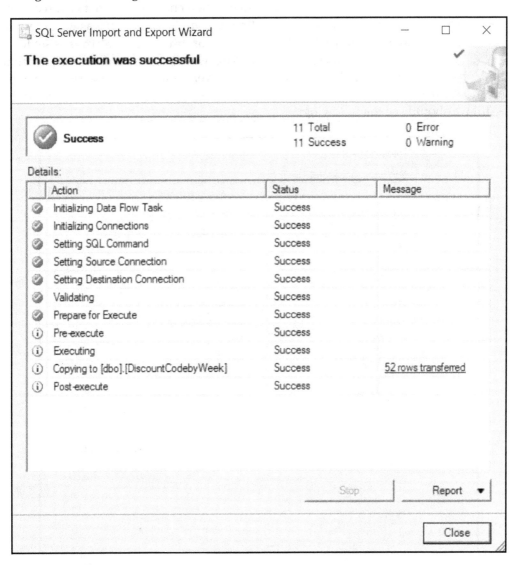

We will now repeat the same process for the other CSV file, CountryRegionBikes.csv.

Importing CountryRegionBikes

Once again we will set our data source to be a flat file and select the CountryRegionBikes.csv file as our data source. When choosing our data source, once again select the **Advanced** tab and rename the first column to index. Just as we did with DiscountCode, we should confirm that the data type for PercentBikeRides is set to numeric data type and not a character data type. Next we want to specify our destination, which will be Microsoft OLE DB Provider for SQL Server. Enter the necessary credentials if needed and make sure that the AdventureWorks2014 database is selected. If everything is successful we should see the following:

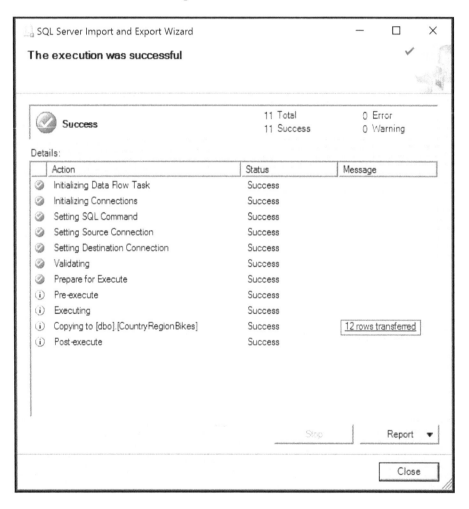

Summary

We have covered quite a bit in this chapter to get us started with both R and Python but our work will pay off as we move along with subsequent chapters. We went through two exercises to scrape data from GitHub using both R and Python. As can be seen, both tools have popular packages that allow for easy scraping of data. Both approaches were described in detail to allow you to find which process works better for you. Python is more generally known as a web scraping software tool; however, R has similar capabilities for similar tasks. Both approaches were presented to offer you more tools to keep in your toolbox. These are not the only packages that either programming language has to offer to allow for web scraping, but they are some of the more popular ones. Further investigation will show many other scraping packages such as `scrapy` for Python.

In the next chapter, we will begin our BI development with Microsoft Excel and PowerBI.

3
Analysis with Excel and Creating Interactive Maps and Charts with Power BI

Microsoft Excel is known by many in the field as the grandfather of business intelligence. This may very well be due to the fact that your grandfather was a member of the first generation of analysts to use Excel. All kidding aside, for many years within the corporate world, Excel was the primary tool used to analyze data from a data warehouse as well as to build reports. This is due to many reasons but primarily due to the fact that almost all companies have licenses with Microsoft and so analysts, developers, and managers can conveniently access Excel's capabilities with minimal effort. Specifically, it is difficult to imagine a finance department not leveraging some form of reporting with Excel.

In the last 20 years there has been a conscious effort to push users away from establishing a BI platform built on top of Excel and instead to move towards other tools, which will be discussed in more detail later on in this book. The primary reason for this has to do with the fact that the delivery of a BI solution using Excel contains both the visualization as well as the data behind the visualization. While some may find no issue with this, it can lead to potential problems in the future when it comes to data integrity. If the recipient of the report is able to get to the data behind the visualization and components that are being used to drive decisions, then the integrity of the report can be called into question.

This does not mean that Excel cannot be embraced within the BI community. There are many areas where Excel can assist an analyst when dealing with a dataset. Additionally, Microsoft has released a new desktop visualization tool called Power BI, which enables charts and map visualizations against shared datasets found in Excel or in databases such as SQL Server.

We will cover the following topics in the chapter:

- Getting to know your data in SQL Server
- Connecting Excel to SQL Server Table
- Connecting Excel to SQL Statements
- Getting started with Microsoft Power BI
- Creating Visualizations with Power BI

Getting to know your data in SQL Server

For the purposes of this book, we will be focusing on Excel 2016. To learn more about where to purchase and/or download the latest version of Microsoft Excel, visit the following website: `https://products.office.com/en-US/`.

Working through the tables that we have inside our SQL Server database can be a bit of a daunting task. There are over 60 tables in the AdventureWorks2014 database, with the majority of them being dimensional or lookup tables, such as `[Person].[CountryRegion]`, as seen in the following screenshot:

```
SQLQuery17.sql - D...RPUKTS\asher (52))*  ✕

  ⊟SELECT TOP 5 [CountryRegionCode]
        , [Name]
        , [ModifiedDate]
    FROM [AdventureWorks2014].[Person].[CountryRegion]
```

100 % ▼

🔲 Results 🔩 Messages

	CountryRegionCo...	Name	ModifiedDate
1	AD	Andorra	2008-04-30 00:00:00.000
2	AE	United Arab Emirates	2008-04-30 00:00:00.000
3	AF	Afghanistan	2008-04-30 00:00:00.000
4	AG	Antigua and Barbuda	2008-04-30 00:00:00.000
5	AI	Anguilla	2008-04-30 00:00:00.000

The previous table is basically a lookup for country names associated with a specific code. The next step would be to identify a table to function as the fact table within this schema. That table would be [AdventureWorks2014].[Sales].[SalesOrderHeader].

To see all the columns in the table, run the following script:

```
SELECT *
FROM [AdventureWorks2014].[Sales].[SalesOrderHeader]
```

As can be seen from the result set, there are several ID columns, such as TerritoryID and CurrencyRateID, as well as several numeric columns (measures), such as:

- SubTotal
- TaxAmt
- Freight
- TotalDue

In order to get a summary of how these measures roll up by TerritoryID, the following script should be written in MS SQL Server:

```
SELECT
TerritoryID as 'Territory ID'
,sum(SubTotal) as 'Sub Total'
,sum(TaxAmt) as 'Tax Amount'
,sum(Freight) as Freight
,sum(TotalDue) as 'Total Due'
FROM [AdventureWorks2014].[Sales].[SalesOrderHeader]
group by TerritoryID
order by 1 asc;
```

The preceding code is fine to write in SQL Server; however, there are more efficient ways of aggregating data directly inside of Excel with much less scripting.

Connecting Excel to a SQL Server Table

Let's go ahead and fire up MS Excel 2016 on our local machine. Select **Blank workbook**, as seen in the following screenshot:

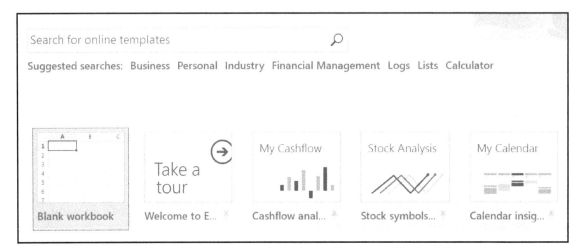

The next step is to click on the **Data** tab and select **New Query** and **From Database**. Then select **From SQL Server Database**, as seen in the following screenshot:

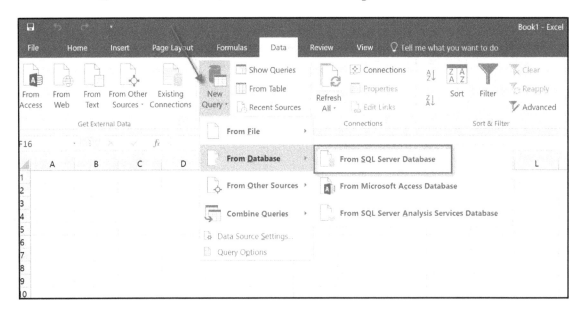

In cases where there is more than one database in the same SQL Server environment, the user will need to specify which database to use (`AdventureWorks2014` in our case).

There will be a prompt for server name credentials from your MS SQL Server. Add your own SQL Server name to the box:

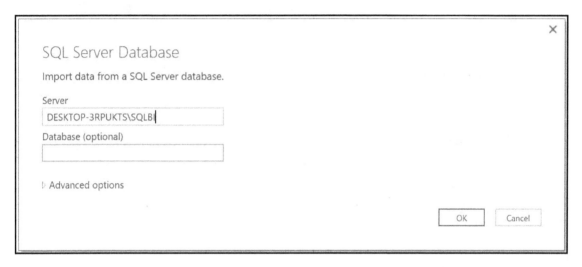

Expand the navigator on the left-hand side to expose all the tables available from the AdventureWorks database and select the table called `Sales.SalesOrderHeader,` as seen in the following screenshot:

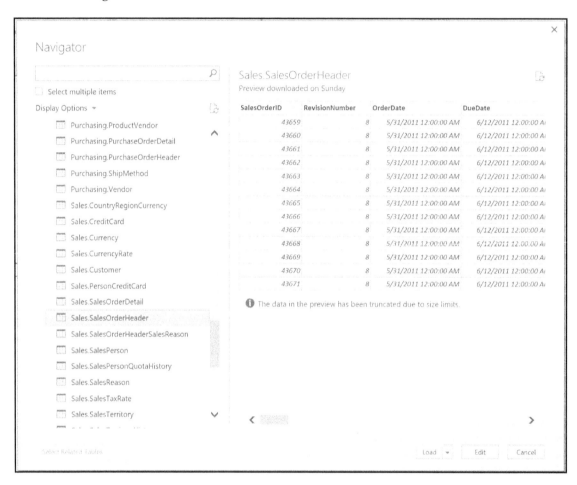

Once the table has been selected, select the **Load** button to retrieve the table into the Excel spreadsheet. The columns will appear on a new sheet, with filterable column headers:

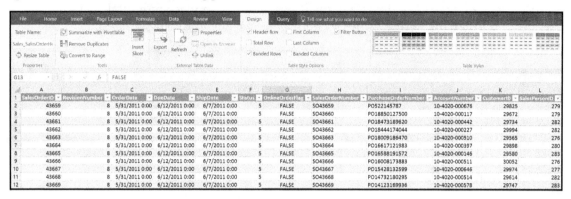

Exploring PivotTables in Excel

The next step is to pivot the columns using a PivotTable inside of MS Excel. In order to perform this, select the **Insert** tab and click on the **PivotTable** icon to select the data that will be pivoted, as seen in this screenshot:

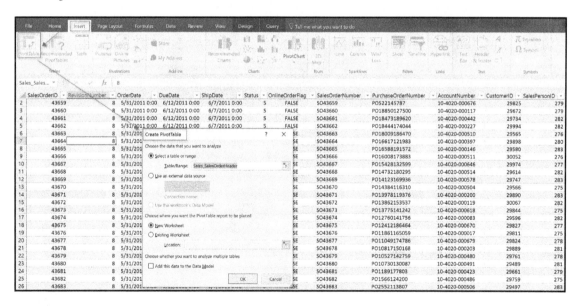

When creating a pivot table, it is ideal to have the new table placed in a new worksheet instead of an existing one as it avoids unnecessary clutter within Excel. Once the PivotTable has been created, place **TerritoryID** in the **Rows** section and place **SubTotal, TaxAmt, Freight**, and **TotalDue** in the **Values** section, as seen in the following screenshot:

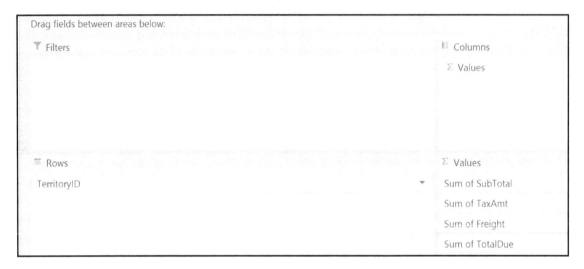

The values for the measures should be identical to the values found when executing the script statement previously used to aggregate numeric fields by territory ID:

```
SELECT
TerritoryID as 'Territory ID'
,sum(SubTotal) as 'Sub Total'
,sum(TaxAmt) as 'Tax Amount'
,sum(Freight) as Freight
,sum(TotalDue) as 'Total Due'
FROM [AdventureWorks2014].[Sales].[SalesOrderHeader]
group by TerritoryID
order by 1 asc;
```

The result set from MS SQL Server is shown in the following screenshot:

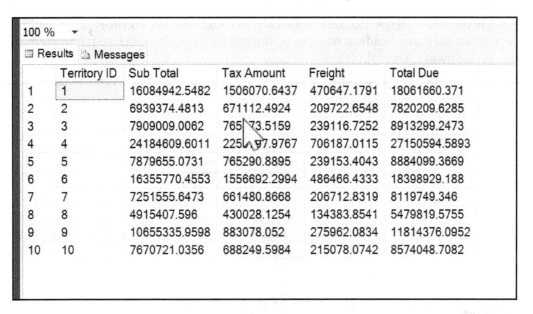

The result set from the PivotTable is show here:

3	Row Labels	Sum of SubTotal	Sum of TaxAmt	Sum of Freight	Sum of TotalDue
4	1	16084942.55	1506070.644	470647.1791	18061660.37
5	2	6939374.481	671112.4924	209722.6548	7820209.629
6	3	7909009.006	765173.5159	239116.7252	8913299.247
7	4	24184609.6	2259797.977	706187.0115	27150594.59
8	5	7879655.073	765290.8895	239153.4043	8884099.367
9	6	16355770.46	1556692.299	486466.4333	18398929.19
10	7	7251555.647	661480.8668	206712.8319	8119749.346
11	8	4915407.596	430028.1254	134383.8541	5479819.576
12	9	10655335.96	883078.052	275962.0834	11814376.1
13	10	7670721.036	688249.5984	215078.0742	8574048.708
14	**Grand Total**	**109846381.4**	**10186974.46**	**3183430.252**	**123216786.1**

The result sets from the PivotTable as well as the SQL Server query should be identical. One of the advantages of PivotTables is that you are not limited to a tabular display of data. If there is a need to look at the **TaxAmt** values across columns with **TerritoryID** as column headers rather than row headers, this can be done with a simple switch of parameters, as seen in the following screenshot:

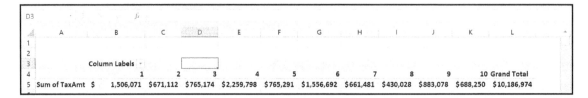

This same data manipulation feature would not be as straightforward in MS SQL Server or any other SQL database as it was in MS Excel. In addition to manipulation of the structure within the dataset, any filters or sorting would be performed using the PivotTable fields and functions and would not require any SQL script, unlike within MS SQL Server.

Connecting Excel to SQL Statements

Just as there are tables in SQL Server within our `AdventureWorks2014` database for us to query on, there are also predefined views that are available for us to use; for all practical purposes, these views behave exactly the same as tables. The views are available at the following location within SQL Server:

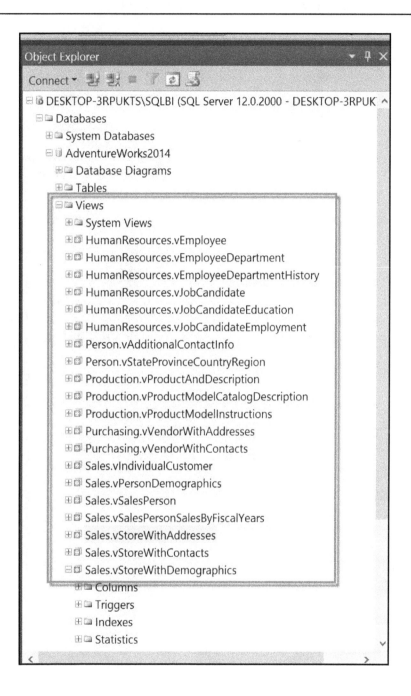

The following script can be used to pull store information such as postal codes and the number of employees:

```
SELECT
StoreAddress.City as 'City'
,StoreAddress.Name as 'Store Name'
,StoreAddress.PostalCode as 'Postal Code'
,sum(StoreDemo.NumberEmployees) as 'Number of Employees'
 FROM [AdventureWorks2014].[Sales].[vStoreWithAddresses] as StoreAddress
 INNER JOIN [AdventureWorks2014].[Sales].[vStoreWithDemographics] StoreDemo
on
 StoreAddress.BusinessEntityID=StoreDemo.BusinessEntityID
 Group by
 StoreAddress.City
,StoreAddress.Name
,StoreAddress.PostalCode
 order by 1 asc;
```

The original connection to Excel from SQL Server was only for a single table. Using the same steps we previously outlined for connecting to SQL Server, we will establish a new connection, an actual SQL statement, as seen in the following screenshot:

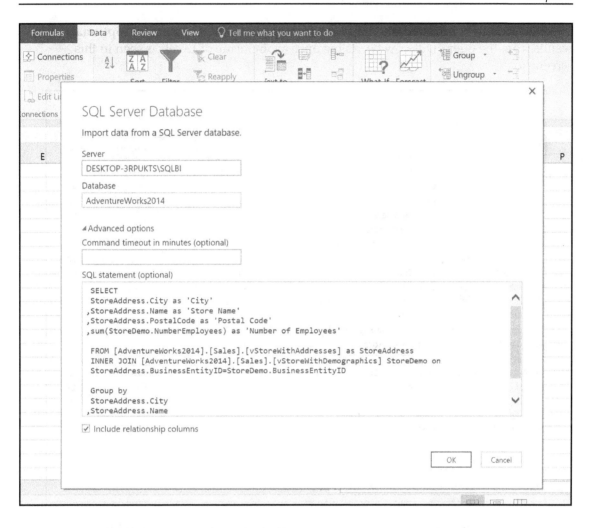

The SQL statement is pasted into the message box labeled **SQL statement (optional)**. The results from the query will now be visible once again inside of Excel, as seen in this screenshot:

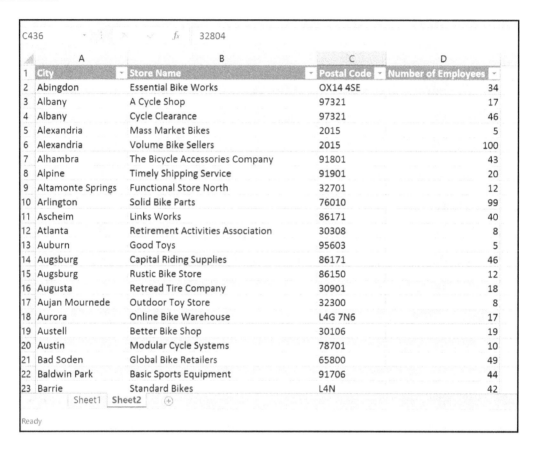

While it is possible to aggregate tabular data using PivotTables, some individuals who are more visual in nature may prefer to see data aggregated using charts instead. Fortunately, Excel gives you the ability to pivot charts just like you can pivot a table.

Exploring PivotCharts in Excel

A PivotChart is pretty much what you would expect it to be, that is, a visual representation of a PivotTable in Excel. We can apply our PivotChart against the same data shown previously by selecting the **PivotChart** icon under the **Insert** tab, as seen in this screenshot:

Once selected with the appropriate data, an interface similar to that of a PivotTable will appear, as seen in the following screenshot:

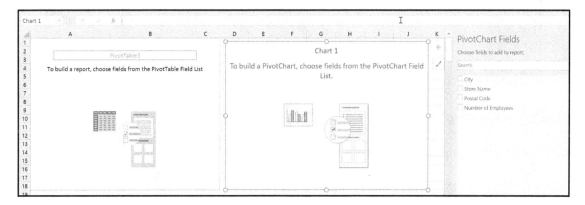

The only difference between this interface and the one for PivotTables is the middle chart, which will dynamically reflect the values selected in the PivotChart fields. The data is initially at the postal code level, but if we were interested in identifying the city that has the highest employee count irrespective of postal code, we would only need to select the **City** and the **Number of Employees** in the PivotChart fields as well as a descending sort on **Number of Employees**, as seen in the following screenshot:

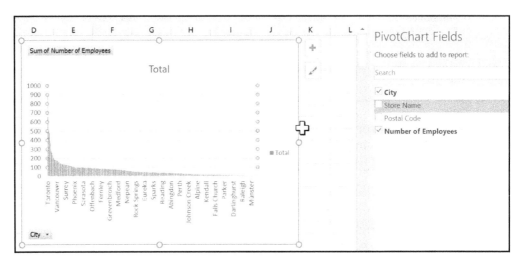

In order to apply a sort on a column chart by descending order, it is first necessary to select a specific column of data, right-click on the column, select **Sort**, and then select **Sort Largest to Smallest** as seen in the following screenshot:

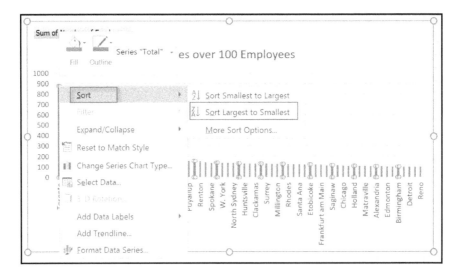

The descending column chart clearly shows **Toronto** as the city with the highest number of employees. Filtering on PivotCharts can help you zoom in on specific values of interest. By selecting the **City** dropdown in the bottom left of the PivotChart, you have the ability to make filter selections:

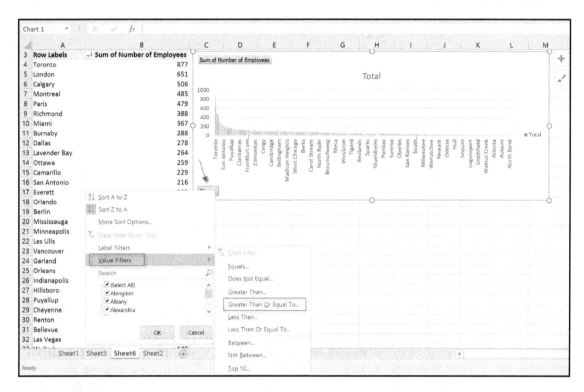

This value filter only pulls back cities with over 100 employees, as shown in the following screenshot:

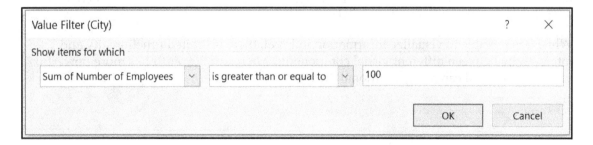

Once the filter has been applied to the dataset, the chart will reflect the updated logic, as seen in this screenshot:

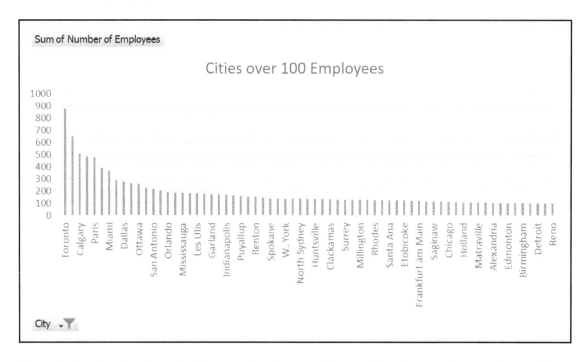

The title for the chart has also been updated manually to reflect the new logic. This can be done by double-clicking on the label and renaming the text. Visualizing data in charts and graphs rather than in tables can better assist in identifying outliers in data or possible anomalies within magnitudes of data. Luckily for us, with this `AdventureWorks` dataset, there isn't a necessity for data scrubbing. **Toronto** being a large metropolitan city would logically have a high employee count; however, if that high number were associated with a place that didn't have bicycle shops, then maybe it would be more of a cause for concern with the data or the query pulling the data.

While it is possible to visualize information in Excel, there is limited functionality and interactivity between different visual components. Microsoft Power BI has more powerful visualizations and can bring additional life to the same dataset.

Getting started with Microsoft Power BI

Microsoft Power BI introduces a familiar interface for those used to working with MS Excel but who are looking for more advanced visualizations and a drag-and-drop user experience for self-service business intelligence.

Downloading and installing Microsoft Power BI

Getting started with Microsoft Power BI is pretty straightforward. The website to download the desktop version from is found here: `https://powerbi.microsoft.com/en-us/desktop`.

Once you are at the website, click on the **Download** button, as shown in the following screenshot:

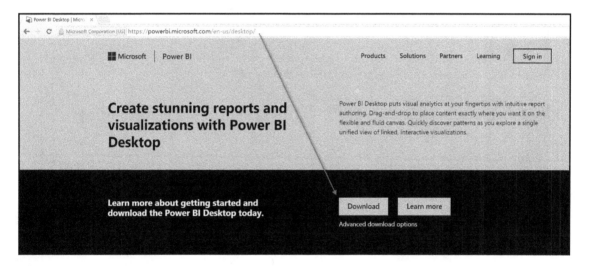

Once the executable file has successfully downloaded, click on the file to begin the installation process, as shown in this screenshot.

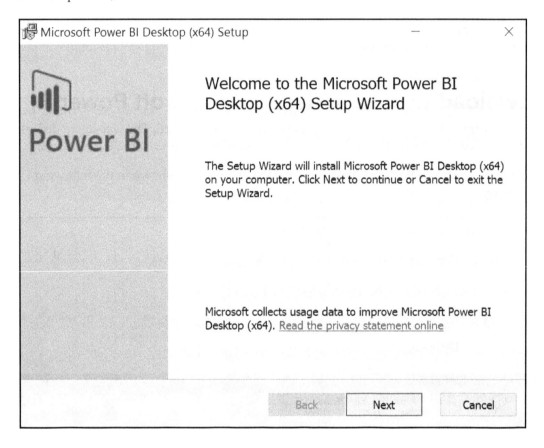

Accept the terms of the license agreement and select **Next**, as seen in the following screenshot:

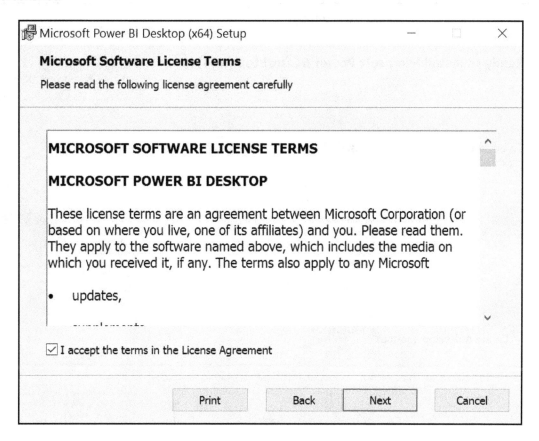

Create a desktop shortcut, if desired, and click on **Install**:

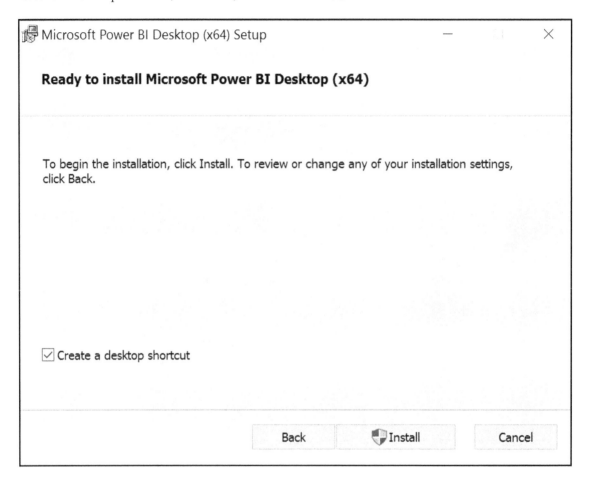

Once the installation is complete, begin the launch of the Power BI desktop application, as seen in the following screenshot:

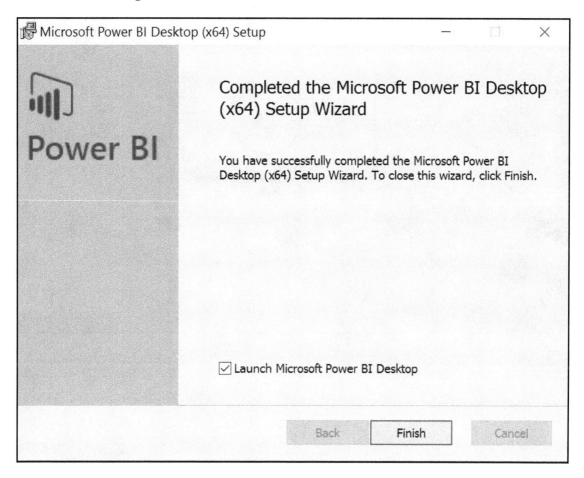

Click on **Get Data** when the startup page for Microsoft Power BI loads up, as seen in this screenshot:

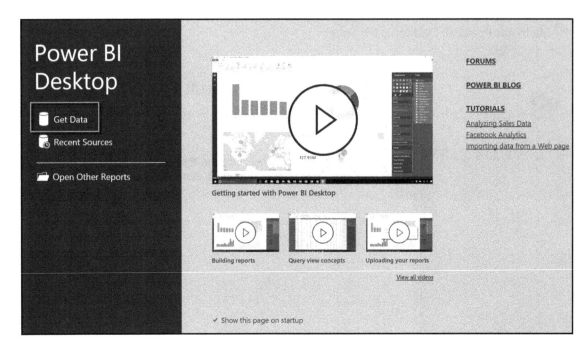

Select a database and SQL Server database to connect to the data source. Once that is completed, you will see a familiar interface to pull in the data once you've entered the SQL **Server** name and **Database**, as seen in the following screenshot:

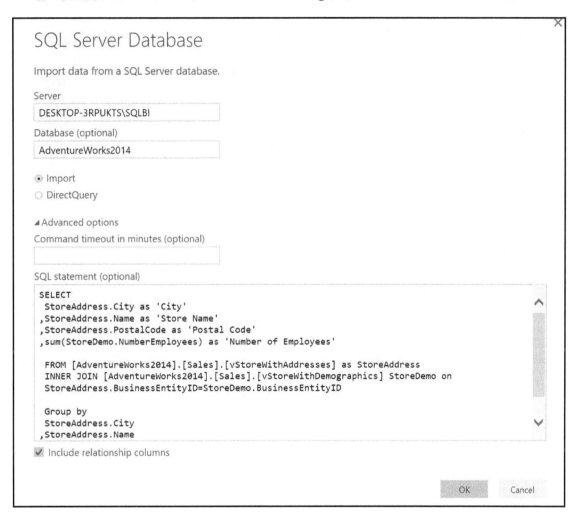

The interface is almost identical to that of Excel. Once the connection has been completed, you can load the data into Power BI:

City	Store Name	Postal Code	Number of Employees
Abingdon	Essential Bike Works	OX14 4SE	34
Albany	A Cycle Shop	97321	17
Albany	Cycle Clearance	97321	46
Alexandria	Mass Market Bikes	2015	5
Alexandria	Volume Bike Sellers	2015	100
Alhambra	The Bicycle Accessories Company	91801	43
Alpine	Timely Shipping Service	91901	20
Altamonte Springs	Functional Store North	32701	12
Arlington	Solid Bike Parts	76010	99
Ascheim	Links Works	86171	40
Atlanta	Retirement Activities Association	30308	8

DESKTOP-3RPUKTS\SQLBI: AdventureWorks2014

Load   Edit   Cancel

Creating visualizations with Power BI

Once the data is loaded into Power BI, we can preview the results by clicking on the Data icon, below the Report icon, as seen in the following screenshot:

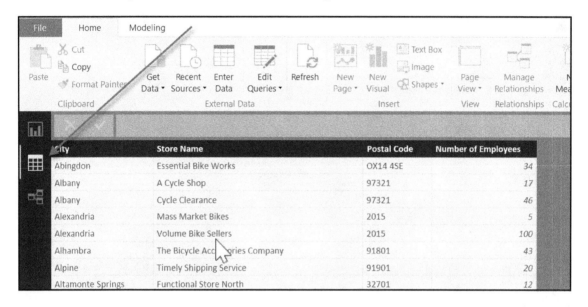

This gives us an opportunity to format the data in a way that will be most suitable to us for building a map chart. While selecting the **Postal Code** column header in the **Modeling** tab, we can change the format type from **Uncategorized** to **Postal Code**, as seen in this screenshot:

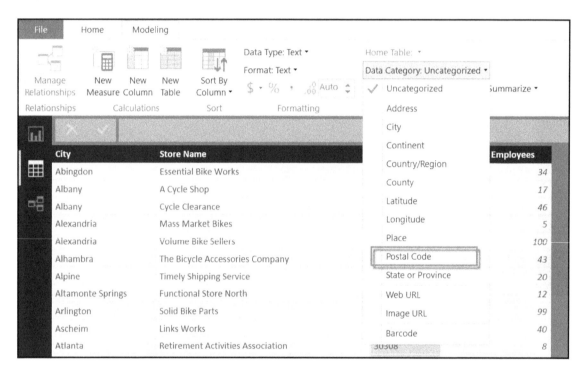

This modification ensures that the **Postal Code** column will be treated as a location identifier within the map. Once that is complete, return to the report mode, which is above the data model, and select the **Number of Employees** and **Postal Code** fields from your query, as shown in the following screenshot:

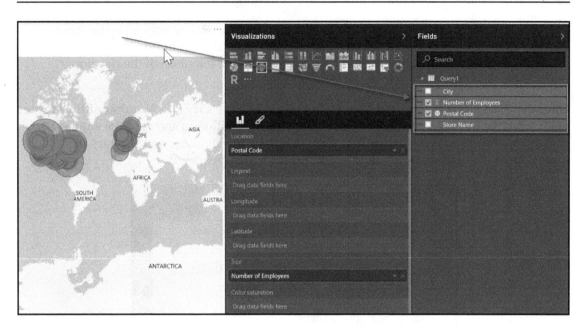

A map is automatically generated with green circles highlighting the volume of employees by postal code.

The next step is to add a new bar chart to the right of the map with the city name as well as the employee count. In order to do this, make some space by minimizing the map to make room for the bar. Then click on the bar chart from the canvas of visualization components available at your disposal, as seen in the following screenshot:

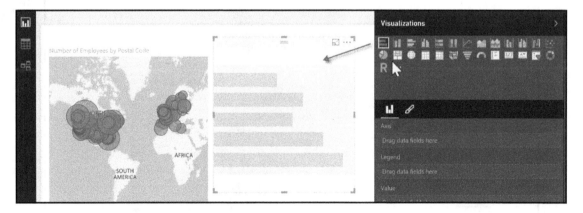

TIP

The developer may have to click first in an empty space inside the canvas. If the map is still selected, when clicking on the bar button the map changes to a bar chart, which may not be the intention of the developer.

Once the chart has been inserted onto the canvas, select the **City** and **Number of Employees** fields from the query to be visible on the bar chart. In addition to showing the values, by clicking on the ellipsis icon on the bar chart, you have the ability to sort the bars in ascending or descending order, as seen in the following screenshot:

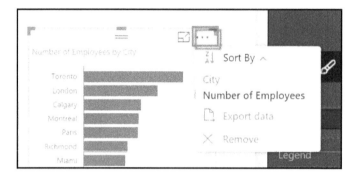

Once the bars have been sorted in descending order, the visualization should look similar to this:

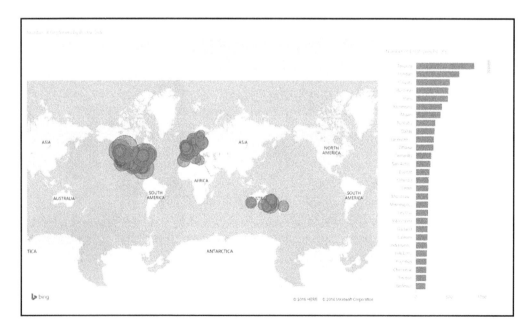

Both charts are interactive with each other without any programming required from the developer. If the user makes a city selection from the bar chart, it will filter the value to the map as seen in the following screenshot:

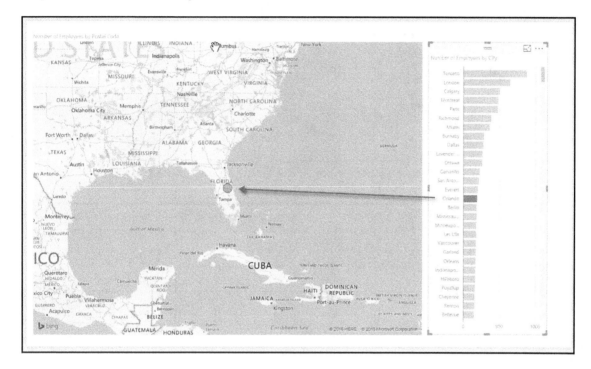

Publishing and sharing Microsoft BI

Microsoft gives users the opportunity to share their reports and dashboards with other users who are interested in the outcome from the report and the interactivity available to them.

Under the **Home** tab, click on the **Publish** icon:

Initially when publishing a document for the first time, you may need to sign up for a Microsoft account or sign in with your Microsoft Office 365 account from work. Once the sign-in is confirmed, the following icon will show up, indicating that the visualization is in the process of being published:

Once the visualization has been successfully published, you may click on the link generated to open up the report or dashboard under the app.PowerBI.com (`https://powerbi.micros oft.com/en-us/`) website, as shown in the following screenshot:

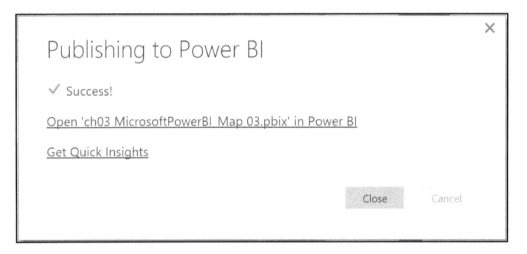

The link will take you to a website that will have a near-identical interface to the desktop Power BI interface. On the website, you will have the opportunity to publish a version of the report to external users by clicking on the **File** button and selecting **Publish to web**, as shown in this screenshot:

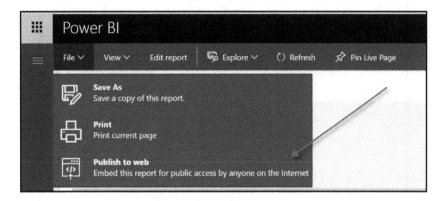

Once the visualization has been published to the Web, a code may be generated that can be used to share it with other users who have access to the Web, as seen in the following screenshot:

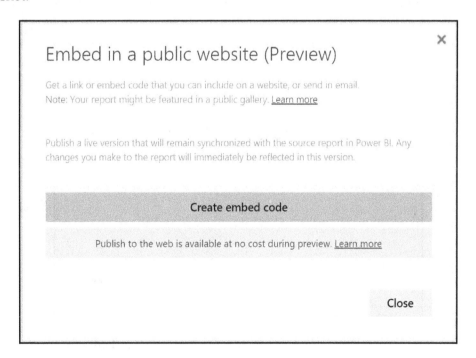

Once you click on **Create embed code**, a message like this will appear:

As the message highlights, this report will become available to anyone on the Internet as it will be viewed in a public gallery. Once the **Publish** button is selected, this is what you see:

Here we end the chapter. Hope you enjoyed reading it as much as I enjoyed writing it!

Summary

In this chapter, we moved forward with BI platforms by expanding our query analysis against the data to build different datasets. These datasets were first analyzed with Excel, with PivotTable and PivotChart manipulations, to get a sense of what type of visualizations are possible as well as the magnitude of the measures behind the datasets. We then built upon our visualizations from Excel with an interactive Microsoft Power BI dashboard on top of a query that showed us the volume of employees located by city and postal code for the AdventureWorks Company.

In the next chapter, we will focus on building bar charts using D3.js.

4
Creating Bar Charts with D3.js

D3.js, or **D3**, stands for **Data-Driven Documents**. The most common method of data connectivity to D3 involves **Comma-Separated Values (CSV)**. D3 uses JavaScript functions to leverage documents such as **SVG (Scalable Vector Graphs)** elements and HTML to render visualizations to a web browser. In addition to HTML, CSS is used to further style web pages with different colors, fonts, and sizes.

Mike Bostock is credited with being the developer of D3. He worked for the NYTimes and in 2011 he developed D3 to help leverage advanced visualizations that were not readily available in existing enterprise tools. Since that time D3 has become available to developers and some of the most amazing visualizations have been developed with D3.

 To learn more about Mike Bostock and D3, visit the following website: https://bost.ocks.org/mike/.

D3.js, or D3, may not seem like a traditional option for a business intelligence solution at first glance. This may be due to the fact that D3 is a JavaScript library used to create visualizations directly for the Web. Often, companies that are leveraging their visualizations based on their BI platform do so within a portal that is exclusive to their own internal users or customers. In recent years, this trend has been slowly changing as companies as well as individuals are beginning to leverage their data on websites using open source software without the need for enterprise licenses. Additionally, mobile-compatible visualizations have also led to a demand for development with D3 and other open source software.

There is one huge advantage that D3 has over other traditional BI software vendors, and that is customizability. As we've seen so far with Microsoft Power BI, there are many vendors with drag-and-drop software solutions to help you visualize your data. This can be done relatively quickly and without writing a single line of code. At the same time, however, the developer is at the mercy of the available components at their disposal. That is not the case with D3. A line chart can be as complex or as simple as the user needs it to be.

> *Business User: Can the lines be dashed alternating between 1 and 2 inches for the plot?*
> *Developer: Yes.*
> *Business User: Can the background be a combination of gray and purple?*
> *Developer: Sure.*
> *Business User: Sweet!*

If you've ever worked with a business user gathering report or dashboard requirements, you have probably received similar questions in terms of customizing a component. However, your response was most likely something like the following:

> *Business User: Can the lines be dashed alternating between 1 and 2 inches for the plot?*
> *Developer: No, that is not available; it's out of stock with the tool.*
> *Business User: Can the background be a combination of gray and purple?*
> *Developer: No, the colors have to be either gray or blue.*
> *Business User: Umm, OK, I guess.*

As a BI developer, one of your goals is to get a buy-in from the business users that you are building these applications for. It's not very inspiring to keep having to tell the users that their vision for the BI product cannot be conceived.

While it may be real fun building visualizations from scratch, it will take more of a learning curve to become self-sufficient as more code will be required up front to get started with the most basic of graphs or charts. Ultimately, the added effort in learning to code for visualizations will reap many rewards down the road, as we will see in this chapter.

Even though this is not a book about learning how to program, it will definitely not hurt to have some background with JavaScript, CSS, and HTML. If any of these languages are sounding foreign to you at the moment, a preliminary introduction to any of them may prove to be quite helpful as you move deeper into the chapter.

In this chapter, we will cover the following items in order to create prototypical charts in D3:

- A background on the D3 architecture
- Loading D3 templates for development
- Setting up traditional HTML components
- Setting up HTML components with D3
- Building a basic bar chart with hardcoded data
- Building a bar chart with CSV data

Some background about the D3 architecture

D3 is a combination of several of the Web's most popular languages and documents. In this section, we will highlight some of the basics within each one as that will ultimately assist with understanding D3 better.

Exploring HTML

Hypertext Markup Language, or as it is commonly known as **HTML**, is the language used for markup on the Web. We see elements in HTML for every web page we visit; we just don't know it. Anytime we see a paragraph title or comments in a text field, that's an example of HTML. However, it is not likely to find a web page that has only HTML content as that would look like a very boring page. If you've been around the block a few times and remember the look and feel of websites from the early 90's, they looked pretty bland because they were primarily built with just HTML. A pretty-looking website needs to have color and style to make it stand out.

To learn more about HTML, visit the following website:
http://www.w3schools.com/html/.

Understanding CSS

Cascading Style Sheets, or **CSS**, is the language used to describe the visual style of a web page. CSS can modify the properties of HTML text to highlight a specific word in a different color, font type, or even font size. Additionally, it can keep the structure consistent so as to minimize manual work. CSS can be maintained directly within the HTML page or it can be maintained separately in its own file with a .css extension.

 To learn more about CSS, visit the following website: http://www.w3schools.com/css/.

Learning JavaScript

Rounding out the trio that makes up the language of the Web is **JavaScript**. Not to be confused with Java, JavaScript is an object-oriented functional programming language that runs on almost every website you visit. For the purposes of D3, JavaScript has many libraries that are used to manipulate the **DOM**, or **Document Object Model**, of a web page. This is how bars and lines can be used to make charts and graphs.

 To learn more about JavaScript, visit this website: http://www.w3schools.com/js/.

Diving into SVG

Scalable Vector Graphs, or **SVG**, is basically an image format that is unique in the sense that it is does not lose resolution or pixilation when expanded, unlike other formats. SVG works seamlessly with CSS and is often used within D3 to design bars, circles, and lines as images.

 To learn more about SVG, visit the following website: http://www.w3schools.com/svg/.

Working with a source code editor

During this chapter, and in subsequent chapters, the code used will be written in a plain text editor. Those who are new to development may only be familiar with Notepad. While notepad is sufficient to write and test scripts, there are better source code editors available that highlight syntax functions, assist with variable auto-completion, and indentation natively. Some of the more popular ones are the following:

- Notepad++ (Compatible with Windows):
  `https://notepad-plus-plus.org`
- Sublime Text 2 (Compatible with both Windows and Mac):
  `https://www.sublimetext.com`
- TextWrangler (Compatible with Mac):
  `http://www.barebones.com/products/textwrangler/`

I am personally a fan of both Sublime Text and Notepad++. I use both of them interchangeably.

Loading D3 templates for development

Unlike the other tools discussed in this book, it is relatively straightforward to get started with D3. We will want to organize our work in a dedicated folder, which we will just call `D3`. We will also go ahead and create a text file inside the `D3` folder; we will save it as `index.html`. This will be our working file throughout this chapter and is often the default naming convention used for the landing page for any website.

There will be two approaches to setting up a file to load D3. One will be an online approach through a link, which will work as long as you are connected to the Internet, and the other approach will work whether you are online or offline. One caveat to keep in mind is that, if you are using the offline approach, you will need to manually update the D3 file with the latest JavaScript file whenever an update to D3 is made available.

Understanding JS Bin

JS Bin (`http://jsbin.com/`) is an online **Integrated Development Environment** (**IDE**) that is quite useful in getting new developers set up with the appropriate syntax for building an HTML page and the necessary libraries automatically loaded.

The first thing that needs to be done upon visiting the site is to click on the **File** icon and select **New**, as seen in the following screenshot:

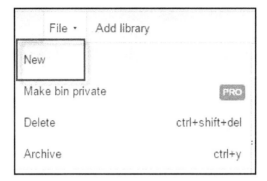

The new file will have the following HTML code as a default template:

```
<!DOCTYPE html>
<html>
<head>
  <meta charset="utf-8">
  <meta name="viewport" content="width=device-width">
  <title>JS Bin</title>
</head>
<body>

</body>
</html>
```

All that is missing in the current file is loading the D3 script. To do so, all that is required is to select the **Add library** icon on the menu and the D3 selection from the dropdown, as seen in the following screenshot:

The library addition of D3 should have only put one additional line of code, which is a script linking to the repository of the latest version of D3:

```
<!DOCTYPE html>
<html>
<head>
<script
src="https://cdnjs.cloudflare.com/ajax/libs/d3/3.5.6/d3.min.js"></script>
  <meta charset="utf-8">
  <meta name="viewport" content="width=device-width">
  <title>JS Bin</title>
</head>
<body>

</body>
</html>
```

At the time of writing this chapter, version **3.5.6** is the latest available release of D3.

Downloading from D3js.org

An alternate method of loading a D3 library to an HTML file is by downloading the latest version directly from the source.

 To download and learn D3, visit the following website: `https://d3js.org/`.

The introductory section of the website will link to a ZIP file that can be downloaded directly to your local folder, as seen in the following screenshot:

D3.js is a JavaScript library for manipulating documents based on data. **D3** helps you bring data to life using HTML, SVG, and CSS. D3's emphasis on web standards gives you the full capabilities of modern browsers without tying yourself to a proprietary framework, combining powerful visualization components and a data-driven approach to DOM manipulation.

Download the latest version

- d3.zip

Once the file has been downloaded and extracted to a specific location, there should be two JavaScript files present:

- `d3.js`
- `d3.min.js`

Both of these files should be copied and placed in your working development folder, which we earlier named `D3`. Either file can be referenced for development as both will produce the same results for our purposes. Since we are in a development phase and we are testing functionality, it is best to work with the `d3.js` file as it contains definitions that are better suited for explanation of any errors should they arise. The `d3.min.js` version is more compressed as it is stripped of any supplemental content. This would make it a better candidate to deploy in a production environment where faster content load times are preferred for a better overall user experience.

The HTML template working file should be updated to reflect the location change of the D3 library in the local folder. All that is required is to change the following code from this:

```
<script
src="https://cdnjs.cloudflare.com/ajax/libs/d3/3.5.6/d3.min.js"></script>
```

To this:

```
<script src="d3.js" charset="utf-8"></script>
```

The new HTML code should look like this:

```
<!DOCTYPE html>
<html>
<head>
<script src="d3.js" charset="utf-8"></script>
  <meta charset="utf-8">
  <meta name="viewport" content="width=device-width">
  <title>JS Bin</title>
</head>
<body>

</body>
</html>
```

We should now be all set with D3 configured in our HTML page. For the rest of this chapter, we will employ the D3 script that is available locally. However, either method should work fine moving forward.

Setting up traditional HTML components

In order to understand the power and flexibility of D3, it would make sense to first understand an example of leveraging HTML without it.

Adding a new paragraph the traditional way

Adding a new paragraph to the body of the HTML page is pretty straightforward. All that is necessary is to include two <p> tags with with the appropriate name of the paragraph, as seen in the following script:

```
<!DOCTYPE html>
<html>
<head>
<script src="d3.js" charset="utf-8"></script>
```

```
    <meta charset="utf-8">
    <meta name="viewport" content="width=device-width">
    <title>First Example</title>
</head>
<body>
<p>This is our first example</p>
</body>
</html>
```

Besides adding a new paragraph, we also changed the title of this page to **First Example**. When viewing the HTML page inside of the browser, the following should appear:

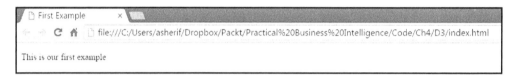

 Anytime we wish to view our HTML file, we can save our results, right-click on the `index.html` file, and choose to view in a browser.

Adding a new paragraph the D3 way

D3 gives developers an alternate method of adding new components to an HTML page. The method is called `d3.select()`. This method allows developers to select an existing document on the page and perform new operations. For example, if we wished to add a second paragraph, underneath the first one, which says `This is our second example`, we would write the following between script tags:

```
<script>
d3.select('body').append('p').text('This is our second example');
</script>
```

Our web page would now look like this:

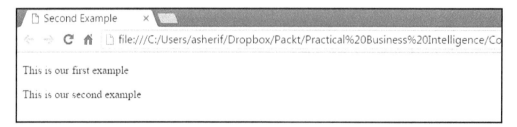

The code inside of the script works identically to the previous code that adds the paragraph tag manually by performing the following operations:

- Selecting the body component
- Appending a second paragraph
- Assigning a text value to the second paragraph that is just below the first paragraph

The full script for the web page so far appears like this:

```
<!DOCTYPE html>
<html>
<head>
<script src="d3.js" charset="utf-8"></script>
  <meta charset="utf-8">
  <meta name="viewport" content="width=device-width">
  <title>Second Example</title>
</head>
<body>

<p>This is our first example</p>

<script>
d3.select('body').append('p').text('This is our second example');
</script>

</body>
</html>
```

In order to further understand the similarities between both paragraphs inside of the actual web page, we can inspect the elements to get further details as to how the two paragraphs are being interpreted by the browser. For this chapter, we will be using Google Chrome. However, if Chrome is not available or you are using a different browser, you can learn more about inspecting the element of that browser by visiting the following website: `http://testingfreak.com/inspect-element-in-firefox-chrome-or-ie-browsers/`.

The easiest way to inspect the element in a Chrome browser is to right-click on the web page and select **Inspect**, as seen in the following screenshot:

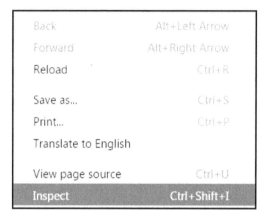

Once your inspection begins, click on the **Elements** tab and expand the <body> section of the HTML, as seen in this screenshot:

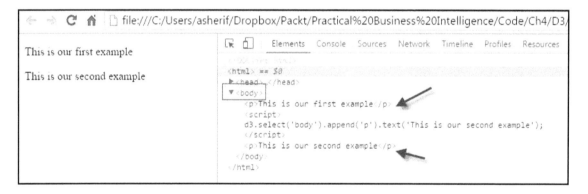

As we can see from the HTML generated in the web page, the first paragraph <p> tag remains unchanged in terms of the way it was scripted inside of our original HTML page; however, the second paragraph <p> tag was generated entirely by the D3 script even though the structure of the second paragraph is identical to the first one. This ability of D3 to manipulate existing documents and create new ones will be the key to creating new visualizations, especially when those documents are SVG.

Adding SVG shapes the traditional way

Many of the components that are available online are generated with SVG and that is primarily due to the fact that SVG elements are easily scalable without any loss in quality. This would make sense since the word *scalable* is part of the acronym that makes up SVG.

The following is an example HTML script for aligning three bars of different colors and different heights side by side inside the body of the web page:

```
<!DOCTYPE html>
<html>
<head>
<script src="d3.js" charset="utf-8"></script>
  <meta charset="utf-8">
  <meta name="viewport" content="width=device-width">
  <title>SVG Example</title>
</head>
<body>

<svg width="5000" height="5000">
  <rect x="0" y="0" width="20" height="100" fill="red" />
  <rect x="40" y="0" width="20" height="200" fill="blue" />
  <rect x="80" y="0" width="20" height="300" fill="green" />
</svg>


</body>
</html>
```

First off, the SVG area is set to have a height of 5,000 pixels and a width of 5,000 pixels inside the browser. Within the SVG area there are three rectangular SVG elements identified as `rect`. Each one of the rectangles has a width of 20 pixels and a varying height between 100 and 300 pixels. They are also spaced apart by 20 pixels each. Finally, each one is given a different color: red, blue, or green.

The HTML script generates the image seen in the following screenshot:

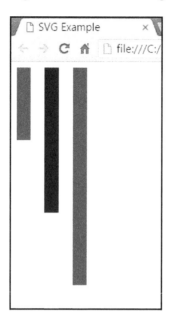

An important note to keep in mind is that within SVG an increase in the value of the *x* and *y* axes will increase x to the right quadrant as expected, but will also increase y to the bottom quadrant and not the top quadrant. This is contrary to what we were taught in grade school for mathematics. There are ways to account for this and we will address this later on in the chapter.

Adding SVG shapes the D3 way

Just as we were previously able to add an extra paragraph in the previous example using D3, we will do the same by adding a fourth bar to the three existing bar charts.

As we can see in the three original SVG elements, each one has a specific `height`, `width`, `x` value, and `y` value. These are all known as attributes and have an `attr` extension. Additionally, they are given a color, which is assigned by a `fill` method. As we did previously when adding a new paragraph, we will select the current `body` and `SVG` components and add a new `rect` object that will be appended to the existing structure, as seen in the following script inside of the body:

```
var newBarRectangle = d3.select("body").select("svg")
        .append("rect")
```

```
.attr("x", 120)
.attr("y", 0)
.attr("width", 20)
.attr("height", 400)
.attr("fill", "purple");
```

In addition to appending the new object to the existing SVG elements, attributes have been added for the height, width, *x* axis, and *y* axis, as well as a purple color for the new bar using the `fill` attribute.

The complete script is as follows:

```
<!DOCTYPE html>
<html>
<head>
<script src="d3.js" charset="utf-8"></script>
  <meta charset="utf-8">
  <meta name="viewport" content="width=device-width">
  <title>SVG Example</title>
</head>
<body>

  <svg width="500" height="500">
  <rect x="0" y="0" width="20" height="100" fill="red" />
  <rect x="40" y="0" width="20" height="200" fill="blue" />
  <rect x="80" y="0" width="20" height="300" fill="green" />
  </svg>
<script>

var newBarRectangle = d3.select("body").select("svg")
                        .append("rect")
                        .attr("x", 120)
                        .attr("y", 0)
                        .attr("width", 20)
                        .attr("height", 400)
                        .attr("fill", "purple");
</script>
</body>
</html>
```

When previewing the existing code, the updated bar chart with a purple fourth bar appears at the rightmost end, as seen in the following screenshot:

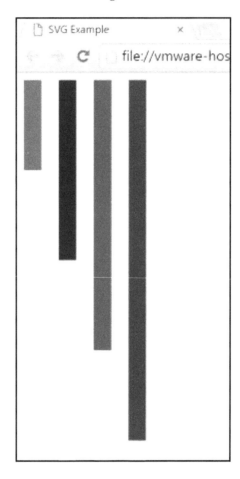

While inspecting the elements of the updated browser with the new purple bar (the rightmost bar), we find that a fourth rectangular bar has been seamlessly added to the existing three bars with the same attribute formatting. The element inspection for the new SVG group can be seen in this screenshot:

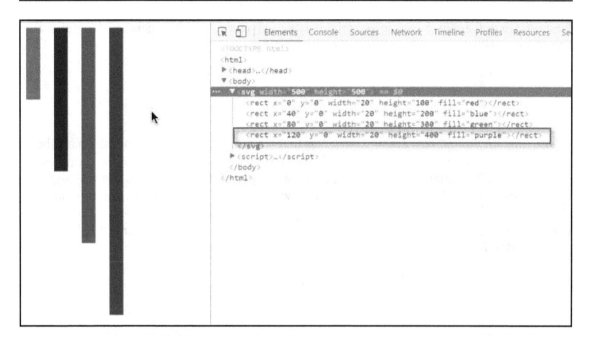

Again we see that D3 can manipulate existing documents by selecting elements within HTML and appending additional specific attributes to those elements. The method of adding attributes one after another is known as *chaining*, and it is useful because it saves time and simplifies code syntax by eliminating the need to write out multiple lines.

Blending D3 and data

The ultimate goal with any visualization is to incorporate actual data elements within the components. Earlier examples showed D3 elements with data points set up inside of the attributes. The next example will highlight creating the same visualization of four bar charts while assigning the height to a variable.

Visualizing hardcoded data

We will start with a new blank template for D3, with only a `<body>` tag and a `<script>` tag. All coding will now be inside the `<script>` tag.

First off, we will assign a couple of variables that will come into play as we put together the bar chart:

```
var svgHeight = 500;
var svgWidth = 500;
var barHeight = [100,200,300,400];
var barDistance = 25;
```

`svgHeight` and `svgWidth` are two variables that we will use to create dimensions for the canvas that we will be working with inside of the browser. Similar to previous examples, it will be a 500 x 500 square. The `barHeight` variable is the data that we will use to assign a specific height to the bars. As we previously saw, we had four bars comprising our bar chart, with each bar being 100 px more than the previous one. Finally, `barDistance` is the variable we will use to create the distance between each bar. Since each bar is 20 pixels in width, that will give us 5 pixels between each bar for some breathing room.

```
var svgBox = d3.select("body").append("svg")
        .attr("height", svgHeight)
        .attr("width", svgWidth);
```

We have created a variable, `svgBox`, that will append an SVG canvas to the body of the page with both height and width 500 px each:

```
var bars = svgBox.selectAll("rect")
        .data(barHeight)
        .enter()
        .append("rect")
        .attr("y", 0)
        .attr("x", 0)
        .attr("height", 100)
        .attr("width", 20)
        .attr("fill", "red");
```

We are now introducing a new function called `selectAll()`, which works similarly to `select()` with some minor differences. The `select()` function only allows us to make changes to one element at a time, which is fine if that is our intent. However, in this exercise, we want to make changes to all of the `rect` elements at once by calling them into our `svgBox` and assigning them attributes. This is where the `selectAll()` functions is more convenient to use. The prior code now assigns a new `rect` SVG element for each element of data in our `barHeight` array. We also assign an x and y value of 0 and a `width` and `height` of 20 and 100 px each. Each bar chart is given the same red color. The visual for the previous code can be seen in the following screenshot:

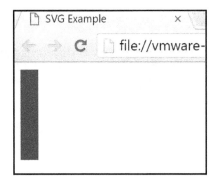

What happened? We have only one bar even though we assigned four data point in our `barHeight` array. Shouldn't we have four bars? Did we do something wrong? We can inspect the elements further to see what is causing this to happen:

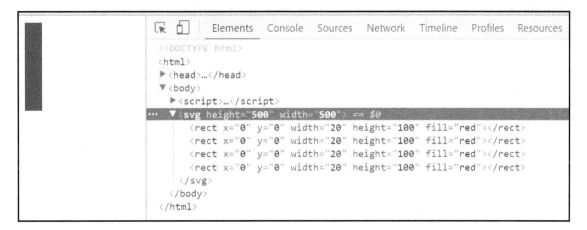

While there are indeed four `rect` SVG shapes attached to the SVG canvas, since they all have the same height and width it appears to the eye as if there is only one bar instead of four. The four bars are superimposed on top of one another. In order to fix this, we will need to apply a JavaScript function into the positioning of the *x* axis as well as to the height of each bar.

D3 and JavaScript functions

JavaScript functions allow us to position the bars at different points along the x axis with varying heights:

```
var bars = svgBox.selectAll("rect")
        .data(barHeight)
        .enter()
        .append("rect")
        .attr("x", function(d,a){
           return a*barDistance;})
        .attr("y", 0)
        .attr("width", 20)
        .attr("height", function(d){
           return d;});
```

We have now replaced the static location of the *x* axis as well as the static height of each bar with an *anonymous* function in JavaScript to return values based on assigned variables.

 To learn more about functions in JavaScript, visit the following website: http://www.w3schools.com/js/js_function_definition.asp.

We first modified the attribute of the *x* axis to be the value of the index denoted as a and multiplied by `barDistance`, which we set at 25 px for each one of the data points, d. This will grant us some separation between each bar and they will no longer be stacked up against each other. Additionally, we added a function of the height attribute to just return the value of each data point, d, as the value for the height of each bar. The visual for the previous code can be seen in the following screenshot:

Reversing the y axis

This is beginning to look similar to our previous bar charts. However, we are still dealing with an upside-down chart that we would like to flip. This requires a slight modification to the *y* axis attribute. We don't want the *y* axis to start at the same point each time, but we do need to end at the same point. This is where the SVG canvas comes into play. We know that the height of the canvas is 500 px, so if we take the first of the four bars as an example, it should start at *y* axis equal to 400 and then end at the 500th pixel. Similarly, for the second bar, it will start at the 300th pixel and end at the 500th.

We can create a function for this by using this formula:

```
y = svgHeight - d
```

We can then replace our old attribute for the *y* axis with the following instead:

```
.attr("y", function(d){return svgHeight-d;})
```

Once the *y* axis attribute has been updated, the bar chart looks like this:

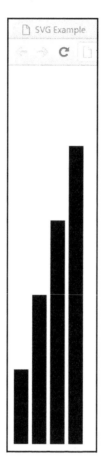

It is now beginning to look a lot more like a vertical bar chart or column chart.

Adding some color

We can continue to customize the bar chart using the four colors we assigned previously by applying a function to the fill attribute of each bar. This can be performed with an `if...then...else` function. The function can be chained to the end of our latest code, as follows:

```
var bars = svgBox.selectAll("rect")
    .data(barHeight)
    .enter()
```

```
.append("rect")
.attr("x", function(d,a){
  return a*barDistance;})
.attr("y", function(d){
  return svgHeight-d;})
.attr("width", 20)
.attr("height", function(d){
  return d;})
.attr("fill", function(d){
  var barColor;
  if (d==100) {barColor = 'red';
  } else if (d==200) {barColor = 'blue';
  } else if (d==300) {barColor = 'green';
  } else {barColor = 'purple';}
  return barColor;});
```

Once the fill function has been applied, the bar chart appears as shown in the following screenshot:

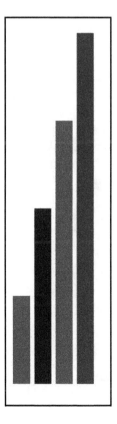

Labeling

Our bar chart is almost complete! Since we are dealing with data, it would be helpful if we could assign actual values to the bars to offer some additional information. These labels are appended to the bar chart as `text` elements similarly to the way we added the `rect` elements to the browser.

Underneath the code for the bars will be the following code for the bar texts:

```
var barTexts = svgBox.selectAll("text")
        .data(barHeight)
        .enter()
        .append("text")
        .text(function(d){return d;})
        .attr("x", function(d,a){
          return a*barDistance;})
        .attr("y", function(d){
          return svgHeight-d+10;})
        .style("font-size", "12px")
        .style("fill", "white");
```

A variable for `barTexts` is created and `text` elements are selected and called into the variable. We then `enter()` the data points that we wish to display on top of each bar and `append()` them as `text` elements. The text is associated with a function that returns the data point, d; and the *x* axis and *y* axis are using similar logic to assign their locations, with the small exception of decreasing the *y* axis by 10 pixels so that the labels show up inside of the bar chart instead of outside. Finally, we make some style additions to the text by setting the color to white and the font size to 12. The updated bar chart will then appear as seen in the following screenshot:

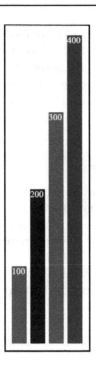

In order to further understand how all the elements play a part in putting together this bar chart, we can inspect the element inside of the browser to get additional details. This can be seen here:

```
    Elements   Console   Sources   Network   Timeline   Profiles   Resources   Securi
<!DOCTYPE html>
<html>
▶ <head>…</head>
▼ <body>
  ▶ <script>…</script>
  ▼ <svg height="500" width="500">
      <rect x="0" y="400" width="20" height="100" fill="red"></rect> == $0
      <rect x="25" y="300" width="20" height="200" fill="blue"></rect>
      <rect x="50" y="200" width="20" height="300" fill="green"></rect>
      <rect x="75" y="100" width="20" height="400" fill="purple"></rect>
      <text x="0" y="410" style="font-size: 12px; fill: white;">100</text>
      <text x="25" y="310" style="font-size: 12px; fill: white;">200</text>
      <text x="50" y="210" style="font-size: 12px; fill: white;">300</text>
      <text x="75" y="110" style="font-size: 12px; fill: white;">400</text>
    </svg>
  </body>
</html>
```

We can now see that, inside our SVG canvas, we have eight elements: four rectangular bars and four text labels comprising the completed bar chart. All of these elements are contained within the 500 px x 500 px SVG canvas. Additionally, we can see that each `text` element has a *y* value that is 10 pixels greater than its `rect` element counterpart. This allows for the text to appear inside of the bar chart as opposed to outside.

Fusing D3 and CSV

Now that we have some background on how to create components with D3 using hardcoded data in variables, we can continue the process by developing D3 components against data in a CSV file. In order to do so, there are two architectural matters that will need to be addressed before any type of development begins:

- Creating and exporting a CSV file to a desired location
- Establishing a server to connect the CSV file to an HTML file to be leveraged by D3

Preparing the CSV file

In `Chapter 2`, *Web Scraping*, we scraped data from a GitHub website, which was extracted to a CSV file and then uploaded to MS SQL Server. The file was called `DiscountCodebyWeek` and contained the following three columns:

- Index
- WeekInYear
- DiscountCode

When the data was originally scraped using R, the contents made it to a CSV file. We can use that same CSV file as our source for this exercise, or we can copy the data from the MS SQL Server database and use that version instead. Either method is fine. Once the data has been secured into a CSV file, all that remains is to save the file into the same folder that has the D3 JavaScript files as well as the HTML file.

Setting up a web server

In order to connect any D3 HTML file with CSV data, we need to set up a basic server. Python gives us the ability to set up a server rather quickly without much architecture, and since we have already installed Python in `Chapter 2`, *Web Scraping* (in the *Downloading and installing Python* section), we will use it as our web server of choice.

There is an option to bypass a web server completely but it requires placing the data directly on a website and then referencing the data as a web link, thereby bypassing any server setup on your end and leveraging the server capabilities of the website. This has its pros and cons. The benefit is that you have less work to build the infrastructure on your end. The drawback is that you are at the mercy of the security and the resources of the website.

If for some reason Python is not an option to set up a server for D3, another popular web server is MAMP. More information about MAMP can be found by visiting the following website: `https://www.mamp.info/en/`.

In order to set up a Python server in Windows, we first navigate to the folder that has the CSV file, and right-click and press *Shift* inside of the folder to get the command window to appear, as seen in the following screenshot:

This is not the only way to open the command window; however, it saves steps by not having to change directories when opening the command window from the default location. We need to run the Python server from the same folder location as the existing one containing the CSV file as well as the D3 scripts.

Once the command window is opened, we can type this:

```
python -m http.server 8000
```

Once the server has connected, a message displaying Serving HTTP on 0.0.0.0 port 8000 ... should pop up inside of the command window, as seen in the following screenshot:

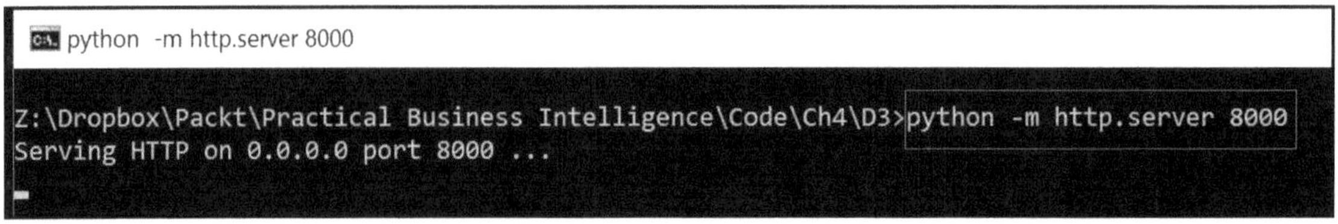

To verify that the Python server is running, create a simple HTML file inside of the same folder and name it index.html.

We can type a simple statement inside of a paragraph tag, such as the following:

```
<!DOCTYPE html>
<html>
<head>
<script src="d3.js" charset="utf-8"></script>
  <meta charset="utf-8">
  <meta name="viewport" content="width=device-width">
  <title>Python Server</title>
</head>
<body>
<p>The Python Server is Running!</p>
</body>
</html>
```

We can then navigate to the following website to see the paragraph displayed: http://localhost:8000.

If the server is running successfully, then the **The Python Server is Running!** message should appear:

Testing the web server

The next sanity check once we have the Python server running is to test that we can connect to the CSV file and view the numbers that we would expect to see. D3 has the ability to load the following file types:

- **Comma-Separated Values (CSV)**
- **Tab-Separated Values (TSV)**
- **JavaScript Object Notation (JSON)**

For purposes of our example we will be loading a CSV file and the D3 method for loading CSV is called d3.csv(). Within the <script> tags, we will insert the following code to bind the two columns for WeekInYear and DiscountCode to arrays and then view the output of the arrays using the console.log() function:

```
d3.csv("DiscountCodebyWeek.csv", function (data) {
  discountData = data.map(function (d) {
    return +d.DiscountCode ;
  });
  weekData = data.map(function (d) {
    return +d.WeekInYear ;
  });
  console.log(discountData);
  console.log(weekData);
  console.log(data);
});
```

JavaScript is not particular about using single versus double quotes within its syntax; however, for better performance and consistency it is recommended to stick with one format over the other. For the purposes of this chapter, we will be employing double quotes as much as possible within in the `<script>` syntax.

The `console.log()` function allows us to view our data results as output in the console of a browser inspector. Once we save this into our `index.html` file, we can navigate to the browser to view the file within the `localhost:8000` site. When we inspect the elements and click over to the console, we should see the data results in an array, as seen in the following screenshot:

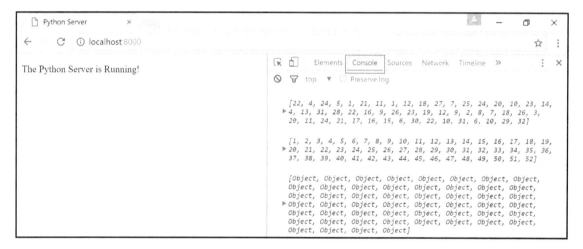

There are three separate arrays. The one on top is the `discount` array, the middle one is the `Week` array, and the bottom one is the entire dataset. There should be 52 object elements inside of each array. Each one represents a week in the year coming from the dataset. If the bottom array is expanded, we can view the actual points for the first week, as seen in this screenshot:

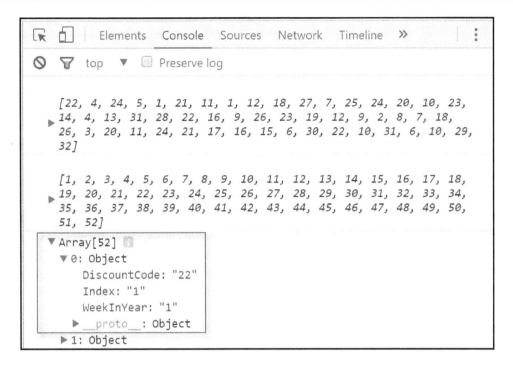

We can now see that, for `Array[0]`, which is the first position in the array, the `DiscountCode = 22`. This is a good sign because we know that the discount for the first week is indeed 22. This is a confirmation that we have successfully connected our CSV file to the HTML page via the Python web server.

Developing a bar chart with CSV data

We are almost ready to begin visualizing actual data with D3. But before we do so, we want to establish an HTML structure that is convenient for us to insert and remove components as we please. The following HTML layout provides that necessary structure for us:

```
<!DOCTYPE html>
<html>
<head>
<script src="d3.js" charset="utf-8"></script>
  <meta charset="utf-8">
  <meta name="viewport" content="width=device-width">
  <title>D3.js Charts</title>

  <style>
    body {
```

```
      background-color: white;
      font-family: Helvetica;
    }
    h1 {
      font-size: 24px;
      font-family:sans-serif;
    }
    p {
      font-size: 20px;
      font-family:sans-serif;
    }
    .axis path{
      fill: none;
      stroke: #000;
    }

    .axis text {
      font-family: sans-serif;
      font-size: 10px;
      stroke: #000;
    }
  </style>
</head>
<body>

<div>
<h1>AdventureWorks Discounts 2016</h1>
<p>Discount Percent by Week  </p>

<script>
//Insert D3.js script here
</script>

</div>

</body>
</html>
```

Inside of the div element we have a comment denoted by a // that guides us to where we should insert our D3 code. Anything that follows a // will not be considered as part of the scripting language and will be ignored. When we view the updated index.html file, we should see the following in our browser:

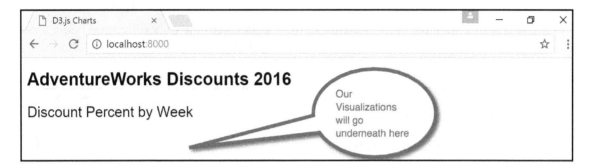

We have assigned the title of **D3.js Charts** to the web page, **AdventureWorks Discounts 2016** as a primary header, and **Discount Percent by Week** as a paragraph header.

We can now insert the following D3 code between the <script> tags in our HTML layout:

```
//begin script
d3.csv("DiscountCodebyWeek.csv", function (data) {
  discountData =  data.map(function (d) {
    return +d.DiscountCode; });
  weekData =  data.map(function (d) {
    return +d.WeekInYear; });
  var w= 750;
  var h = 200;
  var padding = 20;
  var barChartIncrements = 1;

  var svg = d3.select("body")
            .append("svg")
            .attr("width", w)
            .attr("height", h)
            .style("fill", "steelblue")
  svg.selectAll("rect")
        .data(discountData)
        .enter()
        .append("rect")
        .attr("x", function(d, i) {
          return i * (w / discountData.length);
          })
        .attr("y",function(d){
          return h-d - padding-2; })
```

```
            .attr("width", w / discountData.length - barChartIncrements)
            .attr("height", function(d) {
                return d; });
        //close script
    });
```

This code is similar to what we did earlier in the chapter with the only difference being we are using CSV data instead of hardcoded data. When we go to preview the layout in the browser, we see the following:

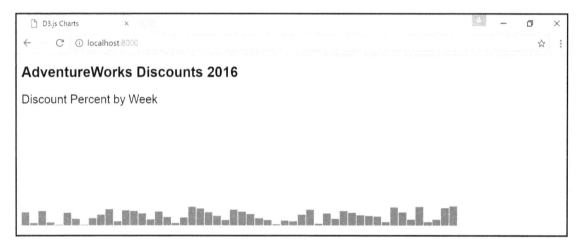

At first glance, the data seems to be accurate, but it never hurts to inspect the elements and make sure the appropriate values are mapped correctly, as seen in the following:

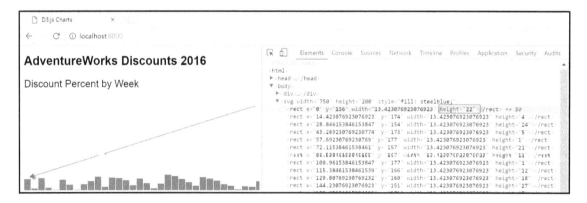

We see that the first `rect` element selected has an *x* value of 0 and a *y* value of 156. This makes sense since the **height** of the `rect` is 22 and the height set for the `svg` canvas is 200. Additionally, we have set aside an additional 20 pixels for padding as well as 2 pixels for scaling purposes that we will get to later on. Since *200 – 22 – 20 – 2* is *156,* we can confirm that the values are accurate. It never hurts to perform a sanity check on the data with the elements to confirm the math is correct.

One more thing to note is that the bar heights are a bit short. We can increase the heights by a factor of 5 by updating the following script:

```
d3.csv("DiscountCodebyWeek.csv", function (data) {
    discountData = data.map(function (d) {
        return +d.DiscountCode;});
```

To this:

```
d3.csv("DiscountCodebyWeek.csv", function (data) {
    discountData = data.map(function (d) {
        return +d.DiscountCode*5;});
```

After executing the script our new bar chart looks like the following:

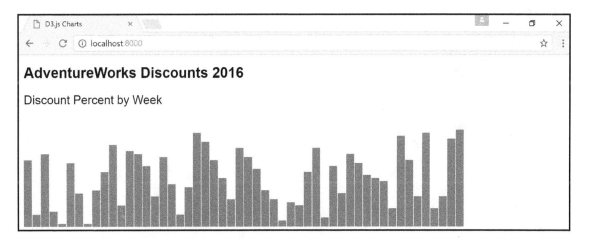

Our bar chart is coming along but we need some additional features that can explain what's going on. At the moment all we have is a bunch of rectangles stacked next to each other. One thing we can do is add some labels to the top of each bar by inserting the following script just above the part that says `//close script`:

```
svg.selectAll("text")
   .data(discountData)
   .enter()
   .append("text")
   .text(function(d) {
     return d/5;
   })
   .attr("x", function(d, i) {
     return i * (w / discountData.length);
   })
   .attr("y", function(d) {
     return h - d -padding -4;
   })
   .attr("font-size", "10px")
   .attr("text-anchor", "left")
   .style("fill", "black");
```

When we preview the new code in the browser we see the following:

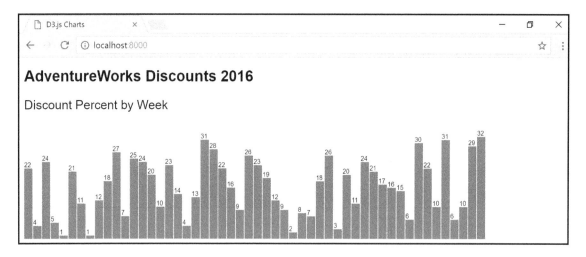

Notice that we needed to divide the value of the text of the discount by 5 to return the value to the original amount.

```
.text(function(d) {
    return d/5;
})
```

While we want the value multiplied by 5 for visual purposes, we wish to keep the original value amount for reporting purposes as part of the labeling.

Our bar chart is starting to look like something more than just a set of rectangles. We can now associate absolute values to each bar on the chart. The last thing that we are missing is a scale for the *x* axis to indicate the week of the year. Fortunately, once again we find that D3 has a function that handles linear scales, `d3.scale.linear()`. We can once again accomplish this by inserting the following script just above the part that says `//close script`:

```
var xScale = d3.scale.linear()
                .range([0,w])
                .domain([1,d3.max(weekData)]);
var xAxis = d3.svg.axis()
                .scale(xScale)
                .orient("bottom");
svg.append("g")
    .attr("transform", "translate(0,"+(h-padding)+")")
    .attr("class", "axis")
    .call(xAxis);
```

After formatting the scale and making sure the labels are aligned properly with the `rects`, we can view the final output:

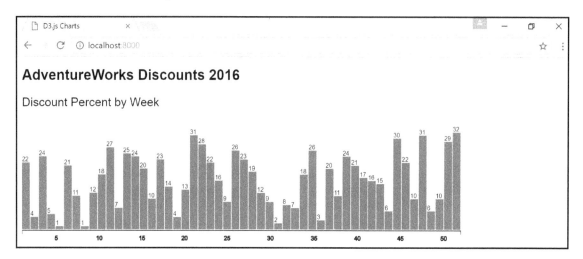

There you have it! Our very own bar chart built with the D3 JavaScript library! We now have a bar chart with text labels and an *x* axis to guide users with regard to **Discount Percent by Week** throughout the entire year. We are able to identify peaks and valleys. One of the advantages to working with D3 is that the visualization is already in a deployable medium for user consumption. Anyone who can access the web server can immediately view the visualization that you have developed for them.

The code is now complete and can be saved as an `index.html` file. The `index` is considered the default page of a website; therefore, it is not inherently necessary to include it inside the link. If a different name were given to the file, such as `chart1.html`, then in order to view that page inside of the server, you would need to navigate to `http://localhost:8000/chart1.html`.

Our bar chart could always be further customized. We have only scratched the surface and so much has been developed in the few years that D3 has been around. However, for the purpose of this chapter, our focus was to get comfortable with pulling data into D3 components and visualizing them.

Summary

This chapter was very heavy with JavaScript and HTML coding and may seem a bit of an overkill at first. However, the process of breaking down individual functions and uses of D3 was done intentionally to ease developers into understanding the basic building blocks that comprise a D3 visualization. While at first it may seem that there is a significant volume of coding needed for a simple visualization, the ability to customize any level of a component will become more valuable as your comfort with D3 increases.

In addition, many templates for D3 are available on D3js (`https://d3js.org/`) and can be used and manipulated with existing data to view new visualizations without needing to understand the underlying code up front. Once a specific need arises within the visualization, there can be modifications of the code, and that is where the understanding of the architecture of D3 will come into play. This is how the D3 community has grown so quickly in such a short amount of time.

While this book dedicates only a single chapter to D3.js, there are many publications out there that dive much deeper into the endless possibilities of D3 visualizations. A few of them are listed here:

- *Data Visualization with d3.js* by Swizec Teller
  (`https://www.packtpub.com/web-development/data-visualization-d3js`)
- *D3.js by Example* by Michael Heydt
  (`https://www.packtpub.com/web-development/d3js-example`)
- *Mastering D3.js* by Pablo Navarro Castillo
  (`https://www.packtpub.com/web-development/mastering-d3js`)
- *Interactive Data Visualization for the Web* by Scott Murray
  (`http://alignedleft.com/work/d3-book`)

In the next chapter, we will expand our focus from bar chart to line chart visualizations developed in R. Developing in R gives us the added benefit of incorporating the forecasting and predictive capabilities of R into line charts and time series.

5
Forecasting with R

R is a popular programming language for statisticians and data scientists. This is primarily due to its popularity with students and professors in the academic world. R is a free and open source language that can be taught in any statistics class with minimal difficulty.

Within the last couple of years, R has creeped into the business intelligence landscape due to the integration of R with enterprise and desktop visualization tools such as Microsoft Power BI and Tableau. During this same period, many academics transitioned from research into the corporate world, and with them came their knowledge of R. While R is known for its predictive capabilities, many are surprised to find that it is a great visualization tool with many libraries, made available by its vast community, such as `ggplot2`.

In addition to the influx of R into the workforce, the introduction of RStudio into the market in 2011 brought added exposure to R. As we noted earlier in `Chapter 2`, *Web Scraping*, RStudio is the IDE of choice for R. Those who are comfortable writing R code within the original editor will not find much difference in writing that same code within RStudio. The difference will lie in presenting results from R to those who need them. Reports for business analysis require a specific format that eliminates or minimizes technical jargon and emphasizes the business aspects of data and information. RStudio has a feature called *R Markdown* that quickly formats technical code into a business-friendly output for reports.

R is also frequently integrated with existing business intelligence tools such as Microsoft Power BI. This is primarily due to, once again, the popular forecasting and predictive packages R has to offer. Therefore, existing R code built outside a particular BI tool can reproduce similar results based on new data consumed by that same BI tool.

In this chapter, we will cover the following topics:

- Configuring an ODBC connection
- Connecting R to a SQL query
- Profiling dataframes in R
- Creating graphs in R
- Time series forecasting in R
- Formatting and publishing code using R Markdown
- Exporting R to Microsoft Power BI

Configuring an ODBC connection

As with all BI tools, our first task will be connecting to data. This process can be accomplished using an ODBC connection. In order to do so, we need to first configure our 64-bit ODBC connection for our SQL Server instance.

ODBC connections can be found in the following location within a typical Windows environment: `C:\ProgramData\Microsoft\Windows\Start Menu\Programs\Administrative Tools`.

Once you've clicked on the ODBC 64-bit connection, select the **System DSN** tab, as seen in the following screenshot:

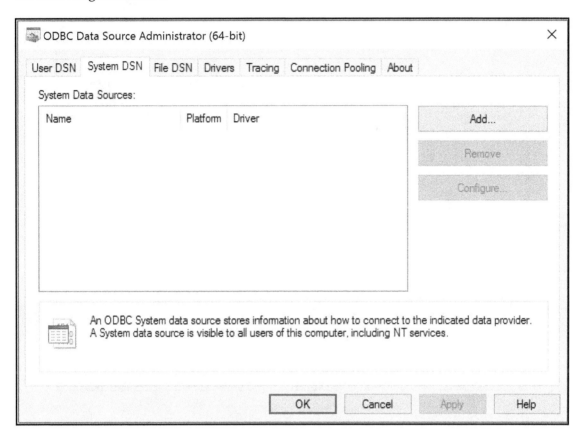

The next step is to create a new connection by clicking on the **Add** button and then selecting the **SQL Server** driver, as seen here:

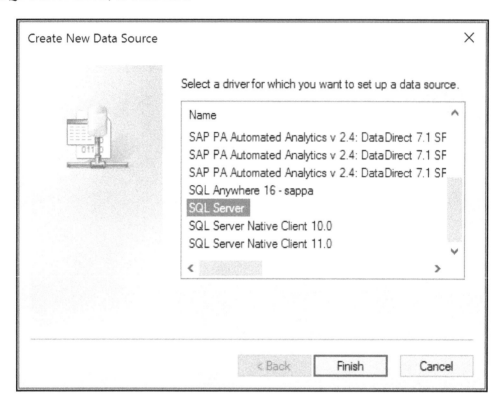

Next we will assign a name to the SQL Server data source. For our purposes, we will name the connection as well as the description as SQLBI, and we will add the server name to complete the configuration process, as seen in the following screenshot:

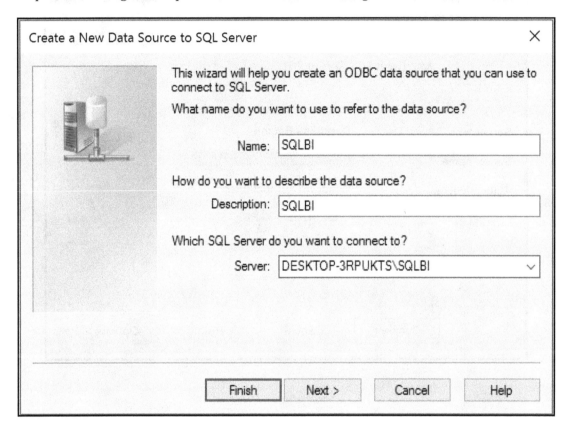

The server name can always be obtained from the login to SQL Server Management Studio, as seen here:

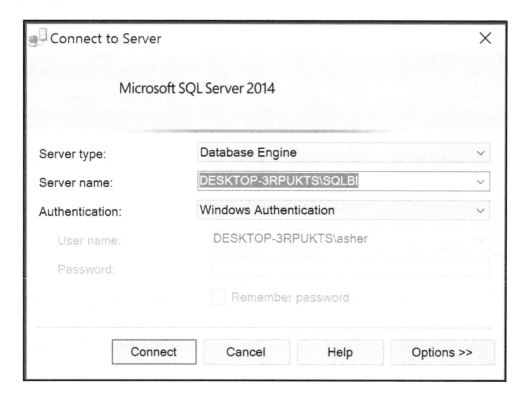

After identifying the server name, the next step is to verify the authenticity of the SQL Server login with either **Windows NT authentication** or **SQL Server authentication**. For our purposes, we will verify with **Windows NT authentication**, as seen in the following screenshot:

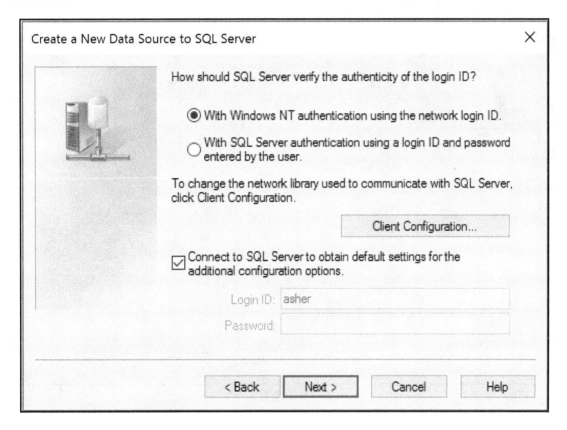

Once the verification is complete, we can assign a default database to our connection. For our purposes, our database is **AdventureWorks2014**:

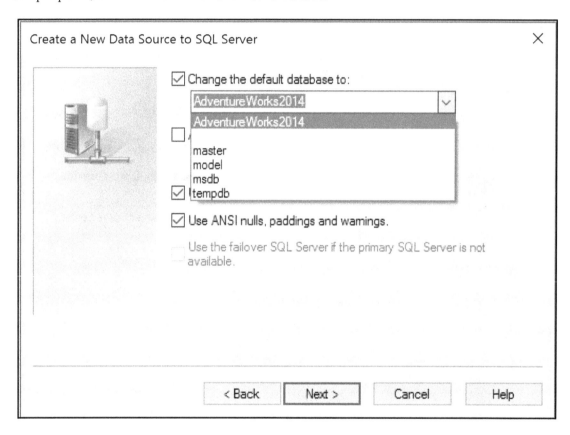

The final configuration message is reserved for language and log file location settings. These can be set to the preference of the user, as seen in the following screenshot:

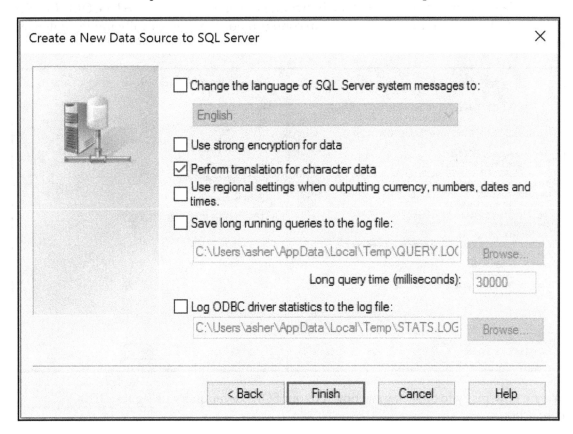

At this point, we can click on the **Finish** button and we are ready to test our connection. The **Setup** message will indicate all the parameters selected during the configuration process and displays a button called **Test Data Source....** If the message says **TESTS COMPLETED SUCCESSFULLY!**, it means the connection configuration was successfully implemented, as shown here:

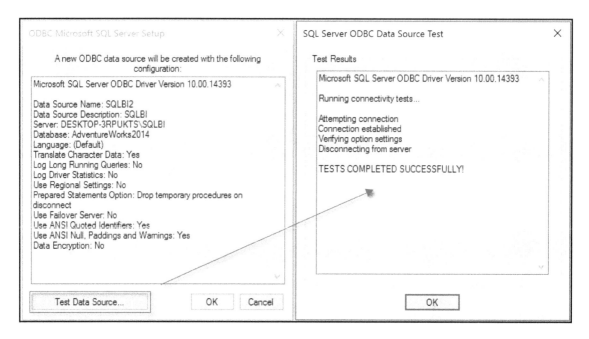

We are now ready to begin connecting R to our SQL Server query using the ODBC connection.

Connecting R to a SQL query

R has a package called `RODBC` that provides access to databases through an ODBC interface. We will continue to use RStudio as our IDE of choice for R. We first run scripts to install and call the `RODBC` library:

```
install.packages('RODBC')
library('RODBC')
```

The next step is to create an R connection that will link to the SQLBI OBDC connection we just created:

```
connection_SQLBI<-odbcConnect('SQLBI')
```

If we are interested in obtaining the connection details for the connection, we can run the following script:

```
connection_SQLBI
```

The output is the parameters for the connection, as seen in the following screenshot:

```
> connection_SQLBI
RODBC Connection
Details:
  case=nochange
  DSN=SQLBI
  Description=SQLBI
  UID=
  Trusted_Connection=Yes
  APP=RStudio
  WSID=DESKTOP-3RPUKTS
  DATABASE=AdventureWorks2014
```

Profiling dataframes in R

We will revisit the same dataset from Chapter 4, *Creating Bar Charts with D3.js*; however, this time it will be retrieved using a SQL statement as opposed to a CSV file. The following SQL statement will return the same data for discount codes by week:

```
SELECT [WeekInYear]
     , [DiscountCode]
  FROM [AdventureWorks2014].[dbo].[DiscountCodebyWeek]
```

We can incorporate this same SQL statement inside of a *dataframe* within R by using the following script:

```
SQL_Query_1<-sqlQuery(connection_SQLBI,
         'SELECT [WeekInYear]
         , [DiscountCode]
         FROM [AdventureWorks2014].[dbo].[DiscountCodebyWeek]' )
```

A dataframe is merely a dataset organized by columns, and the simplest way to get the results of a dataframe is to execute the following script, which will return the first six rows of the dataset:

```
head(SQL_Query_1)
```

In addition to retrieving the first few rows of the dataset, we can identify the structure of the dataset by executing the following script:

```
str(SQL_Query_1)
```

The structure function will return the structure type, number of rows, and variables of the dataset.

After confirming the structure of our dataset, we can begin making some modifications to it, such as renaming the column names to `Week` and `Discount`, by executing the following script:

```
colnames(SQL_Query_1)<- c("Week", "Discount")
```

We will need to convert our `Week` column into an integer from a factor to make logical sense while graphing the dataset. A factor datatype is treated as a character and cannot be graphed as a number until it is converted into a numeric datatype. This can be accomplished by creating a new column, by executing the following script:

```
SQL_Query_1$Weeks <- as.numeric(SQL_Query_1$Week)
```

The dataframe now should contain an extra column called `Weeks` and can be seen once we execute this script:

```
head(SQL_Query_1)
```

The results of the new dataframe are shown in the following screenshot:

```
> head(SQL_Query_1)
  Week Discount Weeks
1 "01"       22     1
2 "02"        4     2
3 "03"       24     3
4 "04"        5     4
5 "05"        1     5
6 "06"       21     6
```

We can get rid of the first column, Week, and reverse the order of Discount and Weeks so that Weeks appears to the left of Discount, using the following script:

```
SQL_Query_1<-SQL_Query_1[,-1] #removes first column
SQL_Query_1<-SQL_Query_1[c(2,1)] #reverses columns 1 and 2
head(SQL_Query_1) #previews first six rows
attach(SQL_Query_1) #environment recognizes dataframe innately
```

Creating graphs in R

Once a dataframe has been set up with the necessary column, we can begin to graph the data and explore visualization options.

Creating simple charts with plot() in R

The most basic graph can be generated with the plot() function using the following script:

```
plot(SQL_Query_1, main = 'Discount Code by Week')
```

The output of the script can be seen here:

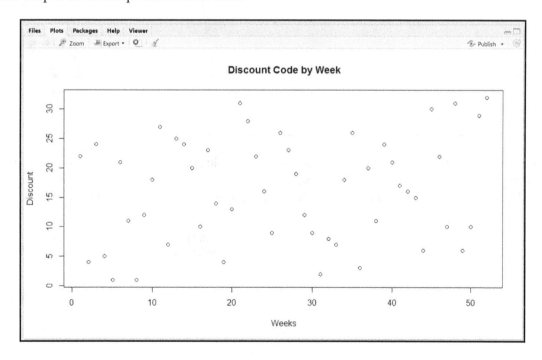

While the plot displays the discount by week, it is difficult to identify the relationship week-to-week without being able to connect the dots.

The following script will connect the dots between each sequential point:

```
plot(SQL_Query_1, main = 'Discount Code by Week', type="o")
```

The output of the script can be seen in the following screenshot:

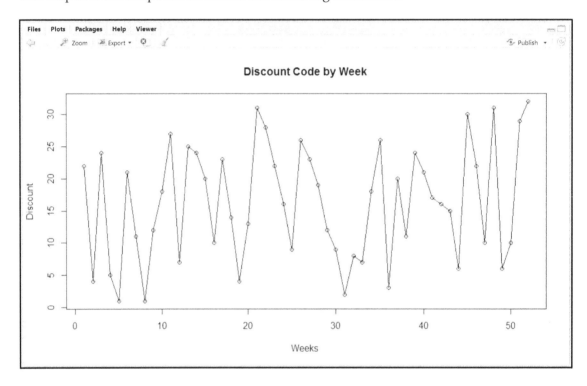

R has the ability to allow developers to combine multiple charts into a larger overall graph by using the par() function. If we choose to display two charts one above the other, we would create a matrix of two rows and one column by running the following script:

```
par(mfrow=c(2,1)) #develops the matrix
plot(SQL_Query_1, main = 'Discount Code by Week')
plot(SQL_Query_1, main = 'Discount Code by Week', type="o")
```

The output of the script can be seen in the following screenshot:

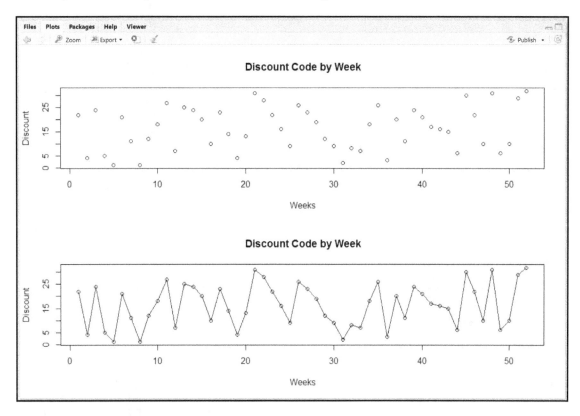

Similarly, if we wished to preview both charts side by side, we would run this script:

```
par(mfrow=c(1,2))
plot(SQL_Query_1, main = 'Discount Code by Week')
plot(SQL_Query_1, main = 'Discount Code by Week', type="o")
```

If we wish to return to the default settings, we just need to run the following script:

```
par(mfrow=c(1,1))
```

Creating advanced charts with ggplot() in R

Building on the previous line chart, we can create gradients of color based on the value of Discount within the line chart. R has a popular plotting library known as ggplot(), which is commonly used to create more complex and elegant charts and graphs with R.

To learn more about the `ggplot()` library for R as well as additional resources to help with designing with `ggplot()`, visit the following website: http://ggplot2.org/.

The following script uses the `ggplot()` function in R to generate a similar line chart plot with a `DiscountCode` legend indicator for the color degree of the line as it relates to the increasing value on the *y* axis:

```
install.packages('ggplot2') #install ggplot() library
library('ggplot2') #call ggplot() library

point_plot <- ggplot(SQL_Query_1, aes(x=jitter(Weeks), y=jitter(Discount),
col=Discount)) +
 geom_line() + geom_point()+
 labs(x="Weeks (1-52)", y="Discount Code", col="Discount Code", )
point_plot + theme_bw()
```

The output of the script can be seen in this screenshot:

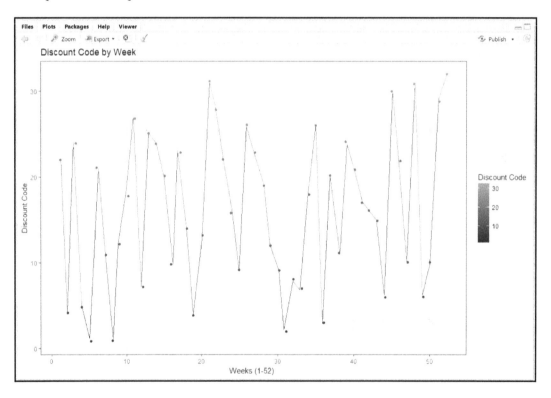

The lighter color shade indicates higher values on the *y* axis while the darker color shade indicates lower values on the *y* axis. The plot uses a black-and-white theme called `theme_bw()`.

 There are several themes available for plots in R; however, the most commonly used ones are `theme_bw()` and `theme_grey()`. To learn more about themes for plots in R, you can execute `help(theme)` inside of the R console.

Creating interactive charts with plot_ly()

R has the ability to create all types of line charts. So far, we have only covered static charts. R also has the ability to create more interactive and beautiful charts with libraries such as `plot_ly()`.

 To learn more about how to use `plot_ly` with R and other languages, visit the following website: `https://plot.ly`.

In order to get started with `plot_ly`, we must first install and call the library using the following script:

```
install.packages('plotly')
library('plotly')
```

We can now graph a simple line chart with `plot_ly()` using this script:

```
plot_ly(data = SQL_Query_1, x = Weeks, y = Discount, type = 'scatter', mode
= 'lines') %>%
layout(title = 'Discount Code by Week',
xaxis = list(title = 'Weeks (1-52)', zeroline = TRUE),
yaxis = list(title = 'Discount Code'))
```

The output of the script can be seen in the following screenshot:

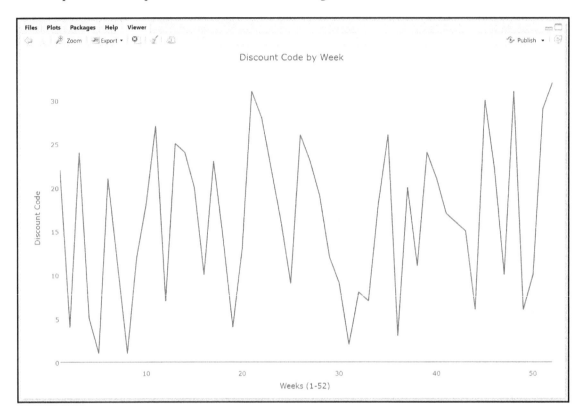

As you hover over any point on the line chart, a mouse-over value will appear as well as a toolbar on the upper right-hand side of the chart to allow you to zoom in and out, scroll left and right, and reset axes, among other activities. The toolbar can be seen in this screenshot:

The initial look of the line chart is similar to the previous versions developed with the `plot()` and `ggplot()` functions in R. We can accentuate the plot by adding a 52-week regression curve that smooths the relationship between points on a week-to-week basis. This function is known as **Locally Weighted Scatterplot Smoother** or **LOWESS**. We can combine the LOWESS curve to our existing line chart into a single visualization by executing the following script:

```
str(p <- plot_ly(SQL_Query_1, x = Weeks, y = Discount,
name = 'Discount',type = 'scatter',  mode = 'lines'))
p %>%
add_trace(y = fitted(loess(Discount ~ Weeks)), x = Weeks,
name = 'Average') %>%
layout(title = 'Discount Code by Week + 52-Week Average',
xaxis = list(title = 'Weeks (1-52)', zeroline = TRUE),
yaxis = list(title = 'Discount Code'))
```

The output of the script can be seen here:

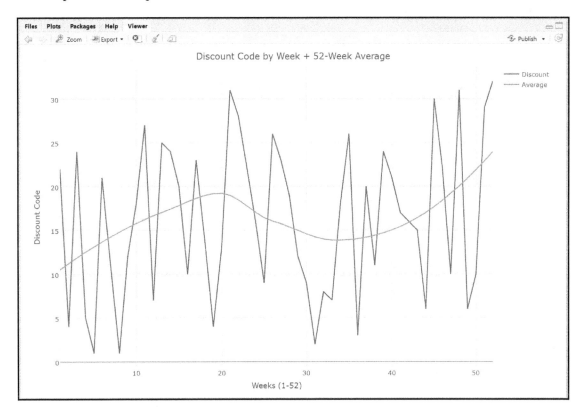

In addition to the line chart produced with `plot_ly`, we can generate a dot plot with `markers` increasing in size and varying in color based on the value of the y-axis using the following script:

```
plot_ly(SQL_Query_1, x = Weeks, y = Discount, mode='markers',
color=Discount, size = Discount)%>%
layout(title = 'Discount Code by Week',
xaxis = list(title = 'Weeks (1-52)', zeroline = TRUE),
yaxis = list(title = 'Discount Code'))
```

The output of the script is as follows:

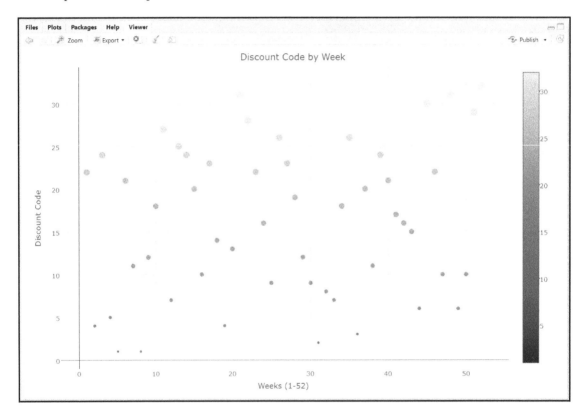

Time series forecasting in R

A time series graph is one that evaluates activity over a period of time. A more specific time series plot can be generated using the `ts()` and `plot.ts()` functions in R, as seen in the following scripts:

```
Query1_TS<-ts(SQL_Query_1$Discount)
plot.ts(Query1_TS, xlab = 'Week (1-52)', ylab = 'Discount', main = 'Time
Series of Discount Code by Week')
```

The output of the time series script can be seen here:

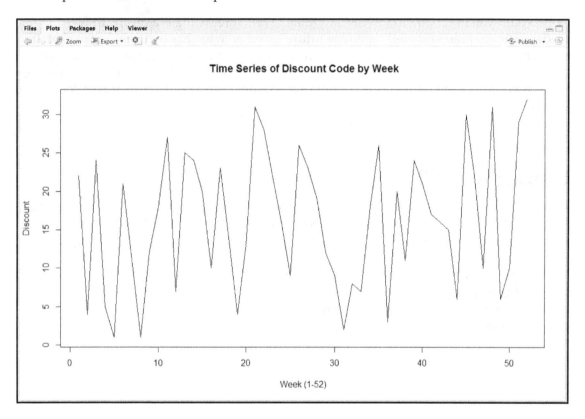

At first glimpse, the time series plot looks no different from earlier line charts developed in this chapter. The difference lies within the inherent qualities of a time series plot, which allows you to view activity over specified intervals over the course of a year. The specified periods can be in hours, days, weeks, months, or even quarters. A time series plot will display *seasonal* activity that repeats around the same time each year. Due to this seasonality, time series plots are strong candidates for forecasting. Let's get a little bit of background on both forecasting and smoothing.

Forecasting 101

Why would you ever want to forecast anything? Well, forecasting is a means to mathematically predict something in the future based on what has occurred in the past. If you can see what is upcoming in your future, then you can be better prepared for it. In our example with discount codes by week, we are trying to forecast what the discount code will be for certain products in the upcoming weeks. By knowing what the discount code may be, we can factor in how much inventory to purchase currently, as opposed to in the future when certain products may be cheaper to purchase.

Smoothing 101

Exponential smoothing is a popular method used to produce a time series while removing any intermittent "noise." This results in a "smoother" line from period to period. In addition to creating a smoother line, different variations of exponential smoothing place a greater emphasis on later time periods than earlier ones when predicting an outcome in the future. This is taking a "what you done for me lately" approach. So, double-exponential smoothing is much better at handling trends than exponential smoothing. Additionally, there is a method known as triple-exponential smoothing, which is known to be even better at handling complex trends.

Forecasting with Holt-Winters

There are several methods for forecasting time series. One common method is known as **Holt-Winters** or **Triple-Exponential Smoothing**. We can incorporate this forecasting method within our time series to extrapolate future time periods (forecasting) as well as to generate a more seamless line between points (smoothing). This script will generate the actual time series plot along with the smoothing line from the Holt-Winters method:

```
discountforecasts <- HoltWinters(Query1_TS, beta=FALSE, gamma=FALSE)
plot(discountforecasts)
```

The output of the script can be seen in the following screenshot:

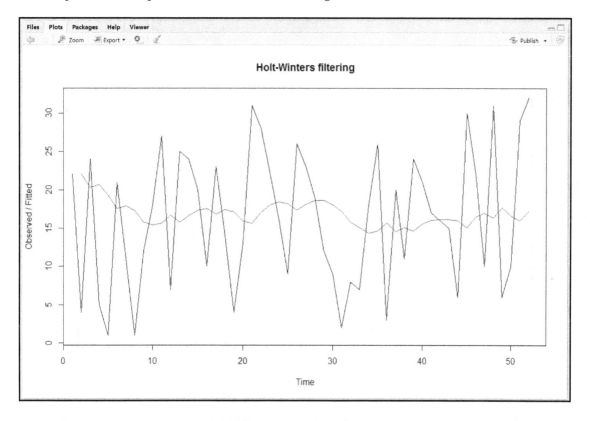

The script to generate the smoothing lines has both the `beta` and `gamma` values set to `FALSE`. The `beta` parameter is used for exponential smoothing when set to `false`. Additionally, the `gamma` parameter is used for seasonal modeling when set to `false` because our model does not have enough data year-on-year to determine if the discount codes are affected by seasonality.

To learn more about the `beta` and `gamma` parameters as well as Holt-Winters forecasting in general within R, execute `?HoltWinters` in the console.

The next step in the Holt-Winters method involves forecasting 2 months of discounts (or 8 periods) based on the previous 52 weeks. This would equate to forecasting eight periods, as seen in the following script:

```
install.packages('forecast')
library('forecast')

discountforecasts_8periods <- forecast.HoltWinters(discountforecasts, h=8)
plot.forecast(discountforecasts_8periods, ylab='Discount', xlab = 'Weeks
(1-60)', main = 'Forecasting 8 periods')
```

The output of the script can be seen here:

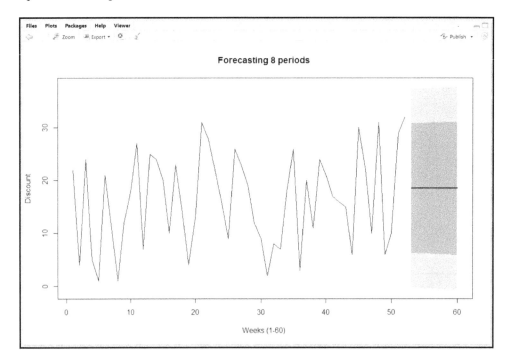

The straight line in the middle of the forecast region represents the mean, with the darker shaded color representing the lower and upper bounds from the mean and the lighter shaded color representing regions closer to the outlier points.

We can compare all three plots using the following script:

```
par(mfrow=c(3,1))

plot.ts(Query1_TS, xlab = 'Week (1-52)', ylab = 'Discount', main = 'Time
Series of Discount Code by Week')

discountforecasts <- HoltWinters(Query1_TS, beta=FALSE, gamma=FALSE)
plot(discountforecasts)

discountforecasts_8periods <- forecast.HoltWinters(discountforecasts, h=8)
plot.forecast(discountforecasts_8periods, ylab='Discount', xlab = 'Weeks
(1-60)', main = 'Forecasting 8 periods')
```

The output of the script is shown here:

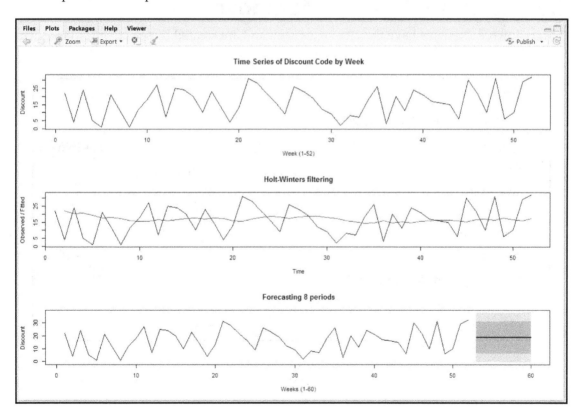

Combining all three charts into one can assist with many features such as standardizing the x axis and allowing for better comparison of patterns.

Formatting and publishing code using R Markdown

We have now reached the part of the chapter where we focus on delivering the fruits of our labor to our consumers, who will take this information back to their users and produce actionable intelligence from it. In order for them to do this, we need to deliver our results inside of a dynamic report. RStudio allows us to do this with *R Markdown*, which is a format that allows for reproducible reports with embedded R code that can be published into slide shows, Word documents, PDF files, and HTML web pages.

Getting started with R Markdown

R Markdown documents have the `.RMD` extension and are created by selecting R Markdown from the menu bar of RStudio, as seen here:

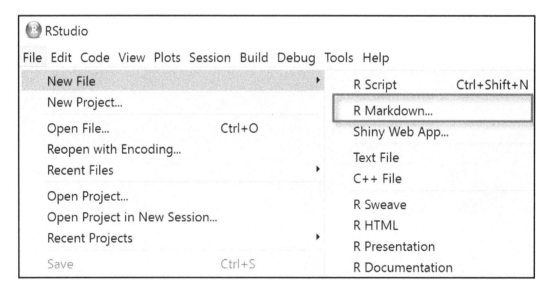

If this is the first time you are creating an R Markdown report, you may be prompted to install some additional packages for R Markdown to work, as seen in the following screenshot:

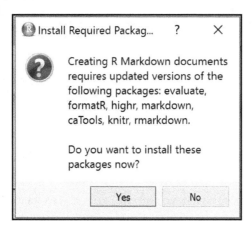

Once the packages are installed, we can define a title, author, and default output format, as follows:

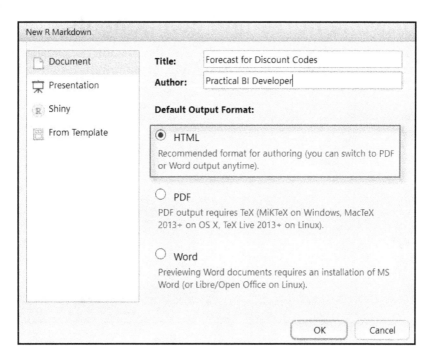

For our purposes we will use **HTML** output. The default output of the R Markdown document will appear like this:

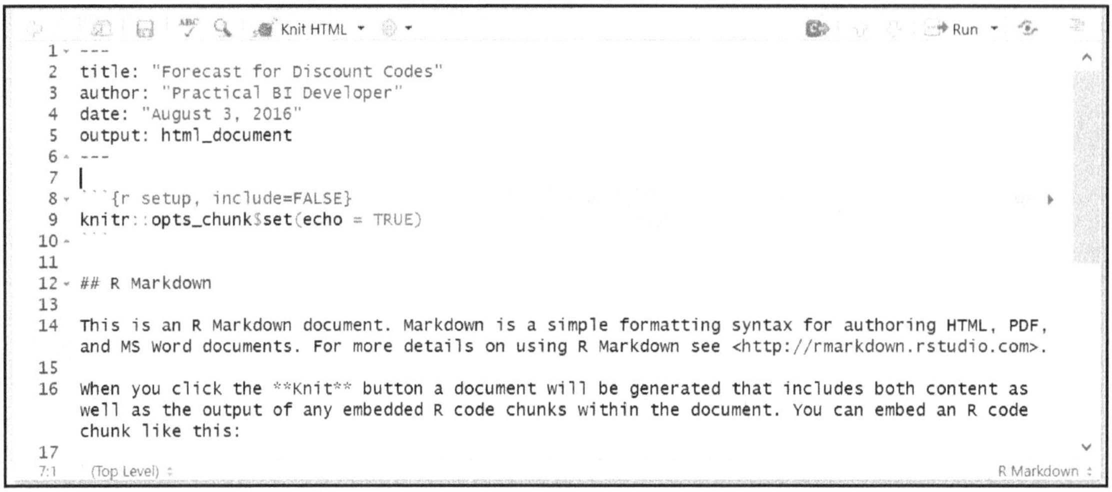

R Markdown features and components

We can go ahead and delete everything below *line 7* in the previous screenshot as we will create our own template with our embedded code and formatting.

Header levels can be generated using # in front of a title. The largest font size will have a single # and each subsequent # added will decrease the header level font. Whenever we wish to embed actual R code into the report, we can include it inside of a code chunk by clicking on the icon shown here:

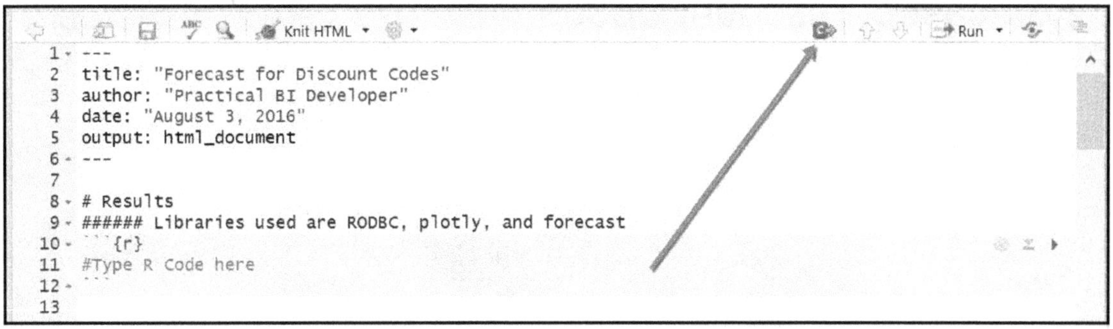

Once that icon is selected, a shaded region is created between two ``` characters where R code can be generated identical to that used in RStudio. The first header generated will be for the results, and then the subsequent header will indicate the libraries used to generate the report. This can be generated using the following script:

```
# Results
###### Libraries used are RODBC, plotly, and forecast
```

Executing R code inside of R Markdown

The next step is to run the actual R code inside of the chunk snippet that calls the required libraries needed to generate the report. This can be generated using the following script:

```
```{r}
# We will not see the actual libraries loaded
# as it is not necessary for the end user
library('RODBC')
library('plotly')
library('forecast')
```
```

We can then click on the **Knit HTML** icon on the menu bar to generate a preview of our code results in R Markdown. Unfortunately, this output of library information is not useful to the end user.

Forecast of Discount Codes

Practical BI Developer

August 3, 2016

Results

Libraries used are RODBC, plotly, and forecast

```
# We will not see the actual libraries loaded
# as it is not necessary for the end user
library('RODBC')
library('plotly')


## Loading required package: ggplot2


##
## Attaching package: 'plotly'


## The following object is masked from 'package:ggplot2':
##
##     last_plot


## The following object is masked from 'package:graphics':
##
##     layout
```

Exporting tips for R Markdown

The report output includes all the messages and potential warnings that are the result of calling a package. This is not information that is useful to the report consumer. Fortunately for R developers, these types of messages can be concealed by tweaking the R chunk snippets to include the following logic in their script:

```
```{r echo = FALSE, results = 'hide', message = FALSE}
```
```

We can continue embedding R code into our report to run queries against the SQL Server database and produce summary data of the dataframe as well as the three main plots for the time series plot, observed versus fitted smoothing, and Holt-Winters forecasting:

```
###### Connectivity to Data Source is through ODBC
```{r echo = FALSE, results = 'hide', message = FALSE}
connection_SQLBI<-odbcConnect("SQLBI")

#Get Connection Details
connection_SQLBI

##query fetching begin##
SQL_Query_1<-sqlQuery(connection_SQLBI,
        'SELECT [WeekInYear]
        ,[DiscountCode]
        FROM [AdventureWorks2014].[dbo].[DiscountCodebyWeek]' )
##query fetching end##

#begin table manipulation
colnames(SQL_Query_1)<- c("Week", "Discount")
SQL_Query_1$Weeks <- as.numeric(SQL_Query_1$Week)
SQL_Query_1<-SQL_Query_1[,-1] #removes first column
SQL_Query_1<-SQL_Query_1[c(2,1)] #reverses columns 1 and 2
#end table manipulation
```

Preview of First 6 rows of data
```{r echo = FALSE, message= FALSE}
head(SQL_Query_1)
```

Summary of Table Observations
```{r echo = FALSE, message= FALSE}
str(SQL_Query_1)
```

Time Series and Forecast Plots
```{r echo = FALSE, message= FALSE}
Query1_TS<-ts(SQL_Query_1$Discount)

par(mfrow=c(3,1))
plot.ts(Query1_TS, xlab = 'Week (1-52)', ylab = 'Discount', main = 'Time
Series of Discount Code by Week')

discountforecasts <- HoltWinters(Query1_TS, beta=FALSE, gamma=FALSE)
plot(discountforecasts)

discountforecasts_8periods <- forecast.HoltWinters(discountforecasts, h=8)
plot.forecast(discountforecasts_8periods, ylab='Discount', xlab = 'Weeks
(1-60)', main = 'Forecasting 8 periods')
```
```

The final output

Before publishing the output with the results, R Markdown offers the developer opportunities to *prettify* the end product. One effect I like to add to a report is a logo of some kind. This can be done by applying the following code to any line in R Markdown:

```
![](http://website.com/logo.jpg) # image is on a website
![](images/logo.jpg)  # image is locally on your machine
```

The first option adds an image from a website, and the second option adds an image locally. For my purposes, I will add a PacktPub logo right above the Results section in the R Markdown, as seen in the following screenshot:

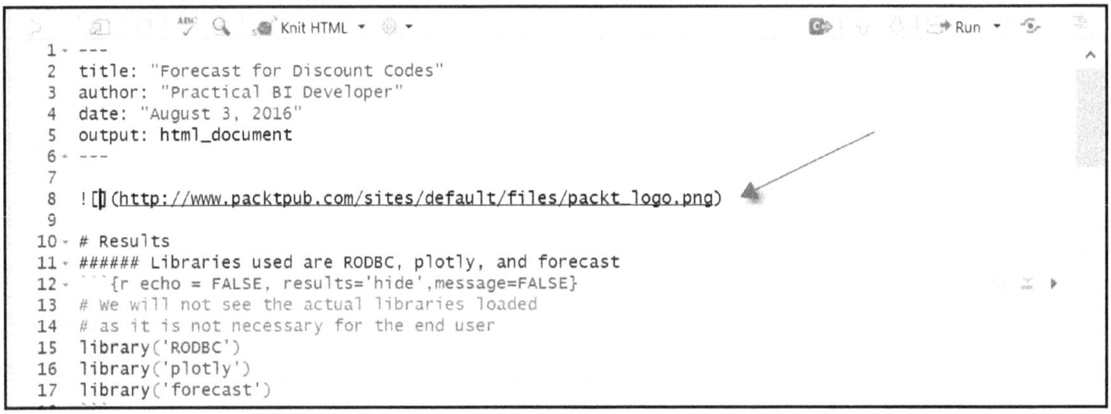

To learn more about customizing an R Markdown document, visit the following website: http://rmarkdown.rstudio.com/authoring_basics.html.

Once we are ready to preview the results of the R Markdown output, we can once again select the **Knit to HTML** button on the menu. The new report can be seen in this screenshot:

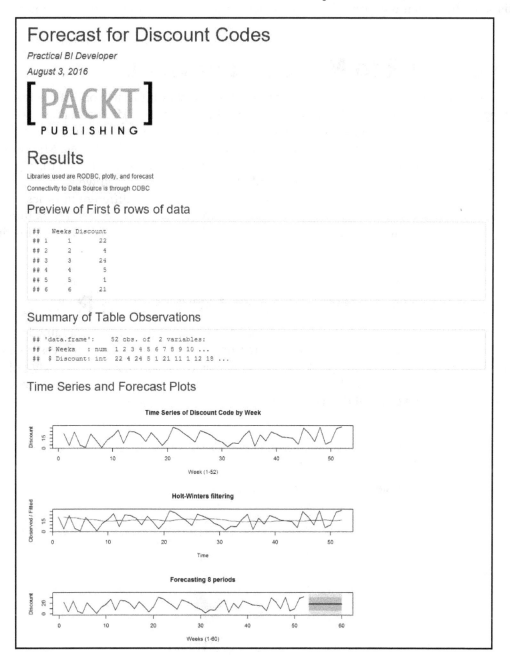

As can be seen in the final output, even if the R code is embedded within the R Markdown document, we can suppress the unnecessary technical output and reveal the relevant tables, fields, and charts that will provide the most benefit to end users and report consumers.

Exporting R to Microsoft Power BI

R is a great standalone tool used to deliver reports to users, but it is also one of the few languages that are incorporated into several other BI tools, such as Microsoft Power BI. When we last explored Power BI in Chapter 3, *Analysis with Excel and Creating Interactive Maps and Charts with Power BI*, we focused on visualizing data pulled in from a Microsoft SQL Server query. You may then ask why it would be necessary to pull in data through R when it can be done directly through Power BI. As we saw earlier when we were forecasting data, R has the ability to generate data points based on different libraries applied to the original dataset. This generated data can then be easily merged back into the original dataset. It is this merged dataset that brings added value to a visualization inside of Power BI.

Merging new columns to dataframes in R

The original dataframe used in this chapter was called SQL_Query_1 and contained Discount Codes by Week. We could choose to implement a simple linear regression model on this dataset to find a straight line that best represented the activity of the weekly points. Once the linear regression model is implemented, the fitted points of the straight line can be merged back into the original dataset, as seen in the following code, which is a **new R script**:

```
library('RODBC')
connection_SQLBI<-odbcConnect("SQLBI")

SQL_Query_1<-sqlQuery(connection_SQLBI,
                      'SELECT [WeekInYear]
                      ,[DiscountCode]
                      FROM [AdventureWorks2014].[dbo].[DiscountCodebyWeek]'
)

attach(SQL_Query_1)

##Change Column Names##
colnames(SQL_Query_1)<- c("Week", "Discount")

SQL_Query_1$Weeks <- as.numeric(SQL_Query_1$Week)
```

```
SQL_Query_1<-SQL_Query_1[c(1,3,2)] #reverses columns 1 and 2

attach(SQL_Query_1)
linear_regression<-lm(Discount~Weeks, SQL_Query_1)

Regression_Dataframe<-cbind(SQL_Query_1, Fitted=fitted(linear_regression))
head(Regression_Dataframe)
```

The original dataframe is still intact, but we have created an additional dataframe where we have merged SQL_Query_1 with a new column for Fitted data from the linear regression model. This new dataframe is called Regression_Dataframe, and the first six rows can be seen in the following screenshot:

```
> head(Regression_Dataframe)
  Week Weeks Discount   Fitted
1 "01"     1       22 13.65602
2 "02"     2        4 13.75775
3 "03"     3       24 13.85947
4 "04"     4        5 13.96120
5 "05"     5        1 14.06292
6 "06"     6       21 14.16465
```

Our next step will be to incorporate the new dataframe into Microsoft Power BI.

Integrating R with Microsoft Power BI

Once we have Microsoft Power BI started up, we can pull in an R data source by selecting **Get Data** from the **Home** tab on the menu bar and choosing R Script, as seen in the following screenshot:

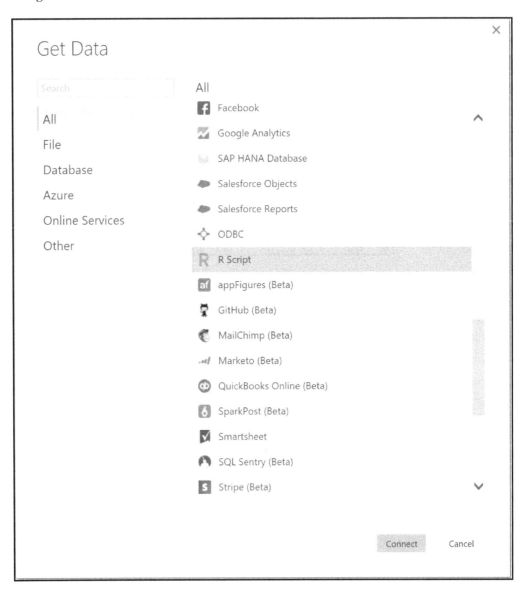

After selecting the **Connect** button, we are prompted with a script editor box to paste in R code:

Additionally, within the **Execute R Script** box, we can see the location for the installation of R: **R is installed at C:\Program Files\R\R-3.2.5.** Once the script is successfully executed, a **Navigator** window will emerge that will allow you to select all of the appropriate dataframes necessary for visualization, as seen in the following screenshot:

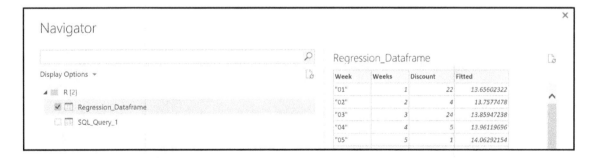

For the purposes of our data, only **Regression_Dataframe** is selected for further visualization. Once selected, all dataframe fields become available to be selected for visualization. You can then select the appropriate fields, as seen in this screenshot:

The default visualization, once the appropriate fields are selected, is a data table, as seen in the following screenshot:

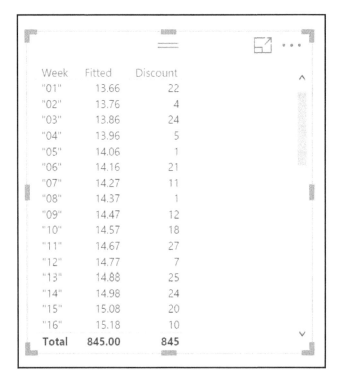

A data table is a good final check to make sure the data is coming through from the source as expected. Once the data has been validated, the default visualization may be selected and then converted into a different visualization, such as a line chart, as seen here:

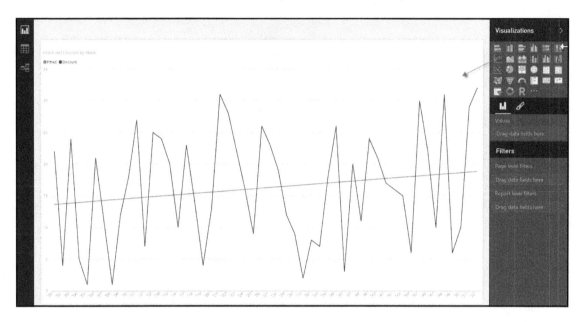

Our final line chart visualizes the familiar weekly `Discount` versus `Week` relationship as well as the `Fitted` line generated by the simple linear regression relationship developed from the model back in R.

Summary

We are at the end of another chapter and we've covered quite a number of topics within R, including maximizing the reporting features of RStudio and R Markdown to fuse common Business Intelligence practices with R Code as well as integrating R with visualization tools such as Microsoft Power BI. We started by connecting our data with a live connection to SQL Server using ODBC and generating our dataframe. We then delved into basic and advanced plot creation within R, which led us to time series graphing with forecasting and smoothing capabilities.

In the next chapter, we will bring a similar BI reporting methodology to Python with the Jupyter Notebook.

6
Creating Histograms and Normal Distribution Plots with Python

Python is a general-purpose programming language that was created in the late 1980s. So, while it has been around for quite a while, it has experienced a popularity surge of late, especially within the data science and data visualization communities. In fact, in a 2016 study performed by CodeEval found that Python was the most popular coding language, as seen in the following screenshot:

2015 Rank		2015	Change%	2014	Change%	2013	Change%
1	Python	26.67%	-14.64%	31.24%	3.10%	30.30%	5.21%
2	Java	22.58%	15.37%	19.57%	-11.85%	22.20%	-13.95%
3	C++	9.96%	1.76%	9.79%	-24.70%	13.00%	3.17%
4	C#	9.39%	27.37%	7.37%	47.37%	5.00%	100.00%
5	C	7.37%	21.37%	6.07%	48.14%	4.10%	-16.33%
6	JavaScript	6.88%	6.09%	6.48%	24.66%	5.20%	33.33%
7	Ruby	5.88%	-17.27%	7.11%	-32.90%	10.60%	10.42%
8	PHP	3.82%	5.45%	3.62%	9.84%	3.30%	-54.79%
9	Haskell	1.77%	17.24%	1.51%	25.83%	1.20%	
10	Go	1.27%	-44.00%	2.26%	50.67%	1.50%	-25.00%

The full evaluation of all the coding languages, as well as the methodology for ranking the study used, can be found at the following website: `http://blog.codeeval.com/codeevalblog/2016/2/2/most-popular-coding-languages-of-2016`.

Python has a strong and passionate community of developers, and much of their innovation within the Python ecosystem has allowed it to branch out into other fields, such as business intelligence.

The greatest gap that has been filled between traditional Python programming and business intelligence has involved the creation of the **IPython Notebook**. Similar to how RStudio introduced interactivity to R, the IPython Notebook introduced interactive computing and visualization to Python programming. This level of interactivity is new to traditional programming languages as it allows a more formatted delivery of results and data.

Even more recently, the IPython Notebook has evolved into the **Jupyter Notebook**, which is the a combination of the Julia, Python, and R programming platforms. The success of the IPython Notebook with Python paved the way for other programming languages to seek similar platforms of interactivity, hence the creation of the Jupyter Notebook. Our entire Python code in this chapter will be built within the Jupyter Notebook (leveraged by PyCharm) and will be delivered using the Jupyter Notebook.

 To learn more about the Jupyter Notebook, visit the following site: `http://jupyter.org/`

In addition to the contributions made by the Jupyter Notebook, there have been significant libraries created that have made Python a powerful tool for data analysis and data visualization. Some of these libraries are as follows:

- `pandas`
- `numpy`
- `matplotlib`

You may have heard the saying, "Python is not great at any one thing, but good at everything". This will become evident as we go through this chapter and develop histograms and normal distribution plots with Python. Histograms are not to be confused with bar charts. Any dataset with a dimension and a measure column can be plotted as a bar chart. The difference with a histogram is the ability to plot the frequency of a single measure continuously to identify any outliers as well as the distribution of the data.

We will cover the following topics in this chapter:

- Preparing SQL Server query for human resources data
- Connecting Python to SQL Server
- Visualizing histograms in Python
- Visualizing normal distribution plots in Python
- Combining a histogram with a normal distribution plot
- Alternative plotting libraries with Python
- Publishing Jupyter Notebook

Preparing a SQL Server query for human resources data

As we've done with previous chapters, we must first prepare our data that we want to visualize inside Python. This dataset will focus on the human resources department for the AdventureWorks company. Our query will pull back the total number of vacation hours that each job title has available. The data for this query is available in the Employee table of the AdventureWorks database, and the following SQL statement will help us generate the results needed:

```
SELECT
[JobTitle]
,sum([VacationHours]) as VacationHours

FROM [AdventureWorks2014].[HumanResources].[Employee]
group by [JobTitle]
order by [VacationHours] asc;
```

The result of the SQL statement for the first ten rows can be seen in the following screenshot:

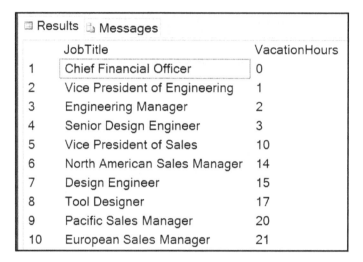

The full dataset from this query result will be the foundation of our histogram as well as our normal distribution plot.

Connecting Python to Microsoft SQL Server

Before we can begin to visualize our data within Python, we must first establish a connection to Microsoft SQL Server from Python. As in Chapter 2, *Web Scraping*, we will continue to use PyCharm as our IDE of choice for development. There are many IDEs that are available free of use to develop Python projects. If you choose to develop with another tool, you should still be able to follow along in this chapter.

Starting a new project in PyCharm

Once you have PyCharm started, you may have your previous project from Chapter 2, *Web Scraping*, still open. We wish to separate the projects, so we will close this project by selecting **File** and **Close Project**, as seen in the following screenshot:

Next, we can start a new project for this chapter by selecting **Create New Project** on the main menu, as seen in the following screenshot:

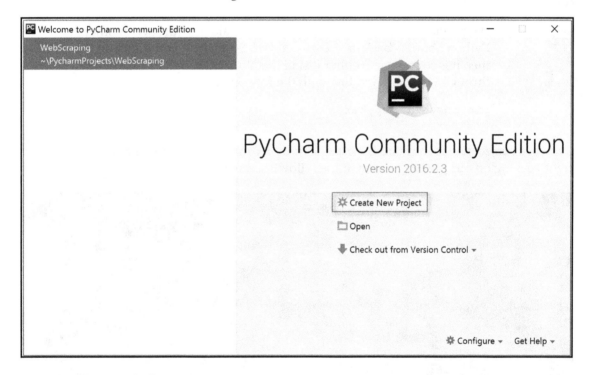

We can then select the Location and the **Interpreter** for this project to save our work, as well as confirming that we are using the necessary version of Python, as seen in the following screenshot:

For this project, we are continuing to use the same version of Python as we did in `Chapter 2`, *Web Scraping*, version 3.4.4. One of the advantages to using an IDE for development is the ability to compartmentalize different versions of Python with different projects without any confusion.

 We previously installed the Jupyter library along with several other Python libraries back in `Chapter 2`, *Web Scraping*. If you didn't do this, then it is necessary to either install the library through PyCharm or through the command line with the following command:

`pip install jupyter`

Once our project has been created, we can start by creating a new **Jupyter Notebook** file by right-clicking on our project, as seen in the following screenshot:

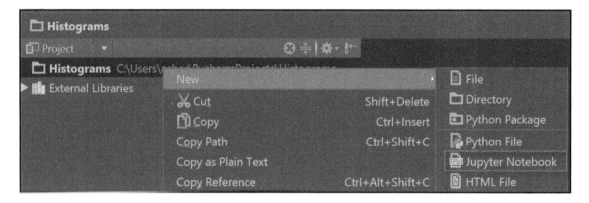

 Keep in mind that if you happen to be using an earlier version of PyCharm, **Jupyter Notebook** may be referred to as **IPython Notebook**.

We can assign any name to the notebook; in our case, we will call it `Histograms.ipynb`. Notebook extensions are denoted by `ipynb`, which refers back to the legacy name of the IPython Notebook, as seen in the following screenshot.

While we will execute an initial line of code in the cell, we will only do so to activate the Jupyter Notebook server. We can do this by running the following line of code:

```
print('Histogram Example')
```

Then we execute the script, as seen in the following screenshot:

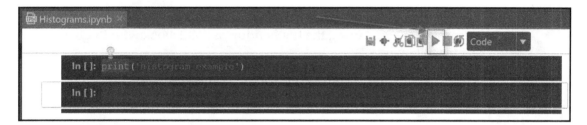

Executing the first line of code automatically triggers the server address for the Jupyter Notebook, as seen in the following screenshot:

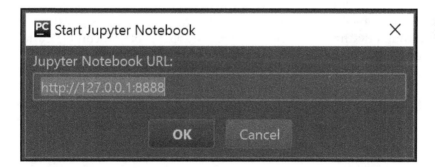

We will need to click on the **OK** button to ensure that the Jupyter Notebook server `127.0.0.1:8888` has been activated.

We can then copy the **Jupyter Notebook URL** and paste into a browser, such as Google Chrome, as seen in the following screenshot:

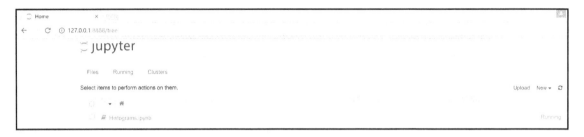

We can see all of the files in our project folder, and since `Histograms.ipynb` is the only file in our project, it is the only one in our list. From this point forward, all of our development will take place in the Jupyter Notebook browser as opposed to directly inside of PyCharm. The Jupyter Notebook server will continue to remain active as long as PyCharm is running locally.

To learn more about using the IPython/Jupyter Notebook with PyCharm, visit the following site:
`https://www.jetbrains.com/help/pycharm/2016.1/tutorial-using-ipython-jupyter-notebook-with-pycharm.html`

Installing Python libraries manually

In `Chapter 2`, *Web Scraping*, we covered installing Python libraries to our local machine, and PyCharm provides a built-in, user-friendly interface to install, uninstall, and upgrade Python libraries. The overwhelming majority of libraries will only need a straightforward installation through PyCharm. However, there are some problem-child libraries that may prove more difficult to install, especially if you are on a Windows machine. One of those problem-child libraries is `SciPy`.

`SciPy` is a popular Python library that is often used for scientific computing in data science algorithms and is also popular amongst engineers, mathematicians, and scientists.

To learn more about `SciPy`, visit the following website:
`https://www.scipy.org`

For our purposes, the `SciPy` library will help us build the normal distribution curve that accompanies a histogram. Occasionally, when we try and install the `SciPy` library through the normal conventions through PyCharm, we receive the error seen in the following screenshot:

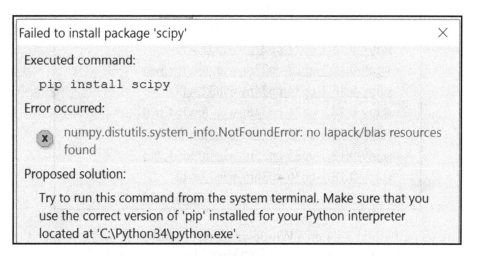

The **Proposed solution** in the error message recommends the developer install the library manually using Command Prompt in the following location: **C:\Python34\python.exe**.

When trying to execute the following command:

```
pip install scipy
```

We may still receive the same error.

If both methods fail, then our only other option is to install the library manually. More often than not, most popular libraries will have their own website that will explain how to perform the installation. For `SciPy`, we can find information on downloading and installing the library from the following website: `https://www.scipy.org/install.html`

As we scroll down the page and get to the **Windows packages** section, we see that an individual named Christoph Gohlke has graciously provided pre-built Windows installers for several Python libraries, including `SciPy`. His repository of Python packages is located at the following website: `http://www.lfd.uci.edu/~gohlke/pythonlibs/`.

As we scroll down his list of packages, we can see all of the `SciPy` versions available for download, as seen in the following screenshot:

SciPy is software for mathematics, science, and engineering.
Requires numpy+mkl.
Install numpy+mkl before installing scipy.

scipy-0.18.1-cp27-cp27m-win32.whl

scipy-0.18.1-cp27-cp27m-win_amd64.whl

scipy-0.18.1-cp34-cp34m-win32.whl

scipy-0.18.1-cp34-cp34m-win_amd64.whl

scipy-0.18.1-cp35-cp35m-win32.whl

scipy-0.18.1-cp35-cp35m-win_amd64.whl

scipy-0.18.1-cp36-cp36m-win32.whl

scipy-0.18.1-cp36-cp36m-win_amd64.whl

Since we are using Python 3.4.4 on a Windows 64-bit machine, we will download the version of `SciPy` that is called **scipy-0.18.1-cp34-cp34m-win_amd64.whl**.

We can then save the build file to the Python interpreter location, which in my instance is located in `C:\Python34\python.exe`. Once the file is saved in the appropriate location, we can then execute the following in the command prompt:

```
C:\Python34> pip install scipy-0.18.1-cp34-cp34m-win_amd64.whl
```

If everything has been successfully executed, we should see the **Successfully installed scipy-0.18.1** message in the command window:

```
C:\WINDOWS\system32\cmd.exe

C:\Python34>pip install scipy-0.18.1-cp34-cp34m-win_amd64.whl
Processing c:\python34\scipy-0.18.1-cp34-cp34m-win_amd64.whl
Installing collected packages: scipy
Successfully installed scipy-0.18.1
```

Any time a library is installed manually outside PyCharm, it is good practice to confirm that PyCharm has identified it and included it within its list of installed packages. One way to validate that `SciPy` or any other Python library has been properly installed manually is to view the **Project Interpreter** list of libraries in PyCharm and look for SciPy. We can reach the Project Interpreter by pressing *Ctrl + Alt + S* inside PyCharm to reach the **Settings** menu, and then expanding the project name to view the **Project Interpreter**, as seen in the following screenshot:

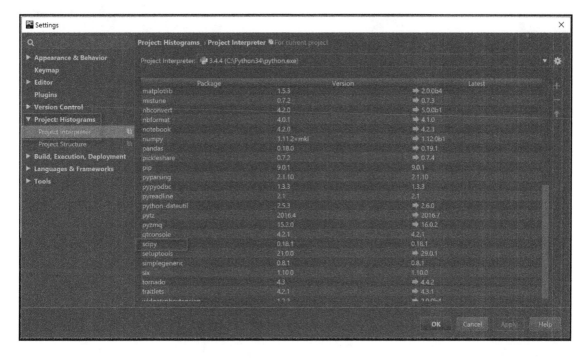

Since `SciPy` is on the list of installed libraries, then we are good to go.

Establishing a connection with the PyPyODBC library

Python has a very powerful library called `PyPyODBC`, which functions as an ODBC interface module. Install it through PyCharm or through the command prompt:

```
pip install pypyodbc
```

Now we will be ready to establish a trusted connection between Python and our Microsoft SQL Server database. Each time we wish to execute a line of code inside of the Jupyter Notebook, we will click on the **Insert** dropdown and select **Insert Cell Below**, as seen in the following screenshot:

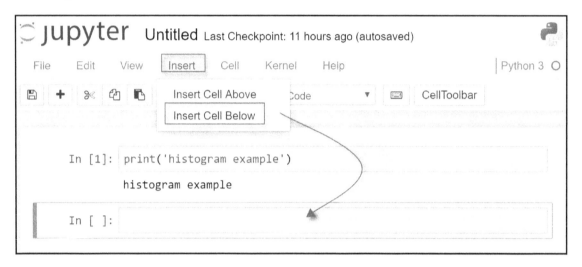

Each block of code is considered a **Cell** within Jupyter, and each cell can be executed individually by selecting **Run Cells** or all at once by selecting **Run All**, depending on the selection made in the **Cell** drop-down menu, as seen in the following screenshot:

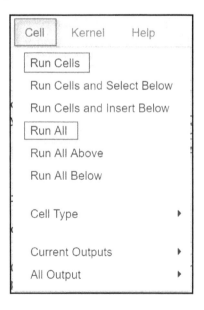

The following script imports the `pypyodbc` library into our notebook and establishes a connection to the SQL Server `AdventureWorks2014` database:

```
import pypyodbc
connection = pypyodbc.connect(driver='{SQL Server}',
                              server='localhost\SQLBI',
                              database='AdventureWorks2014',
                trusted_connection='yes')

connection.getinfo

cursor = connection.cursor()
```

 Note that the server name is using the local instance from MS SQL Server named `SQLBI`. If you defined your instance by a different name, use that name in the server parameter for the connection.

We can insert this script into Jupyter and execute it, as seen in the following screenshot:

Vacation Hours Distribution

```
In [1]:  import pypyodbc
         connection = pypyodbc.connect(driver='{SQL Server}',
                                       server='localhost\SQLBI',
                                       database='AdventureWorks2014',
                         trusted_connection='yes')

         connection.getinfo

         cursor = connection.cursor()
```

Once any script has successfully executed in a Jupyter Notebook, a number in sequential order will appear inside of **In []**, which stands for input.

 To learn more about the `PyPyODBC` package, visit the following site:
`https://pypi.python.org/pypi/pypyodbc`

Building a SQL query inside Python

Our next step is to rebuild the same SQL Server query developed earlier in the chapter using a **Query** variable. We can accomplish this using the following script:

```
Query = ("SELECT [JobTitle],sum([VacationHours]) as VacationHours FROM"
    "[AdventureWorks2014].[HumanResources].[Employee]"
    "group by [JobTitle]"
    "order by [VacationHours] asc")
```

As our third code cell, the script will appear as follows in the Jupyter Notebook:

```
In [3]:  Query = ("SELECT [JobTitle],sum([VacationHours]) as VacationHours FROM"
                "[AdventureWorks2014].[HumanResources].[Employee]"
            "group by [JobTitle]"
            "order by [VacationHours] asc")
```

The SQL statement should remain intact; however, each line in the SQL statement begins and ends with double quotes. This is to ensure that the **Query** variable is aware of how to read the SQL as a string statement that will be understood by the database we are connected to.

The next few lines of script are the following:

```
cursor.execute(Query)
results = cursor.fetchall()
type(results)
```

This will assist with executing the query, saving the query results to a variable called `results`, and then displaying the output type of the `results` variable:

```
In [6]:  cursor.execute(Query)
         results = cursor.fetchall()
         type(results)

Out[6]:  list
```

The `cursor.fetchall()` function allows us to pull in all of the results without any data limitations. If we only want to pull a single component of the query statement, then we would use the `cursor.fetchone()` function instead. In this case, the output of the `results` type variable is a **list**. We can generate this information using the `type()` function. A list in Python is very much what you would expect: a list of values separated by commas within a bracket.

The output of the `results` variable can be viewed simply by executing the following script:

```
print(results)
```

When executed in Jupyter Notebook, we can view the following results:

```
In [5]: print(results)

[('Chief Financial Officer', 0), ('Vice President of Engineering', 1), ('Engineering Manager', 2), ('Senior Design Engineer',
3), ('Vice President of Sales', 10), ('North American Sales Manager', 14), ('Design Engineer', 15), ('Tool Designer', 17), ('P
acific Sales Manager', 20), ('European Sales Manager', 21), ('Marketing Manager', 40), ('Production Control Manager', 43), ('Ma
ster Scheduler', 44), ('Purchasing Manager', 49), ('Benefits Specialist', 51), ('Human Resources Manager', 54), ('Finance Manag
er', 55), ('Senior Tool Designer', 55), ('Assistant to the Chief Financial Officer', 56), ('Accounts Manager', 57), ('Vice Pres
ident of Production', 64), ('Information Services Manager', 65), ('Network Manager', 68), ('Research and Development Manager',
77), ('Document Control Manager', 77), ('Quality Assurance Manager', 80), ('Quality Assurance Supervisor', 81), ('Facilities M
anager', 86), ('Facilities Administrative Assistant', 87), ('Maintenance Supervisor', 92), ('Shipping and Receiving Superviso
r', 93), ('Recruiter', 99), ('Chief Executive Officer', 99), ('Purchasing Assistant', 101), ('Human Resources Administrative As
sistant', 105), ('Accountant', 117), ('Production Supervisor - WC20', 123), ('Research and Development Engineer', 125), ('Marke
ting Assistant', 126), ('Accounts Payable Specialist', 127), ('Database Administrator', 133), ('Network Administrator', 139),
('Control Specialist', 151), ('Document Control Assistant', 157), ('Accounts Receivable Specialist', 183), ('Scheduling Assist
ant', 186), ('Shipping and Receiving Clerk', 189), ('Production Supervisor - WC10', 198), ('Production Supervisor - WC30', 20
7), ('Production Supervisor - WC40', 216), ('Production Supervisor - WC45', 225), ('Marketing Specialist', 230), ('Production T
echnician - WC20', 231), ('Production Supervisor - WC50', 234), ('Production Supervisor - WC60', 243), ('Application Specialis
t', 290), ('Stocker', 291), ('Quality Assurance Technician', 334), ('Janitor', 358), ('Sales Representative', 434), ('Buyer', 5
04), ('Production Technician - WC60', 689), ('Production Technician - WC30', 850), ('Production Technician - WC45', 1200), ('Pr
oduction Technician - WC50', 1213), ('Production Technician - WC40', 1547), ('Production Technician - WC10', 1547)]
```

Building a dataframe with Python

While the `list` format is sufficient for us to view the results and to confirm that our Python query is properly connecting to the original SQL Server query, it is not ideal for us to perform visualizations or data analysis. As we faced in Chapter 5, *Forecasting with R*, we would like to work with a dataframe format that has a tabular structure similar to a spreadsheet. This is where the `pandas` library is very powerful. We can manipulate our `list` into a `dataframe` by importing the `pandas` library and converting the `results list` into a tabular format by using the following script:

```
import pandas as pd
dataframe = pd.DataFrame(results, columns=["Job Title", "Vacation Hours"])
```

The dataframe is appropriately saved to a variable called dataframe. We can use the head() function in Python to view the first five rows of the dataframe variable (including the header), as seen in the following screenshot:

```
In [6]: import pandas as pd
        dataframe = pd.DataFrame(results, columns=["Job Title", "Vacation Hours"]
        dataframe.head()
```

Out[6]:

	Job Title	Vacation Hours
0	Chief Financial Officer	0
1	Vice President of Engineering	1
2	Engineering Manager	2
3	Senior Design Engineer	3
4	Vice President of Sales	10

The dataframe structure is more in line with what we are used to dealing with, especially if you are used to working with databases having a defined number of rows and columns. Even more important than the structure of the dataframe is the ability to compare the first five rows coming from the dataframe and confirm that they are indeed the same first five rows that we retrieved earlier in the chapter when we built the SQL statement within Microsoft SQL Server.

To learn more about pandas, visit the following site:
http://pandas.pydata.org/

Visualizing histograms in Python

We can now begin developing a histogram with Python since we have established an appropriate data structure with a `dataframe`. One of the most popular and powerful plotting libraries in Python is `matplotlib`. If you are familiar with the programming language *Matlab*, then you will find `matplotlib` to be a very quick study.

 To learn more about `matplotlib`, visit the following website: `http://matplotlib.org`

Before we can get started using `matplotlib`, we will first need to install it either through PyCharm or through the command line:

```
pip install matplotlib
```

Next, we will need to import the module and call the `%matplotlib inline` function to view plots directly inside of the Jupyter Notebook:

```
import matplotlib.pyplot as plt
%matplotlib inline
```

We will now create a new `dataframe` based on our existing one using only the column for `VacationHours`. We can now visualize our histogram using `VacationHours` for the plot points, with the `plt.hist()` function from `matplotlib`:

```
VacationHours=dataframe['Vacation Hours']
plt.hist(VacationHours, normed = True)
plt.title('Vacation Hours')
plt.xlabel('Hours')
plt.ylabel('Count')
plt.show()
```

When executed in the Jupyter Notebook, we get the following:

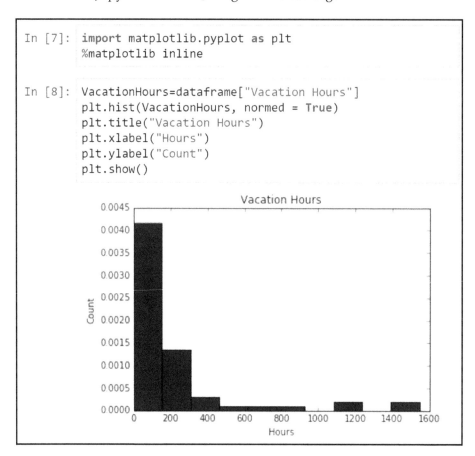

```
In [7]:  import matplotlib.pyplot as plt
         %matplotlib inline

In [8]:  VacationHours=dataframe["Vacation Hours"]
         plt.hist(VacationHours, normed = True)
         plt.title("Vacation Hours")
         plt.xlabel("Hours")
         plt.ylabel("Count")
         plt.show()
```

How do we interpret the x axis of the histogram? Well, the x axis counts the frequency of all of the different VacationHours available for each employee. Each bar of a histogram comprises a specific bin. A bin is a range or an interval of points that are grouped together. The counts comprise the frequency of the points we are measuring. The main characteristics of bins are that they do not overlap and that they are continuous. The overwhelming majority of VacationHours are inside of the first bin of 0-150 hours. There are also some employees who have VacationHours in the **1400** to **1600** range. In addition to that, the y axis for Count has been normalized for when we overlay a normal distribution curve. The following script normalizes the histogram:

```
plt.hist(VacationHours, normed = True)
```

If we were to remove the normalization of the histogram, we would have the following modified histogram:

```
In [9]:  VacationHours=dataframe["Vacation Hours"]
         plt.hist(VacationHours)
         plt.title("Vacation Hours (De-Normalized)")
         plt.xlabel("Hours")
         plt.ylabel("Count")
         plt.show()
```

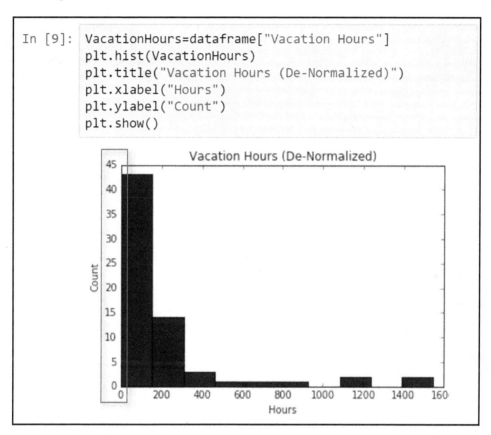

 Note that the scale value does not correspond directly to the start or end of a specific bin but to the scale ticks directly above the value.

The **Count** is now the actual amount and not the normalized count. Therefore, by looking at the first bin we can see there are approximately 43 job titles that have `VacationHours` between 0-150 hours. In the next section, it will become evident why we would want to normalize the count on the *y* axis when we introduce the normal distribution plot.

Visualizing normal distribution plots in Python

The plot most often accompanied by a histogram is a normal distribution plot. These plots come in handy when we are trying to identify averages, outliers, and distributions. Also, they are very easy to produce with Python. They require the following two libraries to be installed:

- numpy
- scipy

 sciPy will help us with producing the normalization parameters of the curve and NumPy, a library that is often associated with linear algebra, will help us perform several mathematical functions.

We installed scipy earlier in the chapter; however, numpy may need to be installed either through PyCharm or through the command line, as follows:

pip install numpy

We can begin by importing both of them into our project, as seen in the following script.

```
import numpy as np
import scipy.stats as stats
```

A normal distribution curve requires two values for its creation:

- Mean
- Standard deviation

 The *mean* sets the center of the curve and the *standard deviation* sets the tails of the curves. A *standard normal distribution* curve is one where the mean is 0 and the standard deviation is 1.

The next step is to create a variable for the *mean* and the *standard deviation* for
VacationHours that will be used in the normalization equation. The following script will
create those variables for us:

```
Vacation_Hours_mean = np.mean(VacationHours)
Vacation_Hours_std = np.std(VacationHours)
```

The value outputs for both the *mean* and the *standard deviation* can be seen in the following
screenshot:

```
In [10]:  import numpy as np
          import scipy.stats as stats

          Vacation_Hours_mean = np.mean(VacationHours)
          Vacation_Hours_std = np.std(VacationHours)

          print('mean = '+str(Vacation_Hours_mean))
          print('standard deviation = '+str(Vacation_Hours_std))

          mean = 219.074626866
          standard deviation = 330.817409775
```

We can already see that our normal distribution curve will not be a standard curve in that
the standard deviation is greater than the mean for VacationHours. We will analyze what
the consequences of this may be later on in the chapter.

sciPy has a function called stats.norm.pdf() that we can use to assign the values to be
plotted, along with the mean and the standard deviation. We can assign this function to a
variable that we will name normal_distribution_curve, as seen in the following script:

```
normal_distribution_curve =
stats.norm.pdf(VacationHours, Vacation_Hours_mean, Vacation_Hours_std)
```

We can then visualize the plot of the normal distribution curve using the `plt.plot()` function:

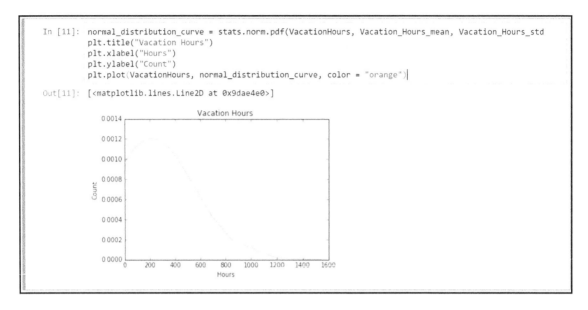

```
In [11]:  normal_distribution_curve = stats.norm.pdf(VacationHours, Vacation_Hours_mean, Vacation_Hours_std
          plt.title("Vacation Hours")
          plt.xlabel("Hours")
          plt.ylabel("Count")
          plt.plot(VacationHours, normal_distribution_curve, color = "orange")
Out[11]:  [<matplotlib.lines.Line2D at 0x9dae4e0>]
```

So, as can be seen in the normal distribution curve, the majority of the data points fall inside of the first 200 hours, which is similar to what we saw with the histogram. In a normal distribution curve, the values underneath the curve should sum up to one.

Combining a histogram with a normal distribution plot

We now have a histogram and a normal distribution plot individually, but it would be nice if we could visualize both them on one graph with the same scales. This can easily be done by referencing both plots in a single cell and then using the `plt.show()` function just once after both plots have been called:

```
plt.hist(VacationHours, normed = True) # plotting histogram
plt.plot(VacationHours, normal_distribution_curve, color = "orange")
#plotting normal curve
plt.title("Vacation Hours") #Assign title
plt.xlabel("Hours") #Assign x label
plt.ylabel("Count") #Assign y label
plt.show()
```

The output of the combined plots can be seen in the following screenshot:

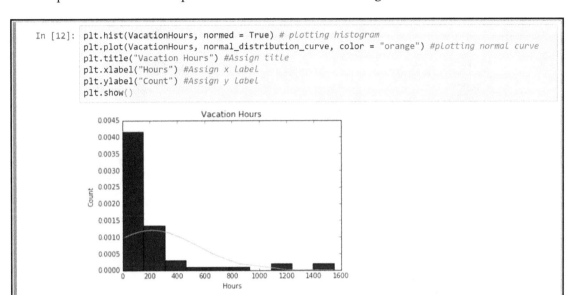

```
In [12]:  plt.hist(VacationHours, normed = True) # plotting histogram
          plt.plot(VacationHours, normal_distribution_curve, color = "orange") #plotting normal curve
          plt.title("Vacation Hours") #Assign title
          plt.xlabel("Hours") #Assign x label
          plt.ylabel("Count") #Assign y label
          plt.show()
```

We now have a combined normal distribution plot and histogram for us to see the distribution of `VacationHours` across different job titles for AdventureWorks.

Annotating in Python

One of the nice features with `matplotlib` is the ability to annotate graphs to help guide users to areas of the graph that we want them to focus on. If we wish to add a vertical line through the mean of the histogram and normal distribution plot, we could do so by using the function `plt.axvline()`. This function allows us to specify the location on the *x* axis for the vertical line to cross, the color of the line, the style of the line, and the width of the line. So, if we would like a red dashed line of width 2 to go through the mean of the histogram, we could add the following code to our existing combination histogram and normal distribution plot:

```
plt.axvline(Vacation_Hours_mean, color = "r", linestyle = "dashed",
linewidth = 2)
```

The updated plot with the addition of the dashed line through the mean can be seen in the following screenshot:

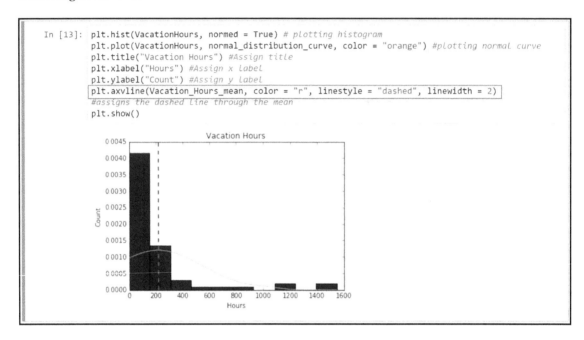

```
In [13]:  plt.hist(VacationHours, normed = True) # plotting histogram
          plt.plot(VacationHours, normal_distribution_curve, color = "orange") #plotting normal curve
          plt.title("Vacation Hours") #Assign title
          plt.xlabel("Hours") #Assign x label
          plt.ylabel("Count") #Assign y label
          plt.axvline(Vacation_Hours_mean, color = "r", linestyle = "dashed", linewidth = 2)
          #assigns the dashed line through the mean
          plt.show()
```

What if we wish to go one step further and indicate with an arrow directly on the graph where the mean is located? And what if we wish to put the actual value of the mean next to the arrow so that the user will know the exact value and won't have to guess what that value is? Both of these features can be accomplished once again with `matplotlib` using the `plt.annotate()` function. The following code can help us generate the annotation, along with the arrow symbol:

```
plt.annotate('Mean = '+ str(round(Vacation_Hours_mean,2)),
            xy=(Vacation_Hours_mean, 0.0013), xycoords='data',
            xytext=(Vacation_Hours_mean*2, 0.0035), textcoords='data',
            arrowprops=dict(arrowstyle="->",
                            connectionstyle="arc3"),)
```

This code starts off by letting us add a text value set to Mean along with the start and end locations for the arrow. Additionally, the code allows us to pick the arc style of the arrow. When we append this code to our existing plot, we get the following screenshot:

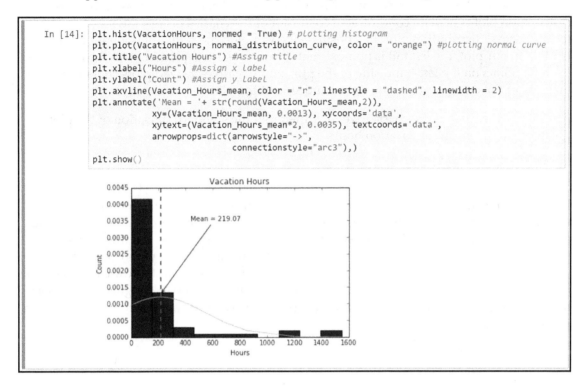

```
In [14]:  plt.hist(VacationHours, normed = True) # plotting histogram
          plt.plot(VacationHours, normal_distribution_curve, color = "orange") #plotting normal curve
          plt.title("Vacation Hours") #Assign title
          plt.xlabel("Hours") #Assign x label
          plt.ylabel("Count") #Assign y label
          plt.axvline(Vacation_Hours_mean, color = "r", linestyle = "dashed", linewidth = 2)
          plt.annotate('Mean = '+ str(round(Vacation_Hours_mean,2)),
                          xy=(Vacation_Hours_mean, 0.0013), xycoords='data',
                          xytext=(Vacation_Hours_mean*2, 0.0035), textcoords='data',
                          arrowprops=dict(arrowstyle="->",
                                          connectionstyle="arc3"),)
          plt.show()
```

We have successfully annotated our VacationHours histogram and normal distribution plot. We can now focus the attention of the user on the average vacation hours for all job titles.

To learn more about annotating in matplotlib, visit the following site:
http://matplotlib.org/1.4.2/examples/pylab_examples/annotation
_demo.html

Analyzing the results

So what? What does this mean for the distribution of the normal plot, or the values of the mean as well as the standard deviation? As we mentioned earlier, the mass of the normal distribution plot is heavily concentrated to the left of the chart. This is known as a *positive-skewed* normal distribution plot. In a positive-skewed plot, the right tail is longer than the left tail. In our plot, the left tail is non-existent. Positive-skewed plots contain the majority of the data points on the left-hand side of the plot, and negative-skewed plots contain the majority of the data points on the right-hand side of the plot.

Additionally, earlier in the chapter we identified that the standard deviation of the plot is greater than the mean for vacation hours:

```
mean = 219.074626866
standard deviation = 330.817409775
```

What does this mean for us? Well, we know that the mean or average is an indication of where the center of the data is located. The standard deviation is more of a measure of the spread of the data overall. Since our standard deviation is larger than our mean, it is a strong indication that some of our data points are significant outliers with values much greater than the mean. Just by glancing at our histogram, we see that there are bins with data around 1,200 hours and 1,400 hours. We can look further into the original `dataframe` to identify the job titles that belong to those bins. We can execute a script to pull the last ten rows of job titles by `VacationHours`:

```
dataframe.tail(10)
```

The outcome of the script can be seen in the following screenshot:

```
In [15]:  dataframe.tail(10)
Out[15]:
```

	Job Title	Vacation Hours
57	Quality Assurance Technician	334
58	Janitor	358
59	Sales Representative	434
60	Buyer	504
61	Production Technician - WC60	689
62	Production Technician - WC30	850
63	Production Technician - WC45	1200
64	Production Technician - WC50	1213
65	Production Technician - WC40	1547
66	Production Technician - WC10	1547

Just as we use `head()` to pull in the top five rows of a dataframe, we can also use the `tail(10)` function to pull in the last ten rows of a dataframe. If we leave it as `tail()`, then it would pull the last five rows by default.

It seems from our results that, if our goal in life is to vacation around the world, then we need to all become Production Technicians. These **Production Technicians** are the cause of the positive-skew of `VacationHours`.

Alternative plotting libraries with Python

`matplotlib` is not the only game in town for plotting with Python. There are several other visualization libraries that are very powerful. One of them is `seaborn`. `seaborn` is actually based on `matplotlib`, so it contains similar functionality but makes more visually appealing plots with minimal coding.

To learn more about `seaborn`, visit the following website: `http://seaborn.pydata.org`

Before we can get started with `seaborn`, we will need to install it using either PyCharm or manually through the command line:

```
pip install seaborn
```

Once it is installed we can call the module into our Jupyter Notebook using the following command:

```
import seaborn as sb
```

We can plot a histogram using `VacationHours` with the following script:

```
sb.distplot(VacationHours, kde = False, rug=True)
```

When the script is executed, we can see the following histogram built with `seaborn`:

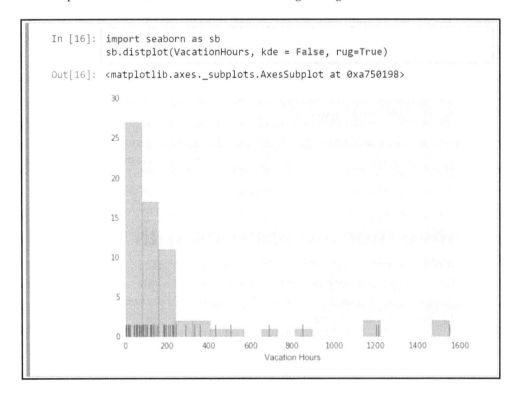

The `rug` parameter is set to `True`. This feature allows for the short rug-like bars at the bottom of the *x* axis to appear. They can be turned off by setting `rug = False`. Additionally, the `kde` parameter is set to `False`. `kde` stands for kernel density estimate, which is the parameter to turn on a normal distribution plot. `seaborn` also has a `kdeplot()` function that allows us to easily plot a normal distribution plot:

```
sb.kdeplot(VacationHours, shade = True)
```

When we execute the `kdeplot()` function we see the following normal distribution plot:

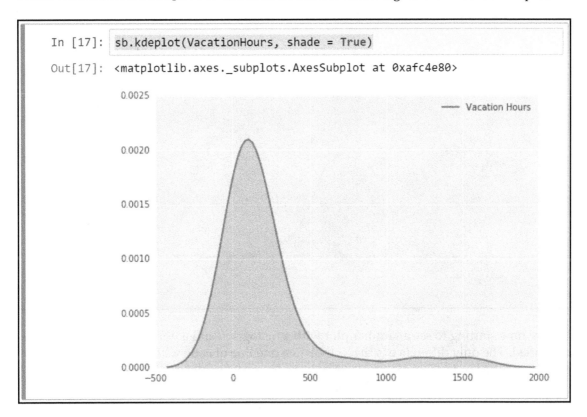

We have the ability to incorporate the `kde` parameter inside of the `distplot()` function, which would combine a histogram with the normal distribution plot. We can turn off the `rug` parameter and turn on the `kde` parameter with the following script:

```
sb.distplot(VacationHours, kde = True, rug=False)
```

When the script is executed we can see the following histogram and normal distribution plot with the updated parameters:

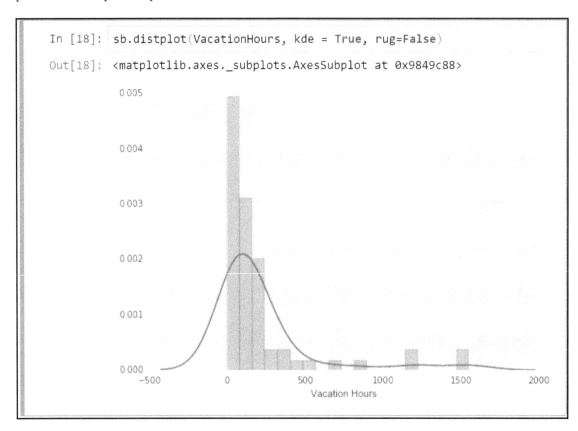

```
In [18]:  sb.distplot(VacationHours, kde = True, rug=False)

Out[18]:  <matplotlib.axes._subplots.AxesSubplot at 0x9849c88>
```

We are now starting to see a familiar plot with a histogram and a normal distribution curve combined. The only difference is that it took just one line of code with seaborn as opposed to a few lines of code with matplotlib.

Additionally, we can use `seaborn` in our existing combined plot built with `matplotlib` and it will enhance the look and feel of the original plot without any additional code other than calling the library, as seen in the following screenshot:

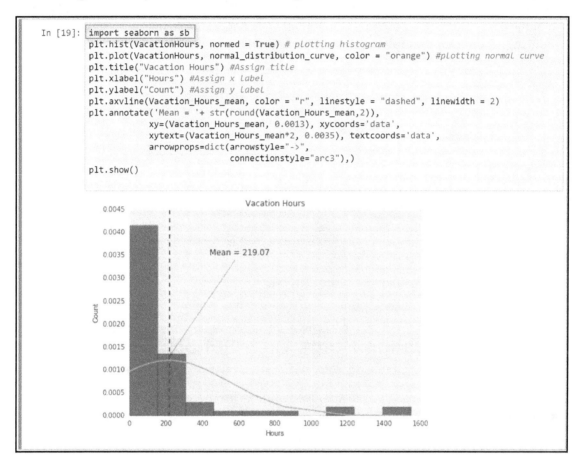

We can see that the `seaborn` library has some built-in features that make plotting straightforward and visually appealing, while `matplotlib` allows for advanced customizations for plots that require detail.

Publishing Jupyter Notebook

Before we share our Notebook with our friends, it might be a good idea to personalize it a bit and add some finishing touches to the look. The first thing that we can do is scroll to the top of the page and click on the first cell. Initially, we had a simple `print()` statement producing **Histogram Example**, as seen in the following screenshot:

```
In [1]:  print('Histogram Example')

         Histogram Example
```

Rather than have a Python script printing out a title for our project, we can use the **Markdown** function in the cell to display a formatted heading, as seen in the following screenshot:

When the **Markdown** is selected, we are given options for the size of the heading, as seen in the following screenshot:

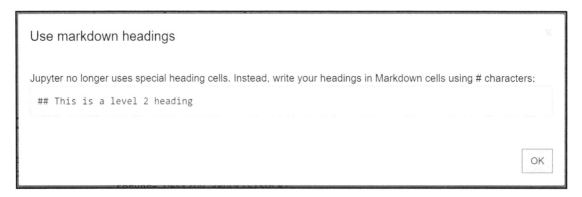

So, we've set our title as `#Vacation Hours Distribution` with a level 1 heading. Now, we just need to execute the cell for the **Markdown** to apply the appropriate formatting, as seen in the following screenshot:

Vacation Hours Distribution

```
In [1]: import pypyodbc
        connection = pypyodbc.connect(driver='{SQL Server}',
                                server='localhost\SQLBI',
                                database='AdventureWorks2014
                    trusted_connection='yes')

        connection.getinfo

        cursor = connection.cursor()
```

We can also add an additional two rows in the cell below the title to indicate the developer and date of the project. The following code is used:

```
## Developer: Ahmed Sherif
### Date: 12/31/2016
```

The result of the formatting code is seen in the following screenshot:

Vacation Hours Distribution

Developer: Ahmed Sherif

Date: 12/31/2016

```
In [1]: import pypyodbc
        connection = pypyodbc.connect(driver='{SQL Server}',
                                server='localhost\SQLBI',
                                database='AdventureWorks2014',
                    trusted_connection='yes')

        connection.getinfo

        cursor = connection.cursor()
```

We are now ready to share our Notebook with others who may be interested in our results. The nice thing about working with the Jupyter Notebook is that we develop directly on the server with a browser. The browser link is sufficient to be used for sharing with other users who are on the same server as you. The link for the Histogram Notebook can be found at the following location:

`http://127.0.0.1:8888/notebooks/Histograms.ipynb`

Additionally, we have the ability to share a local copy of the Notebook with users who do not have access to the server directly. This can be done from the menu of the Jupyter Notebook, by selecting **Download as** and then identifying the format that is most appropriate for sharing our results, as seen in the following screenshot:

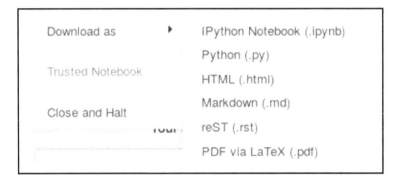

I have found the greatest success with downloading the Jupyter Notebook as a **HTML (.html)** file and then exporting the HTML file to a PDF. While you can save directly to a **PDF via Latex (.pdf)**, this method requires installing plugins and additional packages to your Python project and has been shown to cause some compatibility issues.

Summary

We have covered quite a bit of information in this chapter with Python. We started out by taking a simple dataset from the human resources department for `AdventureWorks` and we were able to show how the vacation hours of each job title were distributed across the entire company using both a histogram as well as a normal distribution plot. We used popular plotting libraries such as `matplotlib` and `seaborn` to quickly visualize the data derived from our human resources query. Finally, we were able to deliver our visualization and analysis easily to others for consumption with the Jupyter Notebook. In the next chapter, we will change gears and move away from programming languages as a means for business intelligence. We will develop a sales dashboard using one of the most popular data discovery and visualization tools, Tableau.

7
Creating a Sales Dashboard with Tableau

Tableau was founded in 2003 as a small company in California specializing in the visualization of relational and OLAP data warehouses and spreadsheets. The goal of Tableau was to empower individuals to build quick and effective visualizations based on spreadsheets and databases. Believe it or not, this was not a common phenomenon in 2003. At the time Tableau entered the market, the business intelligence community was made up of large enterprise offerings such as SAP, Microsoft, and IBM. In 2013, exactly 10 years after the start of the company, Tableau went public with an **initial public offering (IPO)** of over $250M and nothing has been the same ever since.

Tableau is now considered to be a leader ahead of SAP, IBM, and Microsoft when it comes to Business Intelligence and Analytic platforms, according to Gartner:

To learn more about Gartner and how the Magic Quadrant is constructed, visit the following website:
`https://www.gartner.com/doc/reprints?id=1-2XXET8P&ct=160204`

The success that Tableau has seen in the business intelligence arena may be partly due to the fact that it is quite easy for anyone to set up a visualization or a report with minimal effort and resources.

Imagine the following scenario: a data analyst is looking to develop a report with traditional enterprise BI software connected to a data warehouse. Unfortunately, that report is personally requested by the CFO of the company and they are requesting a specific measure to be included in the report that is not currently available in the data warehouse. It is stored in an external file on a different server and is updated manually. The CFO has used this measure in the past to evaluate future costs and is insisting that it be included in this new report. Within the current BI platform, the data analyst does not have the ability to create custom measures within a report. The data analyst puts in a request with IT to get this field included into the current data warehouse so that it may become available for reporting among the current stack of BI tools. This request to IT, however, is not just a simple request that can be completed in an hour. It must go through a ticketing system and a rigorous impact analysis study to determine any effects from releasing such a field out to the overall community. The IT department responds to the ticket a week after receiving it to let it be known that it will take at least one month before the field is tested and it is determined whether this new measure will have a detrimental impact on the health of the company.

The analyst is required to get this report into the hands of the CFO by the end of the week and is on a totally different timeline than the one proposed by IT. So the analyst goes online and reads a blog about how easy and powerful Tableau is at generating reports and dashboards based on data from different sources. The analyst downloads Tableau, connects to his data warehouse as well as the external source, creates a cool-looking interactive report that does even more than what was initially requested, and then publishes it as an internal link that his CFO can easily access. The CFO is impressed with the final product and requests to have this report updated and maintained on a regular basis using Tableau. Additionally, the CFO orders several licenses for the rest of the finance department to fill the reporting gap with the existing BI and data warehouse environment.

This scenario is occurring much more frequently and accounts for the main rise in the use of desktop visualization and exploration tools. We've already discussed one such tool in Chapter 3, *Analysis with Excel and Creating Interactive Maps and Charts with Power BI,* and we will cover another in Chapter 8, *Creating an Inventory Dashboard with QlikSense.*

We will cover the following topics in this chapter:

- Building a sales query in SQL Server
- Downloading Tableau
- Installing Tableau
- Connecting SQL Server to Tableau
- Building a sales dashboard in Tableau
- Publishing dashboard to Tableau Public

Building a sales query in MS SQL Server

Before we can start visualizing our amazing data in Tableau, we must first put together the query that will provide us that amazing data. We have been asked to put together a sales dashboard that highlights sales from different marketing promotions that have been initiated since the start of AdventureWorks. This promotional data is located in the Sales.SalesReason table in the data warehouse, as seen in the following screenshot:

```sql
select
    *
from
    AdventureWorks2014.Sales.SalesReason
```

100 % ▼

◻ Results ▤ Messages

	SalesReasonID	Name	ReasonType	ModifiedDate
1	1	Price	Other	2008-04-30 00:00:00.000
2	2	On Promotion	Promotion	2008-04-30 00:00:00.000
3	3	Magazine Advertisement	Marketing	2008-04-30 00:00:00.000
4	4	Television Advertisement	Marketing	2008-04-30 00:00:00.000
5	5	Manufacturer	Other	2008-04-30 00:00:00.000
6	6	Review	Other	2008-04-30 00:00:00.000
7	7	Demo Event	Marketing	2008-04-30 00:00:00.000
8	8	Sponsorship	Marketing	2008-04-30 00:00:00.000
9	9	Quality	Other	2008-04-30 00:00:00.000
10	10	Other	Other	2008-04-30 00:00:00.000

These results show that there are ten different possible promotions that could have resulted in a sale. The actual sales data is in the `Sales.SalesOrderHeader` table but that table does not have the `SalesReasonID` for us to join sales to promotions. The `SalesOrderHeader` table has a `SalesOrderID`, as seen in the following script:

```
SELECT
distinct [SalesOrderID]
FROM [AdventureWorks2014].[Sales].[SalesOrderHeader]
```

We will need to find a table that can tie `SalesOrderID` to `SalesReasonID`. Fortunately, we have a table that does just that and it is called `SalesOrderHeaderSalesReason`, as seen in the following screenshot:

```
select top 10 * from
AdventureWorks2014.sales.SalesOrderHeaderSalesReason
```

100 %

Results Messages

	SalesOrderID	SalesReasonID	ModifiedDate
1	43697	5	2011-05-31 00:00:00.000
2	43697	9	2011-05-31 00:00:00.000
3	43702	5	2011-06-01 00:00:00.000
4	43702	9	2011-06-01 00:00:00.000
5	43703	5	2011-06-01 00:00:00.000
6	43703	9	2011-06-01 00:00:00.000
7	43706	5	2011-06-02 00:00:00.000
8	43706	9	2011-06-02 00:00:00.000
9	43707	5	2011-06-02 00:00:00.000
10	43707	9	2011-06-02 00:00:00.000

SalesOrderHeaderSalesReason will serve as a link table between SalesOrderHeader and SalesReason, as seen in the following screenshot:

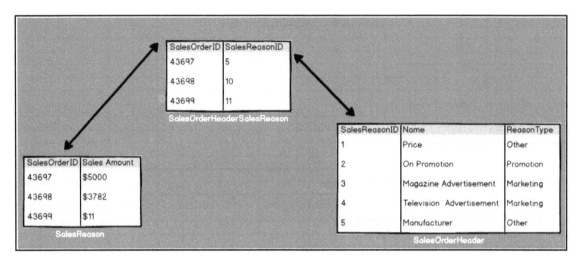

Now that we know the relationship between the different tables to pull in the values that we need, we can generate our SQL statement, as seen in the following script:

```
SELECT
distinct
SalesReason.Name as 'Sale Reason Name'
,SalesReason.ReasonType as 'Sale Reason Type'
,sum(round(SalesOrderHeader.SubTotal,2)) as 'Sales Amount'
,sum(round(SalesOrderHeader.TaxAmt,2)) as 'Tax'
,sum(round(SalesOrderHeader.Freight,2)) as 'Freight Amount'

FROM [AdventureWorks2014].[Sales].[SalesReason] as SalesReason

inner join [AdventureWorks2014].[Sales].[SalesOrderHeaderSalesReason] as
SalesOrderHeaderSalesReason on
SalesOrderHeaderSalesReason.SalesReasonID = SalesReason.SalesReasonID

inner join [AdventureWorks2014].[Sales].[SalesOrderHeader] as
SalesOrderHeader on
SalesOrderHeader.SalesOrderID = SalesOrderHeaderSalesReason.SalesOrderID

Group by SalesReason.Name, SalesReason.ReasonType
Order by 3 desc
```

The results of the previous SQL script can be seen in the following screenshot:

	Sale Reason Name	Sale Reason Type	Sales Amount	Tax	Freight Amount
1	Price	Other	10975842.56	878087.74	274380.29
2	On Promotion	Promotion	6361829.95	508951.68	159044.56
3	Manufacturer	Other	5998122.10	479847.59	149957.80
4	Quality	Other	5549896.77	443989.26	138752.46
5	Review	Other	1694882.19	135589.55	42374.17
6	Other	Other	248483.34	19880.75	6211.85
7	Television Advertisement	Marketing	27475.82	2198.68	687.24

We are now able to relate our `Sales Reason Name` and `Sale Reason Type` with `Sales Amount`, `Tax`, and `Freight Amount`. We have confirmed that this is the level of granularity that is requested to be visualized by executives in a dashboard for the sales team. Our next step is to import that data into Tableau.

Downloading Tableau

Before we can bring data into Tableau, we must first download it onto our local machine. As mentioned earlier in the chapter, it is quite straightforward to get started with Tableau. The first thing we must do is visit their website and download a free version of Tableau, known as Tableau Public: `https://public.tableau.com/en-us/s/download`.

 You may be prompted to enter an e-mail address before you can download the application. At the time of writing, the most recent version of Tableau Public is 10.0.2.

Once the file has been downloaded, we can go ahead and begin the installation process.

Installing Tableau

Running the installation file will trigger the usual setup message asking us to acknowledge the terms and licensing agreement, as seen in the following screenshot:

Once the agreement has been checked, we can begin the installation process by clicking on the **Install** button. As our installation is continuing, we should see its progress, as seen in the following screenshot.

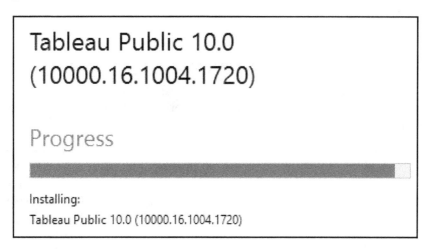

Importing data into Tableau

As we fire up our Tableau Public application for the first time, we are introduced to the different ways that we can bring data in, as seen in the following screenshot:

Unfortunately, there is no direct means to connect to a SQL Server query. Those connections are only available on the licensed version of Tableau that is available for a two-week trial period. Our best option to visualize query results from MS SQL Server is to export the data into a **Text file** and then connect to Tableau.

Exporting to a text file

Exporting from SQL Server is quite straightforward. All that is required is to right-click on the result set from the query statement in MS SQL Server and then select **Save Results As...**, as seen in the following screenshot:

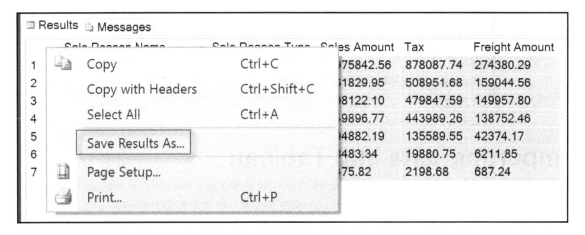

Once the file is saved to a designated location, we can then connect the data results to Tableau Public through the **Text File** method. As our data is loaded into Tableau, we can view the results immediately to confirm that the numbers are consistent with SQL Server, as seen in the following screenshot:

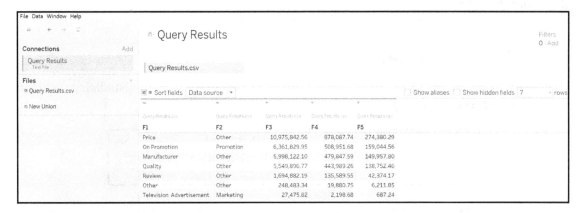

One thing that did not come through was the heading for each column. We can overwrite the default values by double-clicking on **F1**, **F2**, **F3**, **F4**, and **F5** and replacing them with **Sales Reason**, **Sales Reason Type**, **Sales Amount**, **Tax Amount**, and **Freight Amount**, as seen in the following screenshot:

Abc	Abc	#	#	#
Query Results.csv	Query Results.csv	Query Results.csv	Query Results.csv	Query Results.csv
Sales Reason	**Sales Reason Type**	**Sales Amount**	**Tax Amount**	**Freight Amount**
Television Advertisement	Marketing	27,475.82	2,198.68	687.24
Manufacturer	Other	5,998,122.10	479,847.59	149,957.80
Other	Other	248,483.34	19,880.75	6,211.85
Price	Other	10,975,842.56	878,087.74	274,380.29
Quality	Other	5,549,896.77	443,989.26	138,752.46
Review	Other	1,694,882.19	135,589.55	42,374.17
On Promotion	Promotion	6,361,829.95	508,951.68	159,044.56

Building a sales dashboard in Tableau

There are many ways to get started with visualizing in Tableau. One convenient way is to build out several separate visualizations in sheets and then connect them together on a single dashboard canvas later on.

Building a Crosstab

Next to the **Data Source** tab, click on the tab called **Sheet1** to get started visualizing our first component, as seen in the following screenshot:

As we get started with our first visualization, we will primarily see a blank canvas along with access to dimensions, measures, and visualization options. Any object that comes through as a non-numeric field from the data will be labeled under the **Dimensions** header and can be accessed from the upper left-hand side, as seen in the following screenshot:

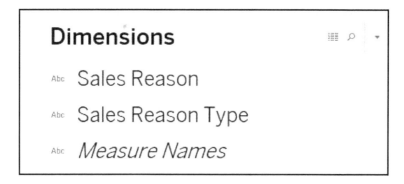

Subsequently, any object that comes through from the data as a numeric field will be interpreted as a measure and will fall under the **Measures** header, as seen in the following screenshot:

Measures

⊹ Freight Amount

⊹ Sales Amount

⊹ Tax Amount

⊹ *Number of Records*

⊹ *Measure Values*

And finally, if you are looking to see what the available options are for visualizing different dimensions and measures, click on the **Show Me** menu on the upper right-hand side of the application, as seen in the following screenshot:

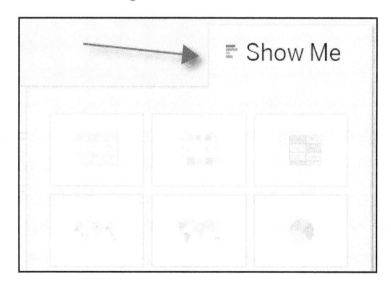

We can start with a simple **Crosstab** that visualizes the three measures we have against the **Sales Reason**. First off, we can drag the three measures onto the **Columns** section and then drag the **Sales Reason** dimension onto the **Rows** section, as seen in the following screenshot:

The default visualization turns the data into a bar chart. Switching the bar chart to a Crosstab is a pretty straightforward process and can be done with a click of a button. We can click on the Crosstab icon, as seen in the following screenshot:

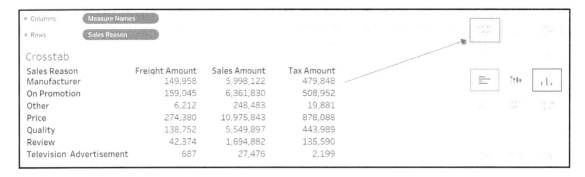

Additionally, we can make some enhancements by double-clicking on **Crosstab** and giving it a more appropriate title, such as `Sales Reason Summary,` as seen in the following screenshot:

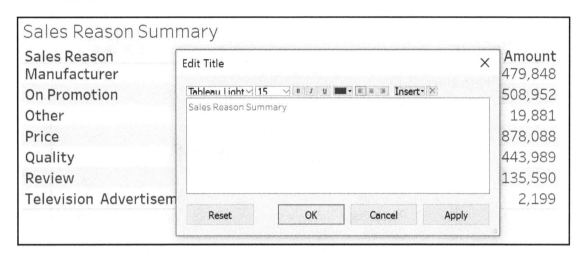

Since we are dealing with sales data, it would be helpful if we could indicate that these numbers are related to a currency value. We can do this by selecting the three measures individually under **Measure Values** and selecting **Format...**, as seen in the following screenshot:

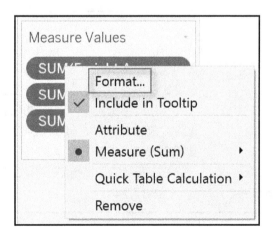

We will see both an **Axis** and a **Pane** tab. We want to select the **Pane** tab and switch the formatting to **Currency (Standard)**, as seen in the following screenshot:

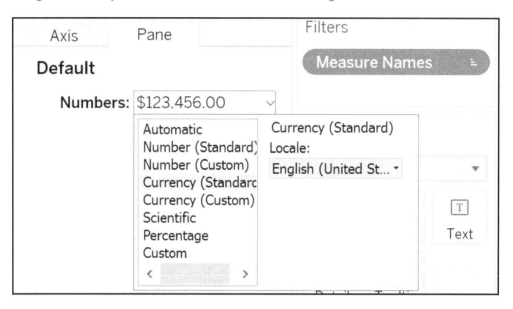

Once we apply the formatting to each measure, our new Crosstab will appear, as the following:

Sales Reason Summary

Sales Reason	Freight Amount	Tax Amount	Sales Amount
Manufacturer	$149,957.80	$479,847.59	$5,998,122.10
On Promotion	$159,044.56	$508,951.68	$6,361,829.95
Other	$6,211.85	$19,880.75	$248,483.34
Price	$274,380.29	$878,087.74	$10,975,842.56
Quality	$138,752.46	$443,989.26	$5,549,896.77
Review	$42,374.17	$135,589.55	$1,694,882.19
Television Advertisement	$687.24	$2,198.68	$27,475.82

Before we move onto our next visualization, let's add one more enhancement to the Crosstab. This first requires us to exit the **Format** section by clicking on the **x** button, as seen in the following screenshot:

If we click on the **Analytics** tab and select **Totals**, we end up having a **Grand Total** summary at the bottom of the Crosstab:

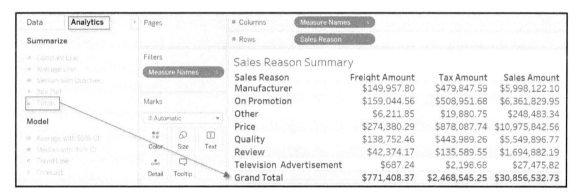

We have just completed our first visualization in the first sheet using a Crosstab.

Building custom calculation fields

Predefined measures come to us directly from the data, such as `Freight Amount` and `Sales Amount`. We also have the ability to create custom measures directly inside of Tableau. For example, we can create the following calculation for `Total Sales Amount`:

    Total Sales Amount = Sales Amount + Tax Amount + Freight Amount

To perform this calculation inside of Tableau, we must first click on **Analysis** on the menu bar and select **Create Calculated Field...**, as seen in the following screenshot:

We can then assign a title to the calculated field, as well as perform the necessary calculation as follows:

    SUM([Freight Amount] + [Tax Amount] + [Sales Amount])

This can be done inside of the calculated field editor:

As long as the message on the bottom left of the calculation screen says **The calculation is valid**, we can apply our custom field to our worksheet. Our new field should now appear along with the other measures, as seen in the following screenshot:

Measures

   ⊕ Freight Amount

   ⊕ Sales Amount

   ⊕ Tax Amount

   ⊕ Total Sales Amount

   ⊕ *Number of Records*

   ⊕ *Measure Values*

In the next section, we will build a visualization that will utilize our newly created custom field.

Creating bullet graphs

Bullet graphs, a relatively new phenomenon within the data visualization community, were spearheaded by Stephen Few, who is regarded as one of the key leaders and influencers in the BI community. Stephen Few was not pleased with many of the visual offerings delivered by BI tools, especially visual components such as gauges and meters that overcomplicated metrics. He ultimately developed the bullet graph as a way to combine several data points in a small amount of space utilizing a familiar component such as a bar chart.

 To learn more about Stephen Few and his visualization philosophy, visit his website:
`https://www.perceptualedge.com`

The benefit of a bullet graph or a bullet chart is that you have the ability to display primary measures such as an actual amount and complementary measures such as a target amount within the same component. In the example that we will tackle, we want to visualize how much of the `Total Sales Amount` is comprised of the `Sales Amount`, `Tax Amount`, and `Freight Amount`.

We can begin by creating a new worksheet as we are building a new visualization component from scratch. In order to create a bullet graph, we are required to have at least one dimension and two measures. For our purposes, we will drag both **Sales Amount** and **Total Sales Amount** onto the **Columns** section and **Sales Reason** to the **Rows** section, as seen in the following screenshot:

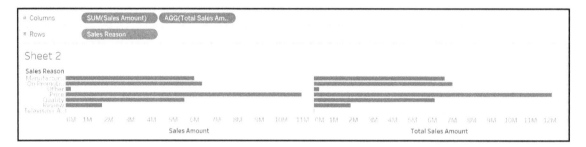

Once again, the default visualization is a bar chart. We can convert to a bullet graph by clicking on the icon in the **Show Me** menu, as seen in the following screenshot:

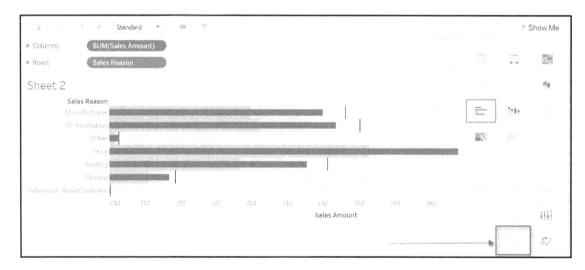

The bars in the bullet chart are not sorted by **Sales Amount** but by **Sales Reason**. We can sort by **Sales Amount** by dragging and dropping the **Sales Reason** dimension onto the **Marks** section, as seen in the following screenshot:

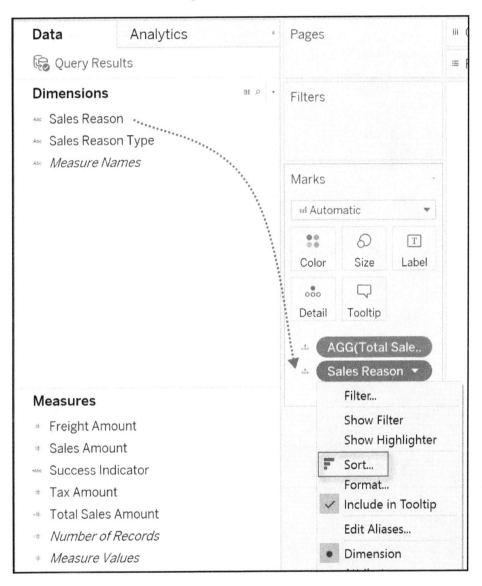

This allows us to access the attributes of the dimension, and we can then right-click on **Sales Reason** to access the **Sort** icon to rearrange our sort order. We can then select **Descending Sort order** and choose to **Sort by** the **Sales Amount** field, as seen in the following screenshot:

Additionally, we can format our bullet graph by giving it a title such as **Sales Amount vs. Total Sales Amount**, as seen in the following screenshot:

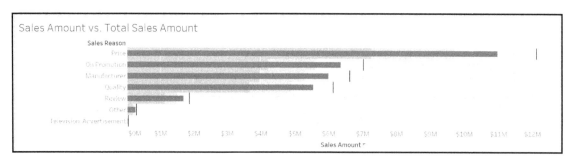

We can see on the bullet graph that there is a vertical tick on the right side of each bar. That tick signifies the value of the **Total Sales Amount**. The actual tip of the bar chart to the left of the tick signifies the value of the **Sales Amount**. Additionally, we see a couple of other ticks, which signify percentages of the **Total Sales Amount**, if we hover over them, as seen in the following screenshot:

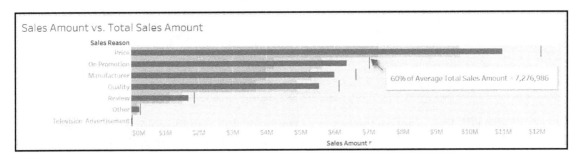

The ticks give 20% intervals to provide an indication of how much the lesser value measure (**SalesAmount**) is of the average amount of the greater value measure (**Total Sales Amount**). These intervals are automatically generated by the bullet graph. What we can gather from the bullet graph is that the gap between **Sales Amount** and **Total Sales Amount** seems to be consistent across the six different values for **Sales Reason**.

One final enhancement we can make to the bullet graph is to apply a different color to each bar representing a different **Sales Reason**. Currently, all six bars represent the same color, but we may get a request to customize each bar with a different color. This can be done by dragging **Sales Reason** underneath the **Dimensions** header and dropping it onto the color palette under the **Marks** header, as seen in the following screenshot:

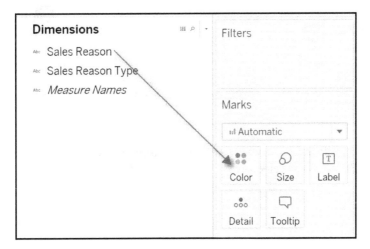

Once we apply the color change based on **Sales Reason**, our bullet graph will appear as seen in the following screenshot:

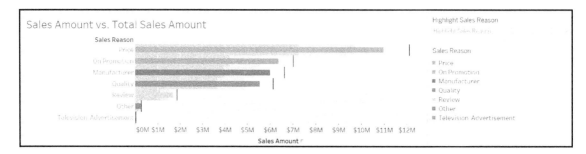

We could also edit the colors on the bullet graph by clicking on the color scheme, selecting **Edit Colors…**, and finally selecting a different **Color Palette** (it is currently set to **Automatic**):

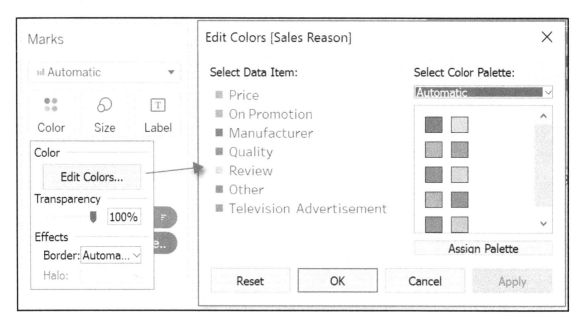

For now, we will remain with our current Color Palette as we move on to our final visualization, a KPI indicator selector.

Creating a KPI indicator selector

Our final component will focus on our higher-level dimension, **Sales Reason Type**, as well as interactivity between components. Once more, we will create a new worksheet and drag the **Sales Reason Type** onto the **Columns** section and the **Total Sales Amount** onto the **Rows** section. We can then select the **Highlight Tables** component from the **Show Me** menu and create the visualization seen in the following screenshot:

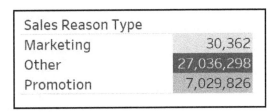

While the highlighted table shows values for the **Total Sales Amount**, what we really need it to do is indicate whether the value is greater than $10M, which is the target for a successful strategy developed by the marketing team. We will call this the `Success Indicator`, and its value will be determined by the following expression within a calculated field:

```
IF [Total Sales Amount] > 10000000 THEN "Success" ELSE "Failure" END
```

Once we've applied the expression to the calculated field and named it **Success Indicator**, we should once again see a **The calculation is valid** message:

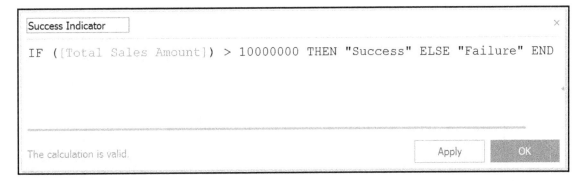

Now we want to apply our `Success Indicator` to our table. We can do this by dragging the **Success Indicator** calculation field on top of the **Shape** marker, as seen in the following screenshot:

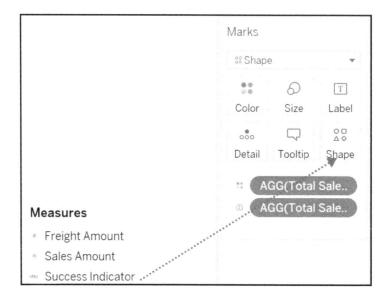

We then click on our **Shape** marker and select **Arrows** as our **Shape Palette**, with the up arrow being assigned to **Success** and the down arrow being assigned to **Failure**, as seen in the following screenshot:

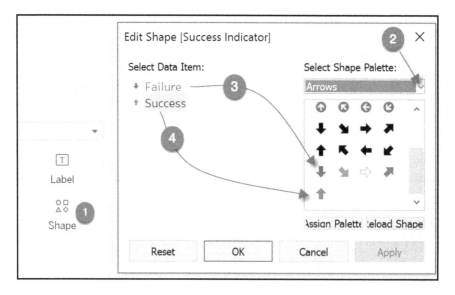

While the arrows have been applied to the table, the color scheme has not yet been applied, as seen in the following screenshot:

In order to apply the correct color scheme, we must also drag the **Success Indicator** on top of the Color marker. We can then edit the **Color Palette** and assign the appropriate colors to both the **Success** and **Failure** indicators, as seen in the following screenshot:

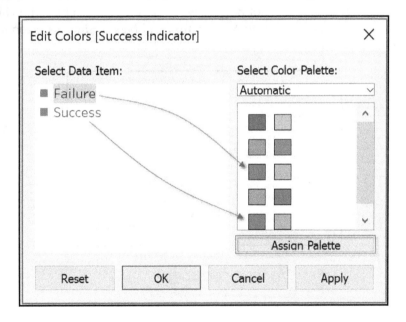

We can now preview our table with the appropriate shape palette and the appropriate color palette, as seen in the following screenshot:

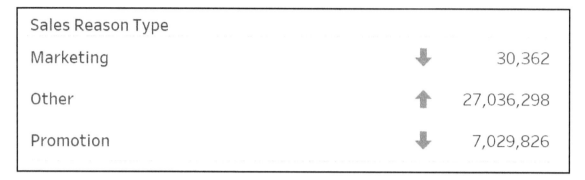

While it is fine to have the value of the indicator available to the right of the indicator, for the purposes of our dashboard it is not necessary. Therefore, we can hide the values by right-clicking on each one and selecting **Mark Label** and **Never Show**, as seen in the following screenshot:

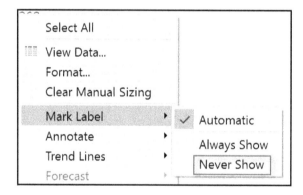

Finally, we can name the component **Success Indicator** and complete the process, as seen in the following screenshot:

We are now ready to put together our dashboard with all of the pieces we've created in the different sheets.

Building a sales dashboard in Tableau

Next to each new worksheet is a tab to create a new dashboard. Let's go ahead and select a new dashboard. But before we connect our worksheets to the dashboard, we want to make the dashboard look a little more user-friendly.

Beautifying the dashboard

On the left-hand side of the dashboard screen, there is a menu that can be used to set the canvas size to **Automatic**, which immediately resets the dashboard to fit any screen it is displayed on:

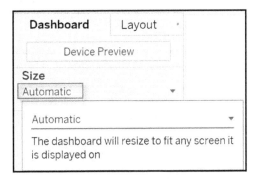

After changing the canvas size, we can next add a title by checking **Show dashboard title** and assigning the **AdventureWorks Sales Dashboard** title. If we right-click on the title and select **Format Title...**, we have the ability to center the title header, as seen in the following screenshot:

We can't have a dashboard without a company logo. Fortunately, someone has already created one online for us to use with the AdventureWorks company. We can download that logo from the following website: `http://i2.wp.com/blog.jpries.com/wp-content/uploa ds/2015/12/AdventureWorks-Logo_blog.jpg?resize=300%2C104`.

At the bottom left-hand corner of the dashboard, we have the ability to drag and drop certain objects onto the canvas, as seen in the following screenshot:

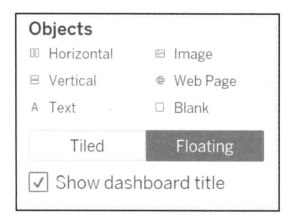

We set all object to be **Floating** as opposed to **Tiled** as it gives us added flexibility in placing objects; we can then drag the **Image** object onto the top right-hand corner of the canvas and upload the logo we downloaded locally to our machine for AdventureWorks, as seen in the following screenshot:

Connecting worksheets to dashboards

The fruits of our labor are beginning to show. Connecting our existing worksheets to our new dashboard is a relatively straightforward process as we can drag and drop each worksheet onto a different part of the canvas, as seen on the following screenshot:

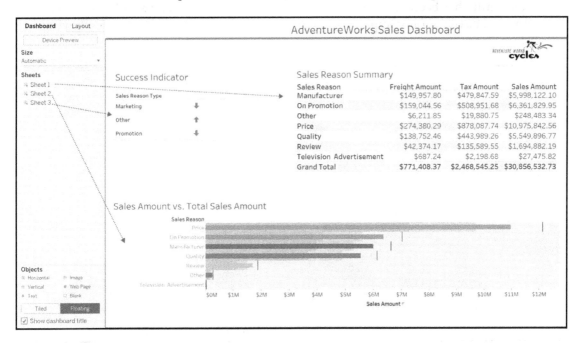

We now have all three components on the dashboard, but there isn't any interactivity between them. None of them are speaking to each other and we need to change that. We can change that by converting the **Success Indicator** visualization into a filterable component by checking the **Use as Filter** icon on the upper right-hand corner of the component, as seen in the following screenshot:

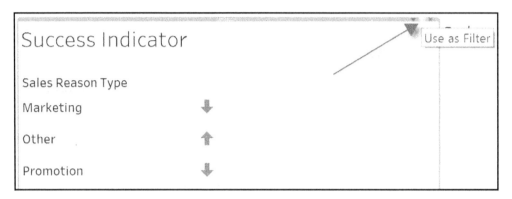

Once that feature has been activated we can select either of the three **Sales Reason Type** indicators and have the filter apply to all filterable components, as seen in the following screenshot:

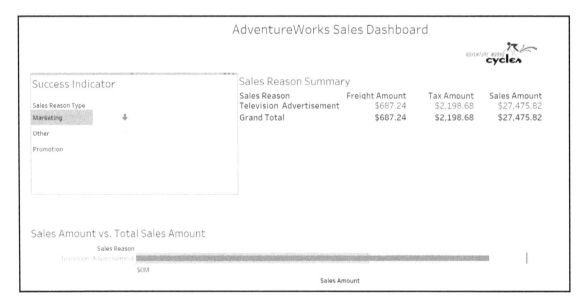

As we can now see, when we select **Marketing** as a **Sales Reason Type** indicator, the other two components then display values for **Television Advertisement** only.

Publishing dashboard to Tableau Public

We are now at the stage where we can share our Tableau dashboard with other interested parties. Thankfully, this process is also pretty straightforward. First and foremost, if we do not already have one, we need to create an account on the Tableau Public website at the following location: `https://public.tableau.com/auth/signup`.

Once we have an account, we can click on the **File** dropdown from the menu and select **Save to Tableau Public...**, as seen in the following screenshot:

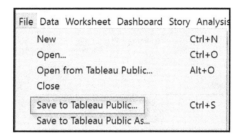

We will then be prompted to log in with our Tableau Public credentials, as seen in the following screenshot:

Once we have logged in we can immediately view our dashboard as it resides on the Tableau Public server, as seen in the following screenshot:

We have the ability to share our dashboard with the public by clicking on the **Share** icon in the bottom right-hand corner, as seen in the following screenshot:

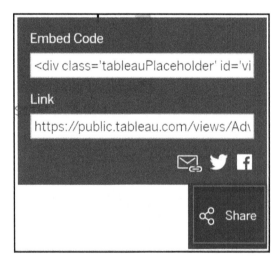

Tableau Public provides us with both the **Embed Code** and the **Link** to the dashboard for sharing purposes.

Summary

We have come to the conclusion of another chapter. We started with a simple MS SQL Server query and turned it into a fully functional dashboard. Our original query only had ten rows of data, but that turned out to be sufficient enough to tell a story about how the sales revenue was distributed amongst different marketing strategies. Tableau helped us isolate different visualizations separately and then combine them into a single dashboard where all three components interacted with each other. Finally, through the Tableau Public portal, we saw how easily we could publish our results and share them with the rest of the world. In the next chapter, we will continue with the desktop discovery genre and focus our attention to the tool that is considered the closest competitor to Tableau: QlikSense. We will build an inventory dashboard for AdventureWorks that will be used to alert managers when certain products are running low and need to be reordered.

8
Creating an Inventory Dashboard with QlikSense

It is hard to imagine another company more closely associated with Tableau than Qlik. They both provide the same data discovery service to customers and are considered direct competitors. The differences between them are few lessen with each new release.

Qlik first emerged on the market in 1996 with QlikView and soon began to find its way into departments looking to quickly capitalize on their data and produce quick and powerful visualizations that could help them answer the pressing questions being asked by their company.

QlikView is the flagship product of Qlik and allows developers to produce guided analytics. More recently QlikSense was developed for business intelligence self-service visualizations and dashboards. While both tools have much to offer to a Business Intelligence department, our focus in this chapter will be on QlikSense because of the ability to deliver a "cleaner" or "finished" product with a dashboard.

In this chapter we will focus on building an inventory dashboard for the AdventureWorks company and help identify the warehouses that are low on inventory and need to stock up on new supplies. In building this dashboard, we will cover the following topics:

- Downloading and installing QlikSense Desktop
- Developing an inventory dataset with SQL Server
- Connecting SQL Server to QlikSense Desktop
- Developing interactive visual components with QlikSense Desktop
- Publishing an inventory dashboard to Qlik Cloud

Getting started with QlikSense Desktop

One of the main advantages with data discovery and visualization tools such as QlikSense is that there is minimal overhead when it comes to getting started with the application whether it be downloading, installing, or configuring components. So let's begin.

Downloading QlikSense

We can download the latest version of QlikSense by visiting the following website: `http://www.qlik.com/us/products/qlik-sense/desktop` and clicking on the **TRY OR BUY** button on the upper right-hand side as seen in the following screenshot:

That will then lead us to a page where we have the option to either download QlikSense Desktop or QlikSense Cloud. We can then go ahead and click on the **FREE DOWNLOAD** button underneath QlikSense Desktop as seen in the following screenshot:

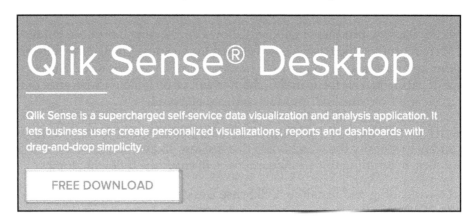

Once selected, the next page will be a registration form to enter contact information, for Qlik to find out something about you before you download QlikSense. Once you submit the form the download process will begin.

Installing QlikSense

When we execute the installation file for the first time, we will see the following message pop up indicating to us whether we have enough space on our local machine to run the file, as seen in the following screenshot:

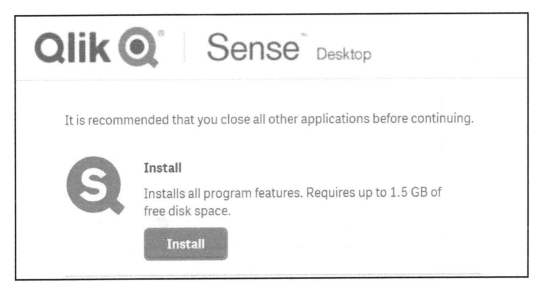

 QlikSense Desktop is available for Windows Vista 64-bit or later versions. It is not currently available on Windows Server or for 32-bit Windows operating systems.

Once we click on the **Install** icon and agree to the terms and conditions, our installation should begin. Once the installation has been successful, a message will appear as seen in the following screenshot:

We have now successfully downloaded and installed QlikSense Desktop and can begin visualizing the data that we will use to build the inventory dashboard.

Developing an inventory dataset with SQL Server

Before we can visualize the dataset for the inventory dashboard, we must first create the dataset. The goal of our dataset is to identify inventory stock within different warehouses and determine if a reorder is necessary.

The following query built in SQL Server is an example of a product, *Adjustable Race*, that has an inventory limit lower than the minimum value required for a reorder:

```
SELECT
loc.Name as WarehouseName
,inv.ProductID
,prod.Name as ProductName
,sum(inv.Quantity) as Inventory
,sum(prod.ReorderPoint) as ReorderPoint
,case when sum(inv.Quantity) > sum(prod.ReorderPoint) then 'N' else 'Y' end
as ReorderFlag
FROM [AdventureWorks2014].[Production].[Location] as loc
inner join [AdventureWorks2014].[Production].[ProductInventory] as inv on
loc.LocationID = inv.LocationID
inner join [AdventureWorks2014].[Production].[Product] as prod on
prod.ProductID =  inv.ProductID

where Prod.Name = 'Adjustable Race'

group by
loc.Name
,inv.ProductID
,prod.Name
```

The output of the query can be seen in the following screenshot:

	WarehouseName	ProductID	ProductName	Inventory	ReorderPoint	ReorderFlag
1	Miscellaneous Storage	1	Adjustable Race	324	750	Y
2	Subassembly	1	Adjustable Race	353	750	Y
3	Tool Crib	1	Adjustable Race	408	750	Y

The last column of the query is the **ReorderFlag** field (built using a case statement), used to indicate whether or not the designated product at a specific warehouse is up for reorder. This will be the query we will use to connect to QlikSense. However, we will remove the following row so that we pull in all products and not just the filter for **Adjustable Race**.

```
where Prod.Name = 'Adjustable Race'
```

Connecting SQL Server query to QlikSense Desktop

We are now ready to connect QlikSense to the inventory query we created in the previous section. When first launching QlikSense we are prompted with a message to **CREATE A NEW APP** as seen in the following screenshot:

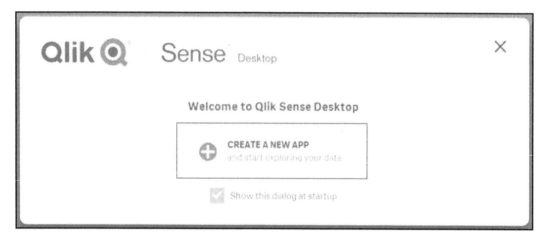

We can go then go ahead and name our application `AdventureWorks Inventory Dashboard` as seen in the following screenshot:

We can then go ahead with creating the application and opening it up. Upon initial load, QlikSense gives developers two different options for adding data, as seen in the following screenshot:

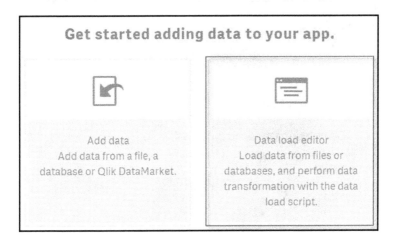

For our purposes we will utilize the **Data load editor** method because it gives us a better opportunity to leverage the existing query we built with SQL Server. Even though it is a bit more of a manual process than the **Add data** method,, which is more of an automated and graphical method, using the **Data load editor** will also help lend insight to how data is loaded into QlikSense.

Once we are in the **Data load editor** method we can click on the **Create new connection** icon on the upper right-hand side and select **ODBC** as seen in the following screenshot:

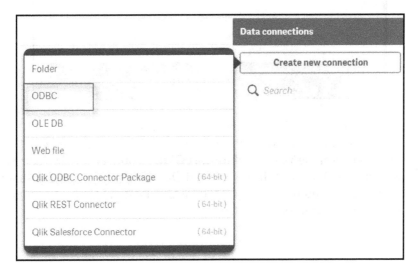

We should be able to find our existing ODBC connection to the SQL Server database, which we named **SQLBI** back in `Chapter 5`, *Forecasting with R*, as seen in the following screenshot:

 The ODBC connection **SQLBI** was created with a Windows NT authentication using the network login ID. Therefore, it is not required to input a username/password for this ODBC connection between SQL Server and QlikSense. If the original ODBC connection had instead been established using SQL Server authentication, then we would need to input a username/password.

Once we have created the connection, we can view some of the default script settings available within QlikSense:

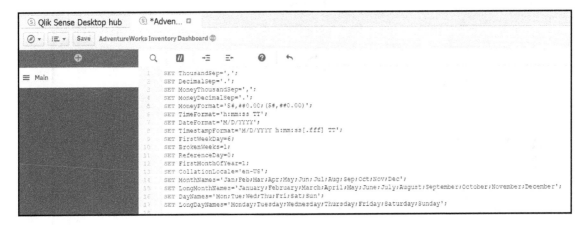

For our purposes we will not be changing any of these default settings. However, this is the location from which to customize settings if required. Underneath these settings, starting on row *19*, we can insert our SQL script from SQL Server to be loaded in QlikSense. The only requirement is to add the following code before the SQL statement to ensure the ODBC connection is used to pull in the script.

```
LIB CONNECT TO 'SQLBI';
```

The complete code will appear in the editor as the following:

```
19    LIB CONNECT TO 'SQLBI';
20
21    SELECT
22    loc.Name as WarehouseName
23    ,inv.ProductID
24    ,prod.Name as ProductName
25    ,sum(inv.Quantity) as Inventory
26    ,sum(prod.ReorderPoint) as ReorderPoint
27    ,case when sum(inv.Quantity) > sum(prod.ReorderPoint) then 'N' else 'Y' end as ReorderFlag
28    FROM [AdventureWorks2014].[Production].[Location] as loc
29    inner join [AdventureWorks2014].[Production].[ProductInventory] as inv on
30    loc.LocationID = inv.LocationID
31    inner join [AdventureWorks2014].[Production].[Product] as prod on
32    prod.ProductID =  inv.ProductID
33
34    group by
35    loc.Name
36    ,inv.ProductID
37    ,prod.Name;
```

We can now load the data generated by the script by clicking on the **Load Data** icon on the upper right hand corner. If the load is successful, we should see a **Data load progress | Data is complete** message as seen in the following screenshot:

Developing interactive visual components with QlikSense Desktop

We've now finished loading data and can begin visualizing within the application. In order to do so, we first need to navigate to the **App overview** icon on the upper left-hand side as seen in the following screenshot:

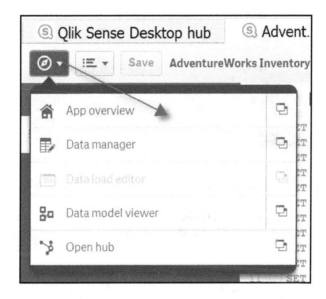

While initially developing applications with QlikSense, we may get lost between the **Data manager** and the **App overview**. Use the icon as your friend to flip back and forth between visualizations and data management.

Building a sheet

Once we are in the **App overview**, we can create a new sheet to begin our application development. We can name our sheet and add the following description:

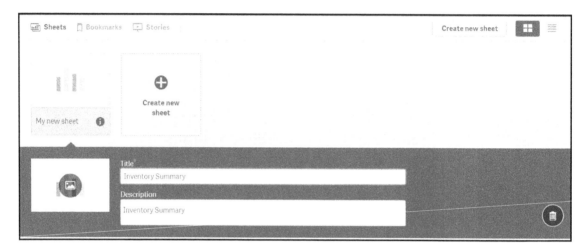

Once we've added the **Title** and **Description**, we will then need to click on the newly created **Inventory Summary** icon to begin development, as seen in the following screenshot:

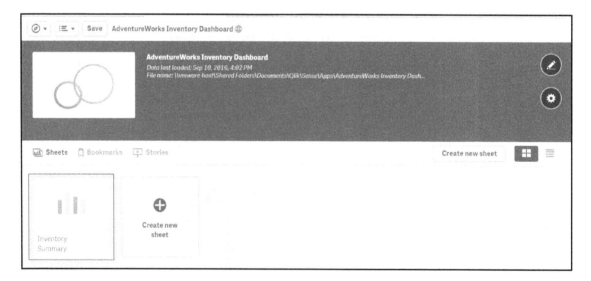

Our **Inventory Summary** sheet is still completely empty with the exception of the message that lets us know where to click to begin modifying our sheet, as seen in the following screenshot:

To make changes to the dashboard, we need to be in **Edit** mode. We can toggle on/off between **Edit** mode by clicking on the following button:

Once we click on **Edit**, we are presented with four icons on the left-hand side of the the menu that allow us to access the following features:

- Charts
- Custom objects
- Master items
- Fields

We will tackle each item on the menu as needed during the visualization development process.

Creating a filter pane component

In our summary sheet we will focus primarily on high-level information at each warehouse. In our dataset we have 14 different warehouses that contain inventory, such as paint and frame welding. Within SQL Server we can identify a distinct list of warehouses by executing the following script:

```
select
distinct
x.WarehouseName
from
(
SELECT
loc.Name as WarehouseName
,inv.ProductID
,prod.Name as ProductName
,sum(inv.Quantity) as Inventory
,sum(prod.ReorderPoint) as ReorderPoint
,case when sum(inv.Quantity) > sum(prod.ReorderPoint) then 'N' else 'Y' end
as ReorderFlag
FROM [AdventureWorks2014].[Production].[Location] as loc
inner join [AdventureWorks2014].[Production].[ProductInventory] as inv on
loc.LocationID = inv.LocationID
inner join [AdventureWorks2014].[Production].[Product] as prod on
prod.ProductID =  inv.ProductID

group by
loc.Name
,inv.ProductID
,prod.Name
) x
```

The output of the query can be seen inside SQL Server:

```
SQLQuery1.sql - DE...RPUKTS\asher (52))*  ×

⊟select
 distinct
 x.WarehouseName
 from
 (
 SELECT
 loc.Name as WarehouseName
 ,inv.ProductID
 ,prod.Name as ProductName
 ,sum(inv.Quantity) as Inventory
 ,sum(prod.ReorderPoint) as ReorderPoint
 ,case when sum(inv.Quantity) > sum(prod.ReorderPoint) then 'N' else 'Y' end as ReorderFlag
 FROM [AdventureWorks2014].[Production].[Location] as loc
 inner join [AdventureWorks2014].[Production].[ProductInventory] as inv on
 loc.LocationID = inv.LocationID
 inner join [AdventureWorks2014].[Production].[Product] as prod on
 prod.ProductID =  inv.ProductID
 group by
 loc.Name
 ,inv.ProductID
 ,prod.Name
 ) x
```

100 %   ▾

▣ Results ▵ Messages

	WarehouseName
1	Debur and Polish
2	Final Assembly
3	Finished Goods Storage
4	Frame Forming
5	Frame Welding
6	Metal Storage
7	Miscellaneous Storage
8	Paint
9	Paint Shop
10	Paint Storage
11	Sheet Metal Racks
12	Specialized Paint
13	Subassembly
14	Tool Crib

The good news is that we do not have to recreate this same query inside QlikSense in order to retrieve the distinct `WarehouseName` values that will be used in the filter. We can just click on the **Charts** icon and drag a **Filter pane** to the left-hand side of the canvas as seen in the following screenshot:

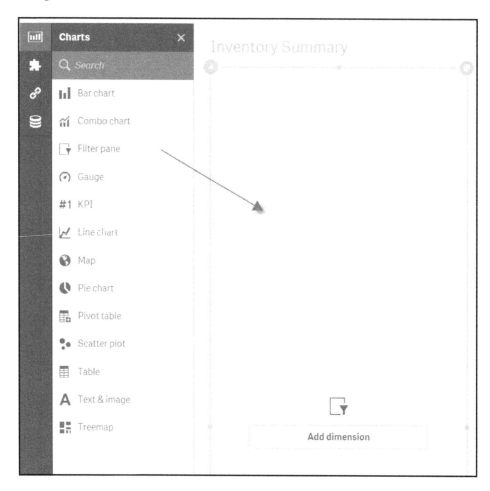

Next we can click on the **Add dimension** icon and select `WarehouseName` as our dimension of choice to show it displayed as a selection. We notice that we get the same 14 unique `WarehouseName` selections that we got earlier in our query.

Underneath the `WarehouseName` filter we repeat the process for creating a filter pane for the `ReorderFlag` indicator. This will give users two filter options for the inventory.

Our selectors are now complete with two filter panes on the left-hand side of the canvas, as seen in the following screenshot:

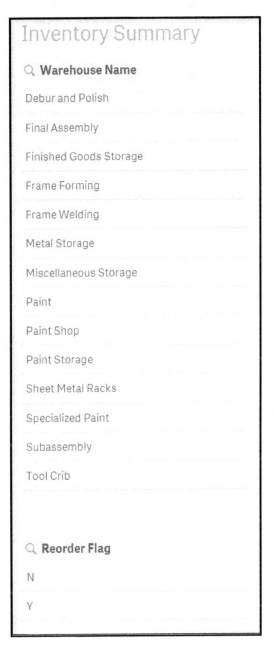

Creating a custom calculation and KPI

We now want to create a measure that will allow us to compare the ratio between the inventory amount and the reorder point amount. We can do that by clicking on the **Master items** icon and selecting **Create new** under **Measures** as seen in the following screenshot:

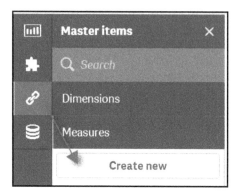

Once we are inside the **Create new measure** function, we can edit the measure inside the **Expression** with the following calculation:

```
Sum(Inventory)/Sum(ReorderPoint)
```

We can assign a name to the calculation of **Inventory Ratio** as seen in the following screenshot:

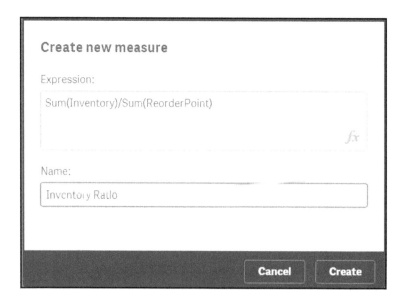

Once we have created the new measure, we can use it just like any other measure from the query. We can now return to our charting components and drag the **#1 KPI** component onto the canvas to the right of the filters, as seen in the following screenshot:

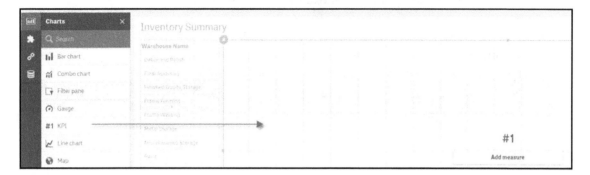

When we select the **Add measure** icon underneath the **#1** label, we now have the option to select the **Inventory Ratio** measure that we've just created, as seen in the following screenshot:

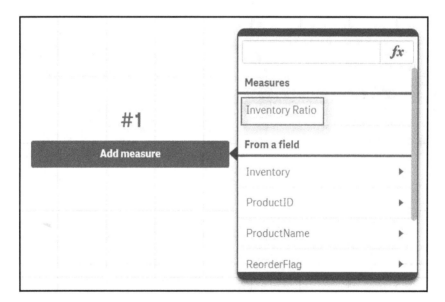

Once we add the measure to the **#1 KPI** component it reflects the value for all warehouses by default. We can begin to test our filters by clicking on **Done** to exit the **Edit** mode, so that we can begin to make selections to the filter pane and see how the input to the filter affects the output in the **#1 KPI** component. For example, if we filter on:

```
Warehouse Name = Paint
```

We get **Inventory Ratio** of **0.29**, as seen in the following screenshot:

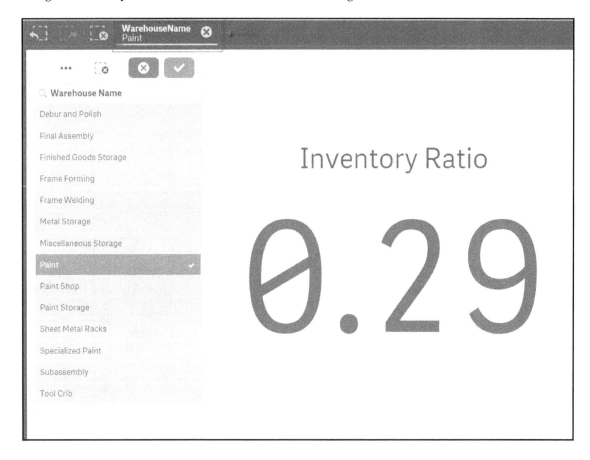

Any selection made in the filter pane additionally shows up on the menu bar as a further indicator that the dashboard is being filtered. The filter pane operates as a multiple selector and the number of selectors made can be seen, as shown in the following screenshot:

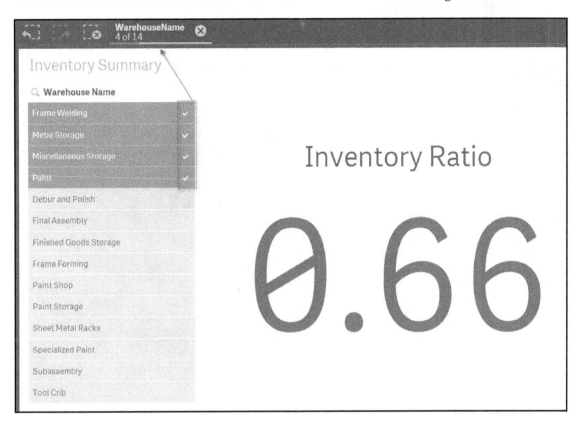

Creating a bar chart with multiple measures

While it is cool that we have a large KPI in the middle of the canvas, it would be even more cool for a user to see a chart component underneath the KPI to provide more substance to that same KPI number. Switching back to **Edit** mode, we can drag and drop a **Bar Chart** component underneath the **Inventory Ratio** component as seen in the following screenshot:

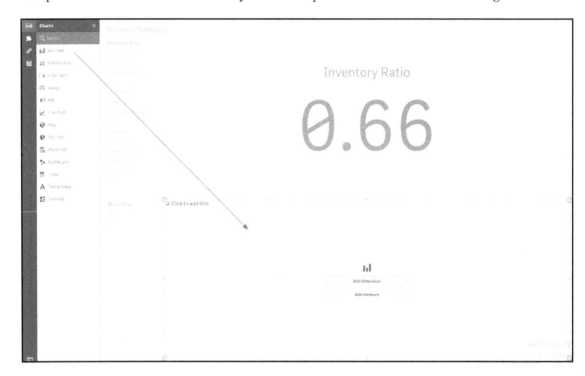

Our goal with this bar chart is to compare the inventory amount with the reorder point amount. We can assign dimensions and measures to the bar chart by first clicking on the **Data** tab as seen in the following screenshot:

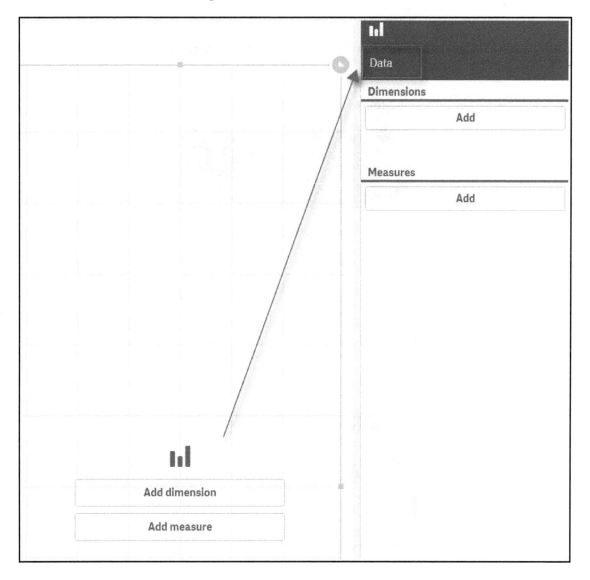

We now have **Add** buttons underneath both **Dimensions** and **Measures**. For **Dimensions**, we will add ProductName from the **Field**. For **Measures**, we will use the **Add** button twice: the first time to add Inventory with a sum aggregation as:

```
Sum(Inventory)
```

And the second time to add ReorderPoint with a sum aggregation as:

```
Sum(ReorderPoint)
```

We can view this output in the following screenshot:

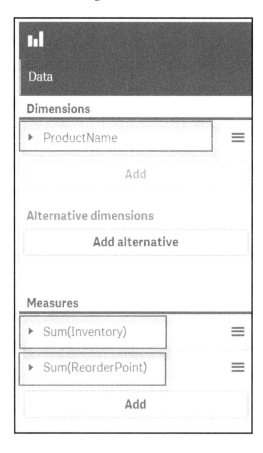

We now have two measures: Sum(Inventory) and Sum(ReorderPoint). We can expand both measures and rename them by changing the labels to the following:

- Inventory
- Reorder Point

Additionally, we can click on the **Click to add title** section on the upper left-hand side of the combo chart and give the chart a name, such as **Inventory vs Reorder Point**. We can also click on the **Appearance | Colors and Legend** tab on the right-hand side and switch the legend title from the **Right** to the **Top**, under **Legend position**, as seen in the following screenshot:

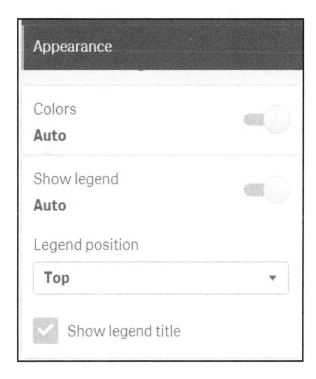

We can now exit **Edit** mode and view the current dashboard as it stands with our current design and with a **Paint Shop** filter, as seen in the following screenshot:

The combination chart shows five products:

- **Paint-Blue**
- **Paint-Silver**
- **Paint-Red**
- **Paint-Yellow**
- **Paint-Black**

The overall **Inventory Ratio** of **0.83**, which means more of the paint is due for a reorder than not. If we apply a secondary filter on the **Reorder Flag = N**, we then only see two products, **Paint-Blue** and **Paint-Silver**, as seen in the following screenshot:

Additionally, we see that, for those two, their overall **Inventory Ratio** is greater than 1.0 with a score of **1.09**. This correctly indicates that we have more inventory than is minimally required to trigger a reorder. We are not in a hurry to place another order for **Paint-Blue** and **Paint-Silver**.

We should expect that, when we set **Reorder Flag** = **Y**, we will see an **Inventory Ratio** less than 1.0 and also see the other three paints show up. The results can be seen in the following screenshot:

Indeed, we do see the remaining three paint colors with a higher **Reorder Point** than **Inventory** for each **Paint Shop** as well as an **Inventory Ratio** of **0.65**.

We have a little bit of white space remaining next to **Inventory Ratio**; we can utilize this to add a scatter plot.

Creating a scatter plot with two measures

A scatter plot is a useful visualization that compares two measures on different axes. We can use a scatter plot to compare both Inventory and Reorder Point. We can begin by dragging a **Scatter Plot** component from the Charts menu and placing it to the right of the **KPI** component as seen in the following screenshot:

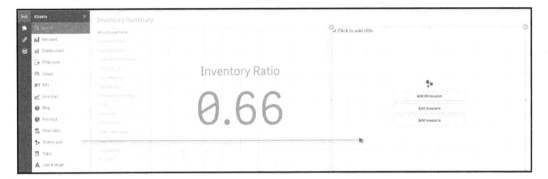

We can now assign **Product Name** to the first dimension, **Inventory**, as the first measure with an aggregation of sum, and **Reorder Point**, as the second measure with an aggregation of sum, as well. The default view of the scatter plot can be seen in the following screenshot:

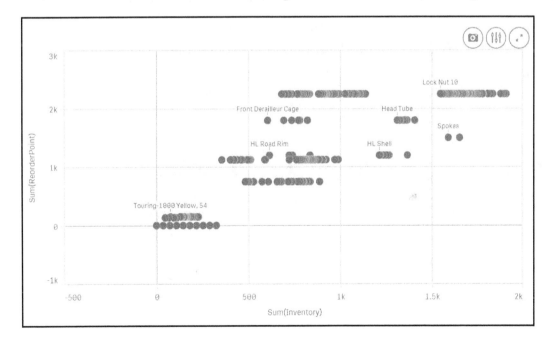

If we set the **Warehouse Name** as **Frame Welding**, we can easily see that the majority of the products have a **Reorder Point** at 375 as seen in the following screenshot:

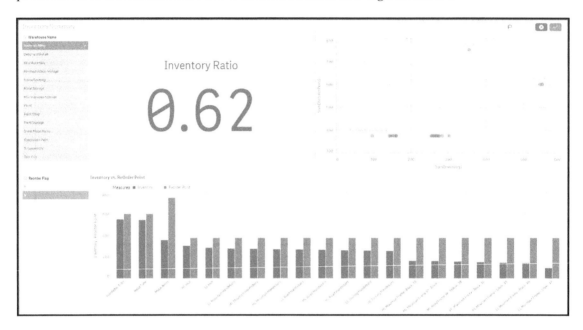

Additionally, the overall **Inventory Ratio** is significantly lower than 1.0 (at **0.62**) and every product has an overall **Inventory** lower than the **Reorder Point**.

We now have a complete dashboard with two selectors and three components all based on a single Microsoft SQL Server query that tells us all we need to know about our inventory. Next we will focus on how to share our dashboard with other users.

Publishing the inventory dashboard

There are different ways to get QlikSense application published to other users. However, depending on the functionality and interactivity required, some methods may be more appropriate than others.

Exporting to a PDF

The quickest and easiest option is to export a document to a PDF, which can be quickly viewed on almost any device. However, the downside to exporting an application to a PDF is that you no longer have access to any interactivity between the different components or even the ability to make a simple selection.

For example, if a user was interested in looking at `Paint Shop` supplies that required an order, we would need to make that selection beforehand. Once the selection was made, we would then click on the **Menu** icon and select **Export sheet to PDF**, as seen in the following screenshot:

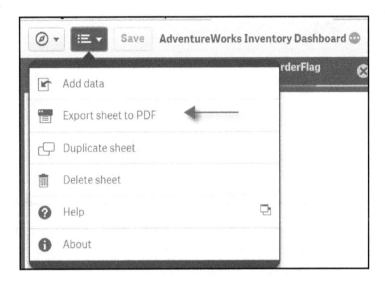

We then have the ability to select the **Paper size**, **Resolution (dots per insch)**, and **Orientation** as seen in the following screenshot:

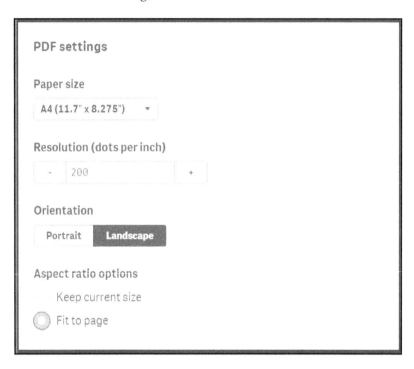

Once we've selected the PDF settings, we can click on the **Export** button and receive a link to download the PDF file, as seen in the following screenshot:

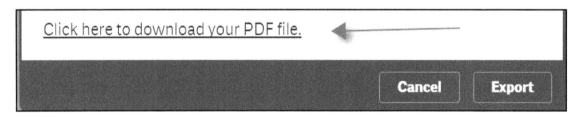

When the file is downloaded and viewed inside of a browser or a PDF reader, the graphical components are viewable but the selector components are invisible, as seen in the following screenshot:

Therefore, if this is a preferred way to deliver QlikSense apps for users, we must keep in mind that any selections must be made prior to delivery.

Exporting to Qlik Cloud

If we are interested in delivering our Qlik Sense application to a user who is requesting full functionality from the dashboard, then our best bet is to publish our app to Qlik Cloud. Additionally, those who have access to our app on Qlik Cloud can also edit the dashboard and modify it to fit their needs if we grant them permissions to do so. Qlik generously allows us to share our app with up to five users for free.

To learn more about Qlik Cloud, visit the following site:
`http://www.qlik.com/us/products/qlik-sense/qlik-cloud`

To get started with Qlik from our desktop application, we can navigate back to our **QlikSense Desktop Hub** and click on the Qlik Cloud icon on the upper right-hand side, as seen in the following screenshot:

We will be taken to `https://qlikcloud.com/` where we can login if we have an account or register to receive an account after filling out some information. Once we've logged in, we will see a browser layout that is similar to what we're used to seeing on the desktop, as seen in the following screenshot:

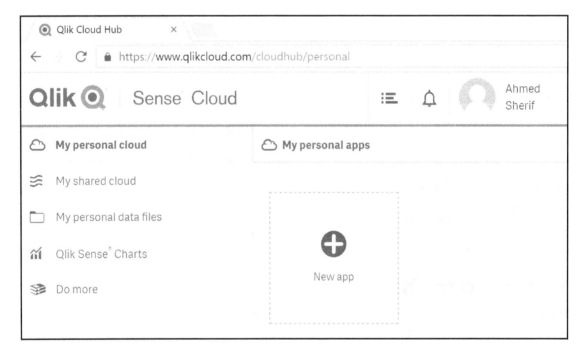

We can click on the **New app** icon under **My personal apps** and select **Upload an app** as seen in the following screenshot:

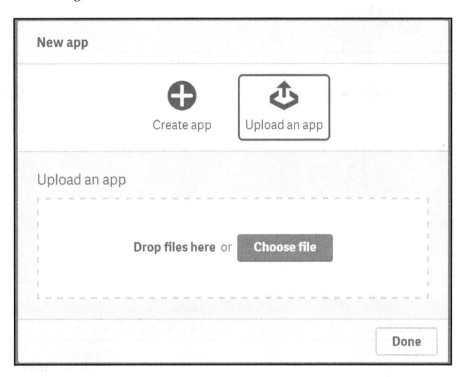

We can then select **Choose file** and select the application file (with the .qvf extension) that we've been working on with QlikSense, as seen in the following screenshot:

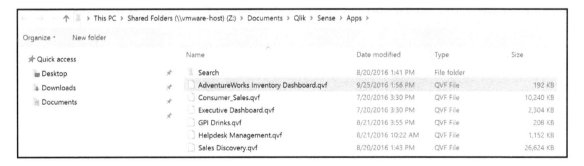

At this point we should now see the name of our dashboard application available as a selection on Qlik Cloud. As we click on it and view the results in the `Inventory Summary` sheet, we should see a familiar-looking dashboard application with all desktop functionality available, as seen in the following screenshot:

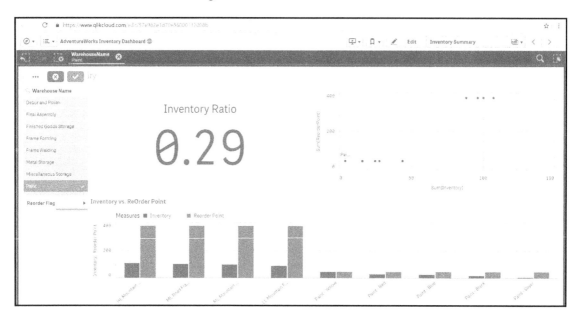

Inside Qlik Cloud, the app has the **Edit** functionality available, which means the user has the ability to edit the dashboard and make further modifications if need be. However, in this case the developer is both the editor and user. If we wish to share the app with users without the ability to edit the dashboard, then we need to go back to **My personal cloud** in Qlik Cloud, right-click on the app, and select **Publish** as seen in the following screenshot:

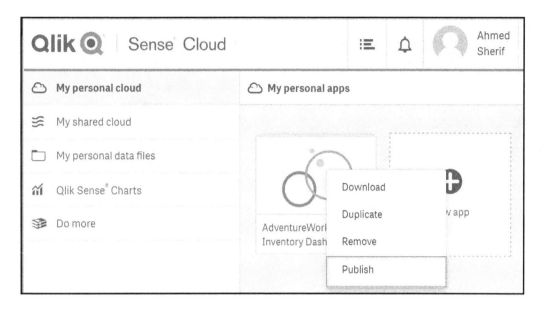

At this point, the app will move from the **My personal cloud** folder to the **My shared cloud** folder as seen in the following screenshot:

The app can now be shared to up to five unique accounts by sending an e-mail to a user using the **Share** button to the right of the app on **My shared cloud**. If a user with a Qlik Cloud account opens up the shared dashboard they will see the same dashboard without the **Edit** function, as seen in the following screenshot:

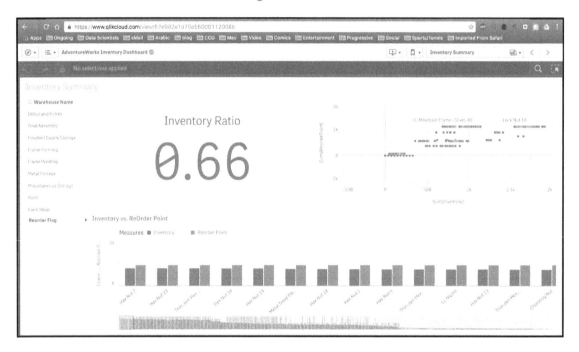

Summary

We have covered quite a bit in this chapter. We started out with a simple query built in SQL Server and then connected it to QlikSense Desktop. We then built several components in QlikSense that interacted with each other. The end result was a finished product of an Inventory Dashboard that made sense to a user looking to understand product availability at the AdventureWorks warehouse. Finally, we explored different methods of sharing our finished application with end users using Qlik Cloud. In the next chapter, we will wrap everything up with an understanding of how to validate our data within SQL Server with some of its built-in tools as well as perform an overall comparison of the entire set of technologies we covered in the book.

9

Data Analysis with Microsoft SQL Server

We have come to the final chapter, and to say that we've covered quite a bit of information would be an understatement. If you've made it this far then you'll notice that business intelligence covers a broad spectrum of interrelated topics, methodologies, and technologies.

> *"The ability to apprehend the interrelationships of presented facts in such a way as to guide actions towards a desired goal."*
>
> *- IBM researcher Hans Peter Luhn*

While the term "business intelligence" was first coined by Hans Peter Luhn of IBM in 1958, it was still only intended for backend folks concentrated on the IT side. BI became commercialized once data warehouses became more readily available in the 1980s and the personal computer became more accessible in the 1990s. Each decade since has seen the introduction of new BI tools by new vendors looking to bridge the gap between business and IT. In the current iteration of BI, there is a concerted effort to integrate social media data into the landscape. Ultimately, the success of a BI venture will hinge upon the database that brings all of the data together.

Microsoft SQL Server is one of the most popular enterprise database managers for many reasons, but primarily due to the accessibility and compatibility of the Microsoft operating system. While the dashboards and reports are what most users interact with directly on a daily basis, a well modeled database and data warehouse will go a long way towards providing consistent results for those same users. Ultimately, the goal is to win the trust of the users with the data. A BI developer can always go back and make any report prettier and flashier, but if the data is not accurate because of an incorrect join in the data warehouse there is not much that can be done to correct that within the actual report.

Very often, a BI developer will get a phone call from a user questioning a specific value that appears on a report or a dashboard. These examples may include any of the following scenarios:

- The user will say that a value appears to have doubled in value compared to that same value the prior month
- The user will say that a field appears to be blank when it should be displaying values
- The user will say that a calculated field does not appear to be accurately summing up the individual parts that add up to the total

The bulk of this chapter will focus on querying techniques that can be used with Microsoft SQL Server to validate results as well as provide data results to users who may not be SQL savvy to build the results needed for their reporting needs. When a question arises about the integrity of the data, it is important to go directly to the source and query the data directly in the SQL Server data warehouse. Hopefully, this chapter will help bridge the gap between the IT nerd and the business analyst. Additionally, we will spend the first part of the chapter doing a comparison of the tools we discussed in the previous chapters.

We will cover the following topics in this chapter:

- Comparing tools head-to-head
- Developing views in SQL Server
- Performing window functions in SQL Server
- Performing stored procedures in SQL Server

Comparing tools head-to-head

We dived deep into six different tools that can be used for BI. As mentioned before, they generally fall under two main categories:

- Data discovery desktop applications
- Traditional programming languages

Deciding on the best tool or methodology for our organization largely depends on our needs as well as our BI maturity. Are the users at a level where they need to be spoon-fed the data in a format that is ready to go out the door? Are the users more tech-savvy that just require us to point them in the direction where the raw data is stored and they can do the rest on their own? These are all good questions and will vary based on the organizations, as well as users within the same organization.

Comparing the data discovery desktop applications

We covered three popular data discovery desktop applications:

- Power BI
- Tableau Public
- QlikSense

As we went through an entire exercise of developing a BI application with each one of these tools, we encountered similarities and differences between each one. We will highlight some of these differences.

Data connectivity

Both QlikSense and Power BI were able to establish a connection directly with SQL Server and import tables and SQL script results. This functionality is quite powerful as we can leverage the latest table updates in a data warehouse automatically through our BI application. Currently, Tableau does not have this feature available in its Public version, only with its licensed version. In order to pull results in, we needed to export a CSV file from SQL Server and import into Tableau Public.

BI maturity

In 2016, Tableau was the market leader for data discovery for many reasons, but primarily for its maturity with components. Tableau has been around the block and has had time on its side to test and fine-tune its visualization offerings of charts, graphs, storyboards, and dashboards.

Qlik is considered by most experts to be the closest competitor to Tableau with a similar offering in terms of visualization components. QlikSense is not the first data discovery desktop tool offered by Qlik. Qlik's flagship product is called QlikView and is primarily known as a tool that lets you dive deep into your data and develop a highly customizable application. If you are a technical person then QlikView can provide limitless opportunities; however, if you are a business person with limited technical skills looking to build a quick and pretty application that answers a specific question with some added interactivity, then QlikSense is a better fit for you.

Power BI has been on the market for the least amount of time but has seen the greatest amount of enhancements since it entered the market in September 2014. As mentioned in `Chapter 3`, *Analysis with Excel and Creating Interactive Maps and Charts with Power BI*, we'd be hard pressed to find a business user who has not used PivotTables or PivotCharts in Excel to answer a business question. So, those users would find a familiar user interface with Power BI. Power BI has an advantage over tools such as Qlik and Tableau, and that is the power of Microsoft. For organizations that already use Microsoft on the frontend with Excel and on the backend with SQL Server, they will very likely find Power BI to be a natural fit for them.

Comparing the traditional programming languages

We covered three programming languages for BI applications:

- D3.js (JavaScript)
- R
- Python

Data connectivity

D3 has the ability to produce some advanced visualizations, but many may find a steep learning curve when producing visualizations attached to actual data. Bringing data into D3 from SQL Server requires several moving parts. First, we exported a CSV file into a folder location, set up a web server that recognizes the folder location, and then used the `d3.csv()` function to call the CSV file from the desired folder location. Python and R both have libraries to directly connect to SQL Server utilizing the ODBC connection, removing the need to deal with CSV files. In our examples, we used the `pypyodbc` library for Python and the `RODBC` library for R.

Delivery

D3 has a built-in advantage over R and Python when it comes to delivering a visualization for user consumption. D3 development occurs within an HTML layout, and JavaScript is known as the *language of the Web*. As soon as we are finished developing a visualization with D3, we can immediately send a link to a user to view in a browser or on a mobile device. Both R and Python require assistance through either of their IDEs (RStudio and Jupyter Notebook) to publish their visualizations.

Developing views in SQL Server

For the remainder of this chapter, we will focus our attention on Microsoft SQL Server functions and procedures that will help us understand and manipulate our data. The more we can manipulate our data to a desired outcome at database level, the less manipulation will be needed by BI developers, data analysts, or business users at the reporting level. This will make for a happy customer.

Quite often, a developer will find themselves querying the same results over and over again with minor changes to a filter a name or a filter a date on regular basis. This type of query is a good candidate to be converted into a view within SQL Server. There are certain advantages to creating a view compared to using the actual table for a query:

- Views can consolidate results from several tables with complex joins into a single location for user access
- Views can apply security on tables by restricting results on what is appropriate for a specific audience on the backend rather than performing the security at the reporting level
- Views can present a consistent structure to the user even if the backend table changes structure by adding or removing columns

When we execute this updated script, we will see the new results minus the row where **Sales Reason Name** is **Other**, as seen in the following screenshot:

	Sale Reason Name	Sale Reason Type	Sales Amount	Tax	Freight Amount
1	Price	Other	10975842.56	878087.74	274380.29
2	On Promotion	Promotion	6361829.95	508951.68	159044.56
3	Manufacturer	Other	5998122.10	479847.59	149957.80
4	Quality	Other	5549896.77	443989.26	138752.46
5	Review	Other	1694882.19	135589.55	42374.17
6	Television Advertisement	Marketing	27475.82	2198.68	687.24

Since this will be a recurring query that will be used my many developers, we can convert it into a permanent view for access to users using the following script:

```
USE [AdventureWorks2014] --Identifies the Database
GO

CREATE VIEW [Sales].[vSalesAmountbySalesReason] AS
SELECT
distinct
SalesReason.Name as 'Sale Reason Name'
,SalesReason.ReasonType as 'Sale Reason Type'
,sum(round(SalesOrderHeader.SubTotal,2)) as 'Sales Amount'
,sum(round(SalesOrderHeader.TaxAmt,2)) as 'Tax'
,sum(round(SalesOrderHeader.Freight,2)) as 'Freight Amount'

FROM [AdventureWorks2014].[Sales].[SalesReason] as SalesReason

inner join [AdventureWorks2014].[Sales].[SalesOrderHeaderSalesReason] as
SalesOrderHeaderSalesReason on
SalesOrderHeaderSalesReason.SalesReasonID = SalesReason.SalesReasonID

inner join [AdventureWorks2014].[Sales].[SalesOrderHeader] as
SalesOrderHeader on
SalesOrderHeader.SalesOrderID = SalesOrderHeaderSalesReason.SalesOrderID

where
SalesReason.Name <> 'Other'

Group by SalesReason.Name, SalesReason.ReasonType
--Order by 3 desc
```

The first time creating a view we use the `Create View` syntax; however, subsequent alterations to that view can use a `Replace View` syntax instead.

When creating a view, certain functions, such as the `Order By` clause, are discouraged and will probably trigger the following error message when executed:

> The `ORDER BY` clause is invalid in views, inline functions, derived tables, subqueries, and common table expressions, unless TOP, OFFSET, or FOR XML is also specified.

These functions will need to be commented out of your script. It is not necessary to include them in the view creation process as they can be used outside of the view itself.

When we proceed to execute the `Create View` statement, we will see the name of our newly created view appear on the list of available views in the **Object Explorer**, as seen in the following screenshot:

Now if we would like to query the results, we can run the following script directly:

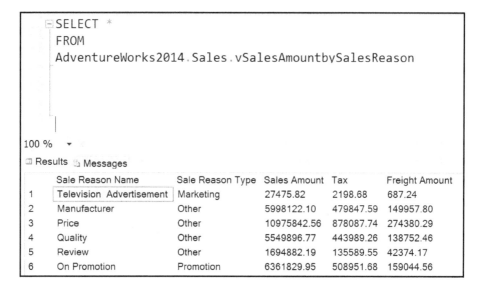

The script is now much simpler to execute while still retrieving the correct number of rows as before. As a BI developer working with business analysts in need of these results, granting them access to a single view may seem more reasonable instead of a more complicated query with several joins that might be out of their comfort zone. While a view has a different structure than a table, as far as a user is concerned there is no difference.

Performing window functions in SQL Server

While most functions and calculations are performed at the reporting level with dashboards and reports, sometimes it may make sense to perform some of these functions at the database level. Some calculation functions are rather complex and can be taxing at the desktop reporting level, but the database on the server level may be more adept at efficiently handling the calculation. Additionally, if the calculation function is performed at the database level, it will provide the same value to all users and maintain consistency. These functions are referred to as *window* functions as they occur over a defined number of rows and columns. The three main window functions we will cover are as follows:

- Rank
- Sum
- Avg

Rank functions in SQL Server

Ranking is fun! Just ask any college football team. One of the most common functions is to rank a dimension based on a measure from best to worst or first to last. We can apply this function using `RANK() over (Order by)` in the `SELECT` statement.

We have the `[AdventureWorks2014].[dbo].[CountryRegionBikes]` table that showcases the percentage of bike riders by country, as seen in the following screenshot:

```
⊟SELECT
        [CountryRegionCode]
        ,[PercentBikeRides]
    FROM [AdventureWorks2014].[dbo].[CountryRegionBikes]
```

100 %   ▾

▦ Results ▱ Messages

	CountryRegionCode	PercentBikeRides
1	AS	32
2	AU	34
3	CA	27
4	DE	23
5	FM	18
6	FR	38
7	GB	35
8	MH	25
9	MP	60
10	PW	45
11	US	22
12	VI	33

We can assign a rank function to each country based on the `PercentBikeRides` value, as seen in the following script:

```
SELECT
   CountryRegion.Name as 'Country Name'
   ,CountryRegionBikes.[PercentBikeRides] as 'Percent Bike Riders'
   ,RANK() OVER (ORDER BY [PercentBikeRides] DESC) AS 'Ranking'
   FROM [AdventureWorks2014].[dbo].[CountryRegionBikes] as
   CountryRegionBikes
   inner join [AdventureWorks2014].[Person].[CountryRegion] as
   CountryRegion on
   CountryRegion.CountryRegionCode = CountryRegionBikes.CountryRegionCode
   order by 3 asc
```

In addition to creating a new column called `Ranking`, we also joined to the `CountryRegion` table to pull in the `Country Name`, as seen in the following screenshot:

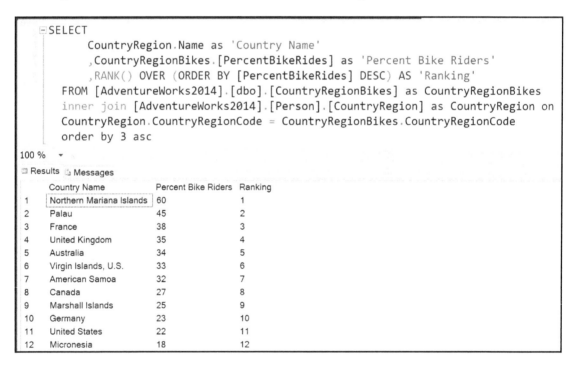

The country with the highest `Percent Bike Riders` is `Northern Mariana Islands`, with a `Ranking` of 1, and the country with the lowest `Percent Bike Riders` is `Micronesia` with a `Ranking` of 12.

We currently have our script with an ascending sort on `Ranking`; however, if we took away that sort order and placed it on `Country Name` instead, we would still keep the same `Ranking` value, as seen in the following screenshot:

```
⊟SELECT
        CountryRegion.Name as 'Country Name'
        ,CountryRegionBikes.[PercentBikeRides] as 'Percent Bike Riders'
        ,RANK() OVER (ORDER BY [PercentBikeRides] DESC) AS 'Ranking'
    FROM [AdventureWorks2014].[dbo].[CountryRegionBikes] as CountryRegionBikes
    inner join [AdventureWorks2014].[Person].[CountryRegion] as CountryRegion on
    CountryRegion.CountryRegionCode = CountryRegionBikes.CountryRegionCode
    order by 1 asc
```

100 %   ▾

▦ Results ▯ Messages

	Country Name	Percent Bike Riders	Ranking
1	American Samoa	32	7
2	Australia	34	5
3	Canada	27	8
4	France	38	3
5	Germany	23	10
6	Marshall Islands	25	9
7	Micronesia	18	12
8	Northern Mariana Islands	60	1
9	Palau	45	2
10	United Kingdom	35	4
11	United States	22	11
12	Virgin Islands, U.S.	33	6

We still observe that `Micronesia` has the lowest `Ranking`, even though it is on row 7. But what happens if we have two countries that share the same value and we want to know what happens to the `Ranking` value? Do they both share the same `Ranking` value? Does one get a tiebreaker over the other? In our current example dataset, we do not have a country that is sharing the same `Percent Bike Riders` as any other country. They are all unique. For the purposes of this exercise, though, we are going to go ahead and fudge the numbers so that two of the countries can share the same `Percent Bike Riders`. We can add a row for `CountryRegionCode` that is `AL` for Albania using the following insert script:

```
USE [AdventureWorks2014]
GO

INSERT INTO [dbo].[CountryRegionBikes]
        ([Index],[CountryRegionCode],[PercentBikeRides])
    VALUES
        (12, 'AL', 32)
```

Our new table for `CountryRegionBikes` will now have 13 rows instead of 12 when we preview the results, as seen in the following screenshot:

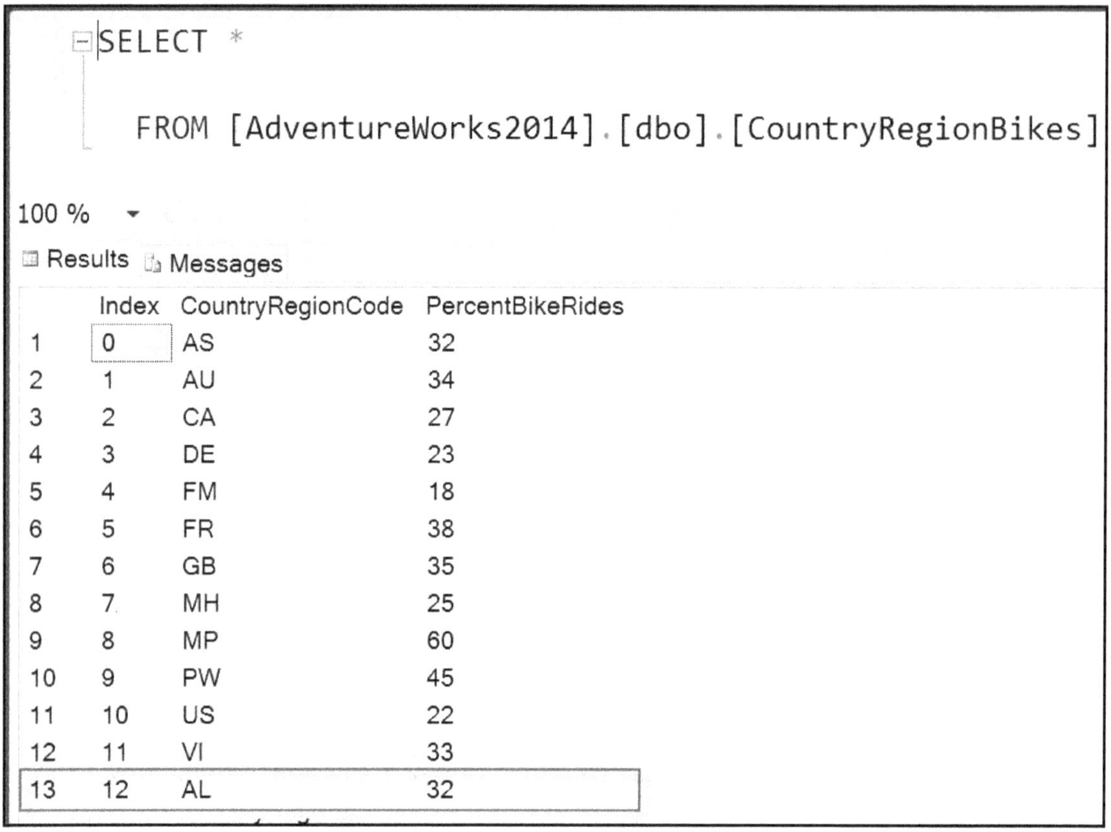

```
SELECT *

    FROM [AdventureWorks2014].[dbo].[CountryRegionBikes]
```

100 % ▾

▦ Results 🗔 Messages

	Index	CountryRegionCode	PercentBikeRides
1	0	AS	32
2	1	AU	34
3	2	CA	27
4	3	DE	23
5	4	FM	18
6	5	FR	38
7	6	GB	35
8	7	MH	25
9	8	MP	60
10	9	PW	45
11	10	US	22
12	11	VI	33
13	12	AL	32

When we execute our full script to pull in `Country Name`, we will now see two countries that have the same `Ranking` for the seventh spot, as seen in the following screenshot:

```
SELECT
        CountryRegion.Name as 'Country Name'
        ,CountryRegionBikes.[PercentBikeRides] as 'Percent Bike Riders'
        ,RANK() OVER (ORDER BY [PercentBikeRides] DESC) AS 'Ranking'
    FROM [AdventureWorks2014].[dbo].[CountryRegionBikes] as CountryRegionBikes
    inner join [AdventureWorks2014].[Person].[CountryRegion] as CountryRegion on
    CountryRegion.CountryRegionCode = CountryRegionBikes.CountryRegionCode
    order by 1 asc
```

100 %   ▾

▢ Results ▯ Messages

	Country Name	Percent Bike Riders	Ranking
1	Albania	32	7
2	American Samoa	32	7
3	Australia	34	5
4	Canada	27	9
5	France	38	3
6	Germany	23	11
7	Marshall Islands	25	10
8	Micronesia	18	13
9	Northern Mariana Islands	60	1
10	Palau	45	2
11	United Kingdom	35	4
12	United States	22	12
13	Virgin Islands, U.S.	33	6

The `Rank()` function will not assign a value of 8 to a `Country Name` because it does not assign a consecutive number if there is a tie. If we wish to incorporate consecutive ranking after a tie, then we must utilize the `Dense_Rank()` function, as seen in the following script:

```
DENSE_RANK() OVER (ORDER BY [PercentBikeRides] DESC) AS 'Dense Ranking'
```

Our new results will appear as follows:

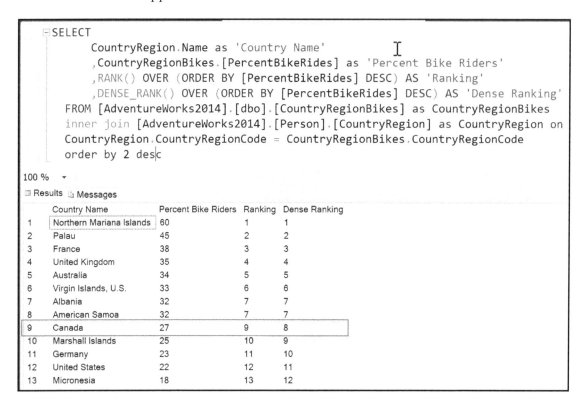

```
SELECT
        CountryRegion.Name as 'Country Name'
        ,CountryRegionBikes.[PercentBikeRides] as 'Percent Bike Riders'
        ,RANK() OVER (ORDER BY [PercentBikeRides] DESC) AS 'Ranking'
        ,DENSE_RANK() OVER (ORDER BY [PercentBikeRides] DESC) AS 'Dense Ranking'
    FROM [AdventureWorks2014].[dbo].[CountryRegionBikes] as CountryRegionBikes
    inner join [AdventureWorks2014].[Person].[CountryRegion] as CountryRegion on
    CountryRegion.CountryRegionCode = CountryRegionBikes.CountryRegionCode
    order by 2 desc
```

100 % ▾

▣ Results ▵ Messages

	Country Name	Percent Bike Riders	Ranking	Dense Ranking
1	Northern Mariana Islands	60	1	1
2	Palau	45	2	2
3	France	38	3	3
4	United Kingdom	35	4	4
5	Australia	34	5	5
6	Virgin Islands, U.S.	33	6	6
7	Albania	32	7	7
8	American Samoa	32	7	7
9	Canada	27	9	8
10	Marshall Islands	25	10	9
11	Germany	23	11	10
12	United States	22	12	11
13	Micronesia	18	13	12

Canada now appears with a Ranking of 9 and a Dense Ranking of 8. Therefore, if we are in need of a Ranking with consecutive counts after a tie, use Dense_Ranking(); otherwise, use Ranking().

Finally, if we want a unique count for each row regardless of whether or not there is a tie, then we need to employ the `Row_Number()` function, as seen in the following screenshot:

```
SELECT
        CountryRegion.Name as 'Country Name'
        ,CountryRegionBikes.[PercentBikeRides] as 'Percent Bike Riders'
        ,RANK() OVER (ORDER BY [PercentBikeRides] DESC) AS 'Ranking'
        ,DENSE_RANK() OVER (ORDER BY [PercentBikeRides] DESC) AS 'Dense Ranking'
        ,ROW_NUMBER() OVER (ORDER BY [PercentBikeRides] DESC) AS 'Row Number'
    FROM [AdventureWorks2014].[dbo].[CountryRegionBikes] as CountryRegionBikes
    inner join [AdventureWorks2014].[Person].[CountryRegion] as CountryRegion on
    CountryRegion.CountryRegionCode = CountryRegionBikes.CountryRegionCode
    order by 2 desc
```

100 %

Results | Messages

	Country Name	Percent Bike Riders	Ranking	Dense Ranking	Row Number
1	Northern Mariana Islands	60	1	1	1
2	Palau	45	2	2	2
3	France	38	3	3	3
4	United Kingdom	35	4	4	4
5	Australia	34	5	5	5
6	Virgin Islands, U.S.	33	6	6	6
7	Albania	32	7	7	7
8	American Samoa	32	7	7	8
9	Canada	27	9	8	9
10	Marshall Islands	25	10	9	10
11	Germany	23	11	10	11
12	United States	22	12	11	12
13	Micronesia	18	13	12	13

We can now observe that `Albania`, `American Samoa`, and `Canada` each have different values depending on the function. `Row_Number()` does allow for a unique assignment of row counts and the row order is based solely on the order of the current configuration of results.

Sum functions in SQL Server

Summarizing data is the name of the game when it comes to reporting with dimensions and measures. When data is summarized to a specific level of granularity, the measures are added up to that same level. There are specific types of summation that can occur within a partition of data, and one that is quite popular is a rolling summation. We will use the following SQL script as a candidate to apply our rolling sum function. The original script appears as the following:

```
SELECT
[FirstName]
,[MiddleName]
,[LastName]
,[EmailPromotion] as 'Email Promotion Count'

FROM [AdventureWorks2014].[HumanResources].[vEmployee]
```

When we execute this script, we see the results in the following screenshot:

	FirstName	MiddleName	LastName	Email Promotion Count
1	Syed	E	Abbas	0
2	Kim	B	Abercrombie	2
3	Hazem	E	Abolrous	0
4	Pilar	G	Ackerman	0
5	Jay	G	Adams	0
6	François	P	Ajenstat	0
7	Amy	E	Alberts	1
8	Greg	F	Alderson	0
9	Sean	P	Alexander	2
10	Gary	E.	Altman	0
11	Nancy	A	Anderson	1
12	Pamela	O	Ansman-Wolfe	1
13	Zainal	T	Arifin	1
14	Dan	K	Bacon	0
15	Bryan	NULL	Baker	0

We would like to include a new column to the right of `Email Promotion Count` that adds up the value of each count as we go down each row. We can do this by applying the following function to the SQL statement:

```
sum([EmailPromotion]) OVER (order BY [LastName], [MiddleName], [FirstName]
asc) as 'Running Sum'
```

Our new result set will appear as seen in the following screenshot:

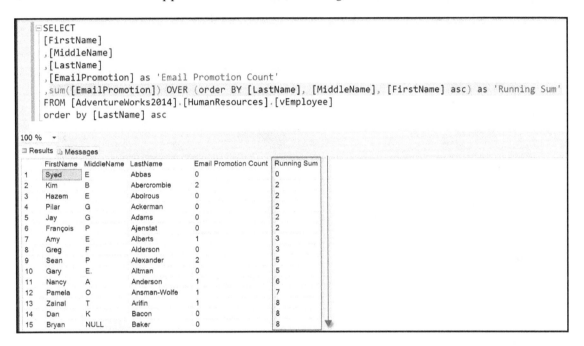

Our new column, `Running Sum`, is now adding the `Email Promotion Count` as we go down the rows with the final row showing a value of 8 for the fifteenth row. Performing running summation calculations come in quite handy, especially when dealing with percentages of total or just wanting to know what the overall total is at any point in time, depending on the order of the partitioned data.

Average functions in SQL Server

Almost as common as the running summation is the running average calculation. We can apply this functionality using a similar format to `Rank()` and `Sum()` with the following:

```
avg() over (partition by, order by )
```

Average calculations over partitions come in handy when dealing with measures over a period of time, such as weeks, months, or even years. A perfect way to apply the avg() functionality would be with the dataset seen in the following screenshot:

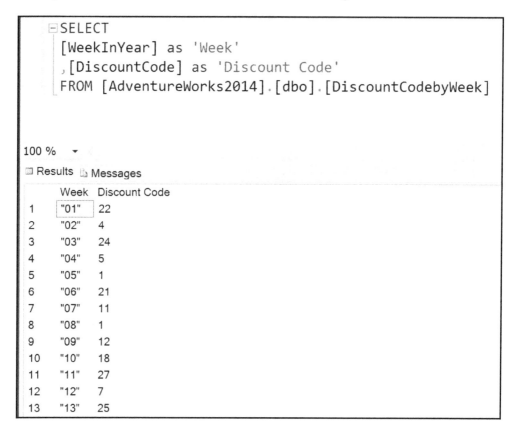

If we'd like to see the rolling average Discount Code as we move from week to week, we can apply the following script to the select clause of the SQL:

```
avg([DiscountCode]) over(order by [WeekInYear]) as 'Running Average'
```

Once we execute the script, we can see the weekly rolling average of the `Discount Code` applied:

```
SELECT
  [WeekInYear] as 'Week'
  ,[DiscountCode] as 'Discount Code'
  ,avg([DiscountCode]) over(order by [WeekInYear]) as 'Running Average'

  FROM [AdventureWorks2014].[dbo].[DiscountCodebyWeek]
```

100 %   ▼

Results Messages

	Week	Discount Code	Running Average
1	"01"	22	22.000000
2	"02"	4	13.000000
3	"03"	24	16.666666
4	"04"	5	13.750000
5	"05"	1	11.200000
6	"06"	21	12.833333
7	"07"	11	12.571428
8	"08"	1	11.125000
9	"09"	12	11.222222
10	"10"	18	11.900000
11	"11"	27	13.272727
12	"12"	7	12.750000
13	"13"	25	13.692307
14	"14"	24	14.428571
15	"15"	20	14.800000

It is always a good idea to test out the calculated numbers manually as a sanity check. The first value for the `Running Average` is **22**. The second value is **13**. If we take the first two values for `Discount Code`, add them up and then divide by two, what do we get?

```
Running Average for Week 02 = (22 + 4) /2 = 13
```

Rolling averages are good for detecting trends because the values are not easily affected by one or two outlier values but account for an overall movement of numbers.

Building crosstabs with case logic

As we've discussed previously, crosstabs are a very popular way of slicing tabular data, especially when trying to evaluate the relationship between two dimensions with a single measure. Many people are addicted to Excel primarily for the sole purpose of being able to create crosstabs with PivotTables. For the most part, data warehouses store information in a tabular format, but there are ways to create crosstab functionality within SQL Server using the `Case` expression. The `case` function serves the same purpose at the database level as `if-then` logic does at the reporting level.

 To learn more about the `Case` expression in Microsoft SQL Server, visit the following website: `https://msdn.microsoft.com/en-us/library/ms 181765.aspx`.

Imagine the following conversation between a data analyst and a BI developer:

> *Data analyst: Hi! Listen, I totally hear you that I should be using Tableau to build my dashboard instead of using Excel, but I just don't know how to manipulate data in Tableau to get the data the way it currently looks in a PivotTable.*
> BI developer: Ok, so how about if I send you a view that already has the data formatted in a Crosstab, would you use Tableau instead of Excel?
>
> Data analyst: You betcha!
>
> BI developer: *rolls eyes* Fine, please submit a ticket.

The dataset that is of interest pulls unit counts for all countries in a tabular format from the view called `vIndividualCustomer`, as seen in the following script:

```
SELECT
[CountryRegionName]  as 'Country'
,[StateProvinceName] as 'State'
,count([BusinessEntityID]) as 'Unit Counts'

FROM [AdventureWorks2014].[Sales].[vIndividualCustomer]
Group by
[CountryRegionName]
,[StateProvinceName]
```

The output of the first ten rows of this SQL script can be seen in the following screenshot:

```sql
SELECT Top 10
    [CountryRegionName] as 'Country'
    ,[StateProvinceName] as 'State'
    ,count([BusinessEntityID]) as 'Unit Counts'

FROM [AdventureWorks2014].[Sales].[vIndividualCustomer]
Group by
    [CountryRegionName]
    ,[StateProvinceName]
```

100 %   ▼

▢ Results ▣ Messages

	Country	State	Unit Counts
1	Canada	Alberta	11
2	France	Pas de Calais	16
3	France	Charente-Maritime	21
4	France	Val d'Oise	30
5	United States	Montana	1
6	United States	Arizona	2
7	United States	Alabama	1
8	United States	Kentucky	1
9	United States	Illinois	6
10	United States	Georgia	3

The user is requesting that the output of the SQL script be presented in the following format instead:

Row Labels	Canada	France	United Kingdom
Alberta	11		
British Columbia	1559		
Charente-Maritime		21	
England			1913
Essonne		150	
Garonne (Haute)		30	
Hauts de Seine		195	
Loir et Cher		17	
Loiret		60	
Moselle		56	
Nord		284	
Ontario	1		
Pas de Calais		16	
Seine (Paris)		386	
Seine et Marne		60	
Seine Saint Denis		285	
Somme		22	
Val de Marne		30	
Val d'Oise		30	
Yveline		168	

The user is looking to replicate a PivotTable in Excel where the column fields are for the countries of `Canada`, `France`, and the `United Kingdom` and the rows are for all of the associated cities for those three countries. The user works with international customers only and therefore has no need for the remaining countries. After seeing this format, it becomes evident that three `case` expressions using the `CountryRegionName` will be sufficient to recreate this format in SQL Server.

Once we apply the three `case` expressions, we are left with the following script:

```
SELECT
[StateProvinceName] as 'State'
,case when [CountryRegionName] = 'Canada' then count([BusinessEntityID])
else 0 end as 'Canada'
,case when [CountryRegionName] = 'France' then count([BusinessEntityID])
else 0 end as 'France'
,case when [CountryRegionName] = 'United Kingdom' then
```

```
count([BusinessEntityID]) else 0 end as 'United Kingdom'

FROM [AdventureWorks2014].[Sales].[vIndividualCustomer]
Group by
[CountryRegionName]
,[StateProvinceName]
Order by 1 asc;
```

The output of the script can be seen in the following screenshot:

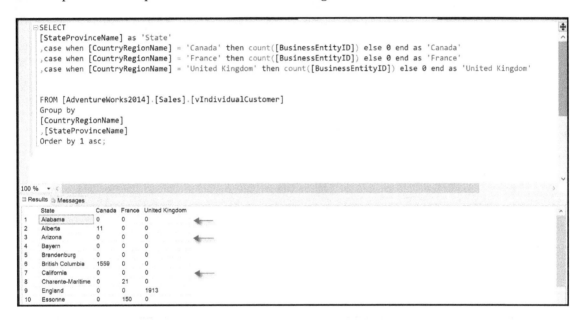

We are now seeing the correct column values for Canada, France, and the United Kingdom; however, we are also seeing row values for Alabama, Arizona, and California that we do not want included in our crosstab.

We can exclude these unnecessary rows by applying the following filter in a where clause:

```
where [CountryRegionName] IN ('Canada', 'France', 'United Kingdom')
```

When we preview this updated script, we should see the same desired outcome we received from the PivotTable:

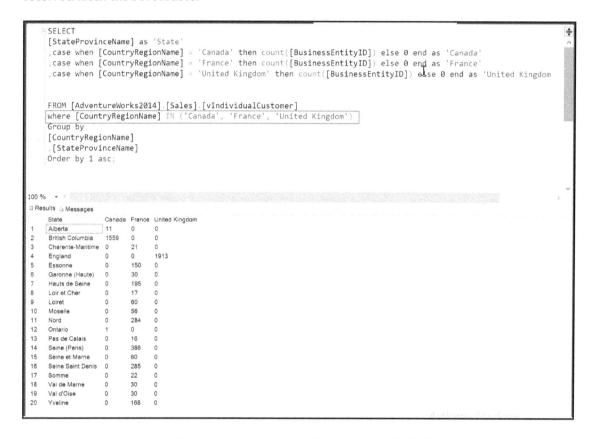

`Case` expressions are not the only way we can build crosstabs in SQL Server.

Building crosstabs with pivot in SQL Server

The `pivot` function is another powerful SQL Server method of converting rows to columns. It performs similarly to a PivotTable in Excel where it rotates a list of unique values of a certain dimension and converts them into multiple column value headers.

To learn more about pivot in Microsoft SQL Server, visit the following website:
`https://msdn.microsoft.com/en-us/library/ms177410.aspx`

We can proceed with the following steps to put together a crosstab using the `pivot` function:

First, we can build the original query with all of the necessary fields without aggregation from the `vIndividualCustomer` view:

```
SELECT
[CountryRegionName]
,[StateProvinceName]
,[BusinessEntityID]
FROM [AdventureWorks2014].[Sales].[vIndividualCustomer]
where CountryRegionName IN ('Canada', 'France', 'United Kingdom')
```

Next, we will use this query as a subquery and run a main query pulling in all fields, as seen in the following script:

```
SELECT *
FROM
(SELECT
[CountryRegionName]
,[StateProvinceName]
,[BusinessEntityID]
FROM [AdventureWorks2014].[Sales].[vIndividualCustomer]
where CountryRegionName IN ('Canada', 'France', 'United Kingdom')
) as tabular
```

We will name the subquery `tabular`. When we execute the script, we will see the following output for the first 10 rows:

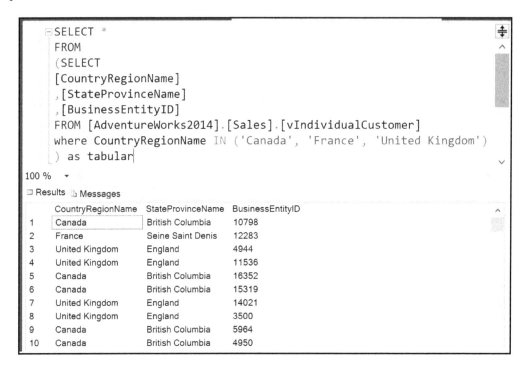

Now we need to develop the remaining part of the script, which will aim to pivot [CountryRegionName] across columns by Count([BusinessEntityID]):

```
PIVOT (
Count([BusinessEntityID])
FOR [CountryRegionName]
IN
([Canada],[France],[United Kingdom])) as NewPivot
```

We can append the `NewPivot` portion underneath the `tabular` portion to reach our final script:

```
SELECT *
FROM
(SELECT
[CountryRegionName]
,[StateProvinceName]
,[BusinessEntityID]
FROM [AdventureWorks2014].[Sales].[vIndividualCustomer]
where CountryRegionName IN ('Canada', 'France', 'United Kingdom')
```

```
) as tabular

PIVOT (
Count([BusinessEntityID])
FOR [CountryRegionName]
IN
([Canada],[France],[United Kingdom])) as NewPivot
```

Once the final script is executed, we can view the output in SQL Server:

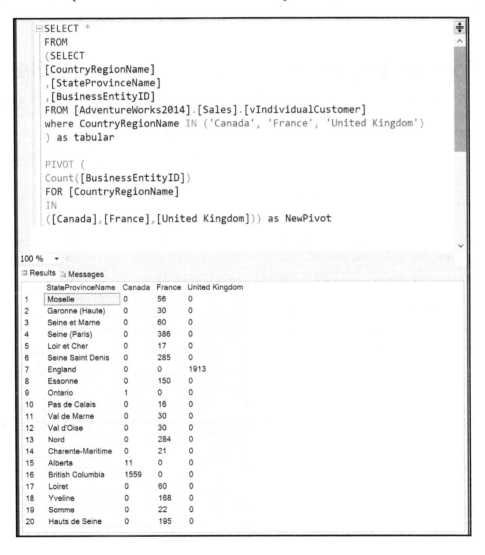

Once again, we can see that we successfully accomplished our goal of putting one dimension as a column and the other dimension as a row. This is just what we would see in a PivotTable in Excel.

The downside to using this method is that it requires manual entry of the specified countries with the `pivot` function. This may be sufficient to use with just a few selections; however, what do we do if the requirement is to include every single country as a column? That would be a significant amount of manual work. Luckily for us, there are procedures in place that can automate these things and make our lives a bit easier.

Performing stored procedures in SQL Server

Stored procedures are a set of scripts that can run at a click of a button to perform a specific task. Stored procedures are great to use for many reasons, especially when it comes to manual tasks. They help automate manual tasks and make things run more efficiently.

 To learn more about stored procedures in Microsoft SQL Server, visit the following website:
`https://msdn.microsoft.com/en-us/library/ms345415.aspx`.

In the previous example, we had to manually enter the values for the three countries that were to be used as columns. Additionally, we had to format them in the following manner:

```
[Canada], [France], [United Kingdom]
```

Well, what if the database had an update and changed the naming for `United Kingdom` to `UK` instead? Our script would need to be updated. Also, if we wanted to include all of the countries as columns, we would need to use the following list:

```
[Australia],[Canada],[France],[Germany],[United Kingdom],[United States]
```

If a new country was added to the list, we'd need to manually update our list to include. It would be ideal to develop a stored procedure that would dynamically generate a unique list of countries.

SQL Server has a great function called `quotename()` that is used to pull back the delimiters to make our list contain the appropriate identifier, which in this case is brackets. If we apply `quotename()` to a distinct SQL statement we can generate a unique list of countries:

```
SELECT DISTINCT quotename(CountryRegionName)+','
FROM [AdventureWorks2014].[Sales].[vIndividualCustomer]
```

The output from this SQL statement can be seen in the following screenshot:

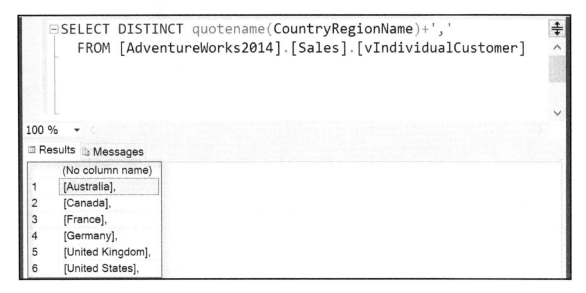

So, we now have our countries in a list wrapped around brackets as we would need them for the `pivot` function. The next few steps will seem a bit reminiscent of what we've done in earlier chapters with D3, R, and Python. We are going to begin assigning values to variables.

The first variable we will assign, `@CountryNames`, will be used for storing a unique list of countries in the appropriate format:

```
Declare @CountryNames NVARCHAR(4000)= ''

SELECT @CountryNames += quotename(CountryRegionName)+','
  FROM [AdventureWorks2014].[Sales].[vIndividualCustomer]
group by CountryRegionName
```

We can then view the output of the variable by using the `print` function in SQL Server:

```
print @CountryNames
```

The output of the variable with the `print` function can be seen in the following screenshot:

```
Declare @CountryNames NVARCHAR(4000)= ''

SELECT @CountryNames += quotename(CountryRegionName)+','
    FROM [AdventureWorks2014].[Sales].[vIndividualCustomer]
    group by CountryRegionName

print @CountryNames
```

100 % ▾

Messages

```
[Australia],[Canada],[Germany],[France],[United Kingdom],[United States],
```

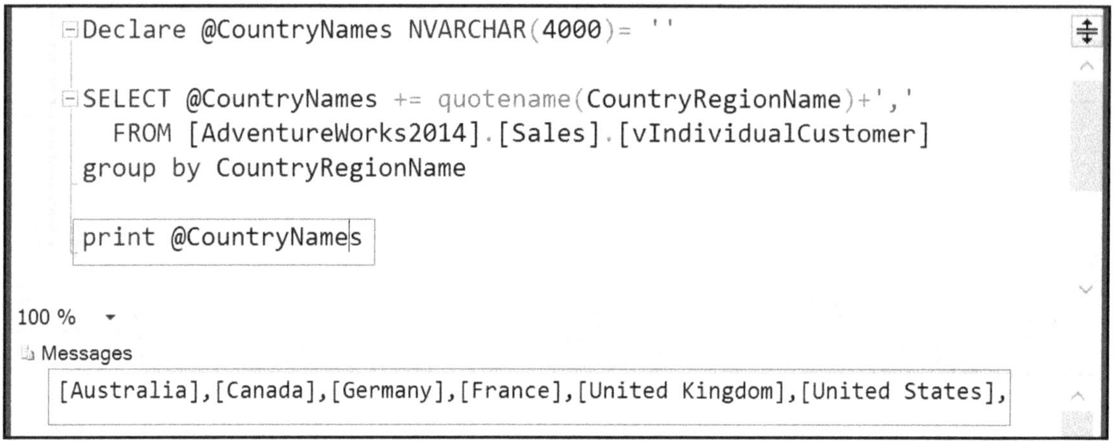

The variable, `@CountryNames`, is pulling back the same distinct list of countries that we need. The only issue is that we have an extra comma at the end of the list that we need to remove. We can do so with the following script:

```
set @CountryNames = substring(@CountryNames,1, len(@CountryNames)-1)
```

The script sets the variable to itself with the caveat of subtracting the last character using the `substr()` function, which is the comma, as seen in the following screenshot:

```
Declare @CountryNames NVARCHAR(4000)= ''

SELECT @CountryNames += quotename(CountryRegionName)+','
    FROM [AdventureWorks2014].[Sales].[vIndividualCustomer]
    group by CountryRegionName

set @CountryNames = substring(@CountryNames,1, len(@CountryNames)-1)

print @CountryNames
```

100 % ▾

Messages

```
[Australia],[Canada],[Germany],[France],[United Kingdom],[United States]
```

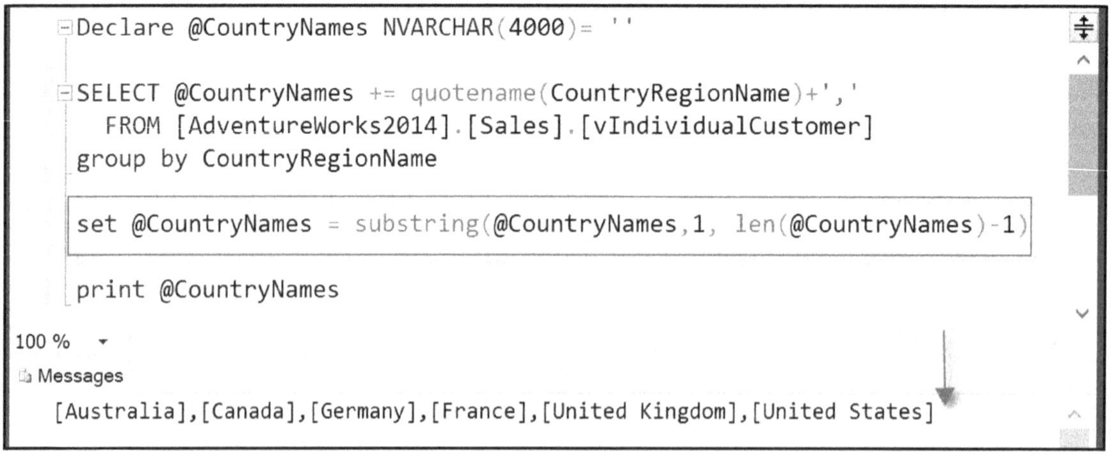

We will next create a second variable, @SQL_Statement, that will be used to store the entire SQL statement:

```
Declare @SQL_Statement NVARCHAR(4000) = ''
```

We will assign @SQL_Statement to the entire script used in the previous section to create the pivot function:

```
set @SQL_Statement =
'SELECT *
FROM
(SELECT
[CountryRegionName]
, [StateProvinceName]
, [BusinessEntityID]
FROM [AdventureWorks2014].[Sales].[vIndividualCustomer]
) as tabular

PIVOT (
Count([BusinessEntityID])
FOR [CountryRegionName]
IN
('
+@CountryNames+
')) as NewPivot '
```

This variable will store the script as a string, and we can view the output of the string by using the print function:

```
print @SQL_Statement
```

The output of the script can be seen in the following screenshot:

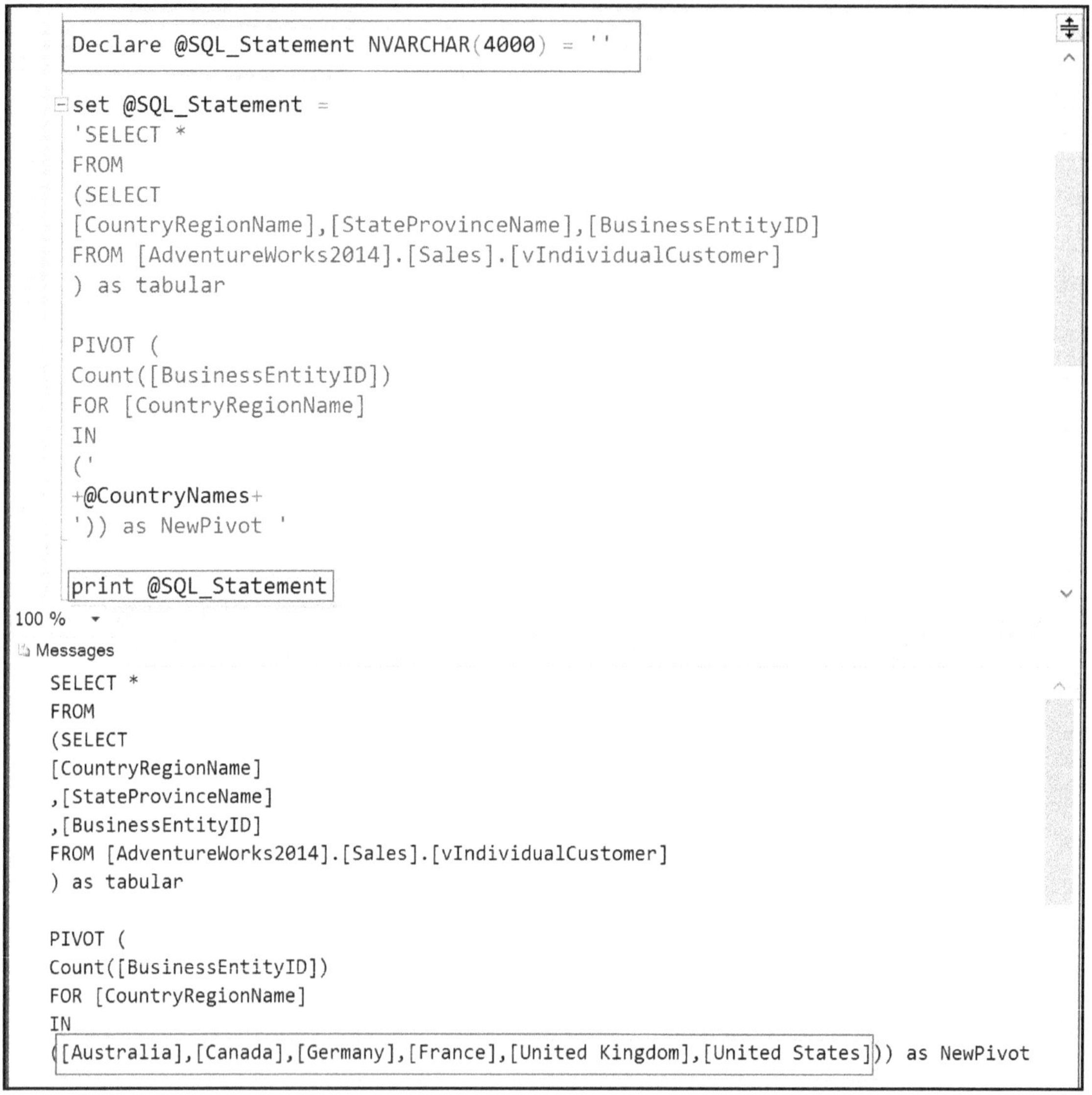

```
Declare @SQL_Statement NVARCHAR(4000) = ''

set @SQL_Statement =
'SELECT *
FROM
(SELECT
[CountryRegionName],[StateProvinceName],[BusinessEntityID]
FROM [AdventureWorks2014].[Sales].[vIndividualCustomer]
) as tabular

PIVOT (
Count([BusinessEntityID])
FOR [CountryRegionName]
IN
('
+@CountryNames+
')) as NewPivot '

print @SQL_Statement
```

100 % ▾

Messages

```
SELECT *
FROM
(SELECT
[CountryRegionName]
,[StateProvinceName]
,[BusinessEntityID]
FROM [AdventureWorks2014].[Sales].[vIndividualCustomer]
) as tabular

PIVOT (
Count([BusinessEntityID])
FOR [CountryRegionName]
IN
([Australia],[Canada],[Germany],[France],[United Kingdom],[United States])) as NewPivot
```

The `print` function shows us the script in its entirety and we can see that the `@CountryNames` variable is showing the values for the countries inside of the other variable, `@SQL_Statement`. We can now remove the `print` function and instead insert the following script to execute the stored procedure:

```
execute sp_executesql @SQL_Statement
```

The entire script for the stored procedure is as follows:

```
Declare @CountryNames NVARCHAR(4000)= ''
Declare @SQL_Statement NVARCHAR(4000) = ''
SELECT @CountryNames += quotename(CountryRegionName)+','
   FROM [AdventureWorks2014].[Sales].[vIndividualCustomer]
group by CountryRegionName

set @CountryNames = substring(@CountryNames,1, len(@CountryNames)-1)

set @SQL_Statement =
'SELECT *
FROM
(SELECT
[CountryRegionName]
,[StateProvinceName]
,[BusinessEntityID]
FROM [AdventureWorks2014].[Sales].[vIndividualCustomer]
) as tabular

PIVOT (
Count([BusinessEntityID])
FOR [CountryRegionName]
IN
('
+@CountryNames+
')) as NewPivot '

execute sp_executesql @SQL_Statement
```

We can now view the entire crosstab for every country:

```
execute sp_executesql @SQL_Statement
```

100 % ▾

Results Messages

	StateProvinceName	Australia	Canada	Germany	France	United Kingdom	United States
1	Moselle	0	0	0	56	0	0
2	Garonne (Haute)	0	0	0	30	0	0
3	Illinois	0	0	0	0	0	6
4	Seine et Marne	0	0	0	60	0	0
5	Brandenburg	0	0	30	0	0	0
6	Hessen	0	0	377	0	0	0
7	Massachusetts	0	0	0	0	0	1
8	Ohio	0	0	0	0	0	4
9	Seine (Paris)	0	0	0	386	0	0
10	Oregon	0	0	0	0	0	1073
11	Wyoming	0	0	0	0	0	2
12	Arizona	0	0	0	0	0	2
13	Saarland	0	0	442	0	0	0
14	Loir et Cher	0	0	0	17	0	0
15	Seine Saint Denis	0	0	0	285	0	0
16	Virginia	0	0	0	0	0	1
17	England	0	0	0	0	1913	0
18	Essonne	0	0	0	150	0	0
19	New York	0	0	0	0	0	3
20	Maryland	0	0	0	0	0	1
21	New South Wales	1559	0	0	0	0	0
22	Ontario	0	1	0	0	0	0
23	Queensland	793	0	0	0	0	0
24	Pas de Calais	0	0	0	16	0	0
25	California	0	0	0	0	0	4445
26	Val de Marne	0	0	0	30	0	0
27	Missouri	0	0	0	0	0	1
28	Val d'Oise	0	0	0	30	0	0
29	Nord	0	0	0	284	0	0
30	Nordrhein-Westfa...	0	0	406	0	0	0
31	Minnesota	0	0	0	0	0	1
32	Florida	0	0	0	0	0	3
33	Charente-Maritime	0	0	0	21	0	0
34	Washington	0	0	0	0	0	2285
35	Alberta	0	11	0	0	0	0

Anytime we have an update to the `[CountryRegionName]` field in the table, the list of countries will dynamically update once we execute this script.

We can turn this script into a stored procedure called `Crosstab` by including the following script at the very top before we declare any variables:

```
CREATE PROCEDURE dbo.Crosstab as
```

We can now view the stored procedure in our **Object Explorer** within Management Studio anytime we expand **Stored Procedures** under **Programmability**:

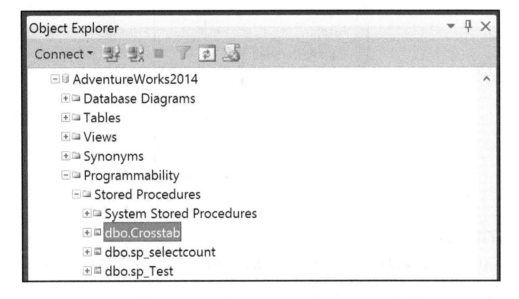

Anytime we need to view our new crosstab, we can simply right-click and execute the stored procedure:

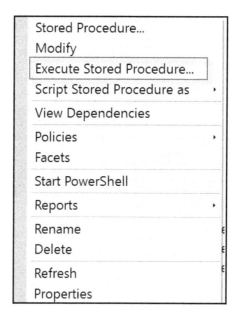

Summary

We have come to the end of the chapter, as well as the end of the book. This chapter has focused on advanced data preparation, manipulation, and calculations to assist end users who will consume these datasets in the various BI tools that we covered in the earlier chapters of the book. We focused our attention at the database level, as opposed to the previous chapters where we did much of the heavy lifting at the reporting level. More focus on the database server side will minimize the resources needed at the desktop level for users and developers. Ultimately, the goal of a BI developer is to get user adoption and user trust.

Index

www.ingramcontent.com/pod-product-compliance
Lightning Source LLC
Chambersburg PA
CBHW062055050326
40690CB00016B/3101